Hallowquest

Hallowquest

Tarot Magic and the Arthurian Mysteries

Designed and written by
CAITLÍN & JOHN MATTHEWS

Illustrated by
MIRANDA GRAY

THE AQUARIAN PRESS

First published 1990

British Library Cataloguing in Publication Data

Matthews, Caitlín
Hallowquest: tarot magic and the Arthurian mysteries.
1. Tarot cards
I. Title II. Matthews, John
133.3'2424

ISBN 0-85030-963-8

The Aquarian Press is part of the Thorsons Publishing Group, Wellingborough, Northamptonshire, NN8 2RQ, England

Typeset by Harper Phototypesetters Limited, Northampton, England
Printed in Great Britain by Woolnough Bookbinding Limited, Irthlingborough, Northamptonshire

1 3 5 7 9 10 8 6 4 2

acknowledgements

The making of this book and the *Arthurian Tarot* pack is the summation of years of meditative and mythological work. It would be impossible to fully acknowledge our debt to our many teachers, both Inner and Outer, but we would like to thank the following by name.

The Servants of the Light course, conceived by Gareth Knight, written by W.E. Butler and supervised by Dolores Ashcroft-Nowicki, has helped inspire much of this work. The many hours of delight and 'holy terror' experienced as part of the Company of Hawkwood brought many things into being which might otherwise have lain fallow. To all those scholars and dreamers who first set our feet on the paths of Brocéliande and who guided our steps through the trackless forest, many thanks.

To Simon Franklin, under whose aegis this work began, and to Eileen Campbell who helped it to its final shape: thank you for the opportunity to share our vision.

Lastly, to Miranda Gray, our heartfelt gratitude for conveying our vision in pictorial form so patiently.

To the Company of the Hallows

'if skill be of work or of will
in the dispersed homes of the household, let the Company
pray for it still.'

— *Charles Williams,* Taliesin Through Logres

'We must create once more the pure work.'

— *W.B. Yeats*

'Here is an old pack of cards has done its work many a night before this, and old as it is, there has been much of the riches of the world lost and won over it.'

— *W.B. Yeats,* Red Hanrahan

contents

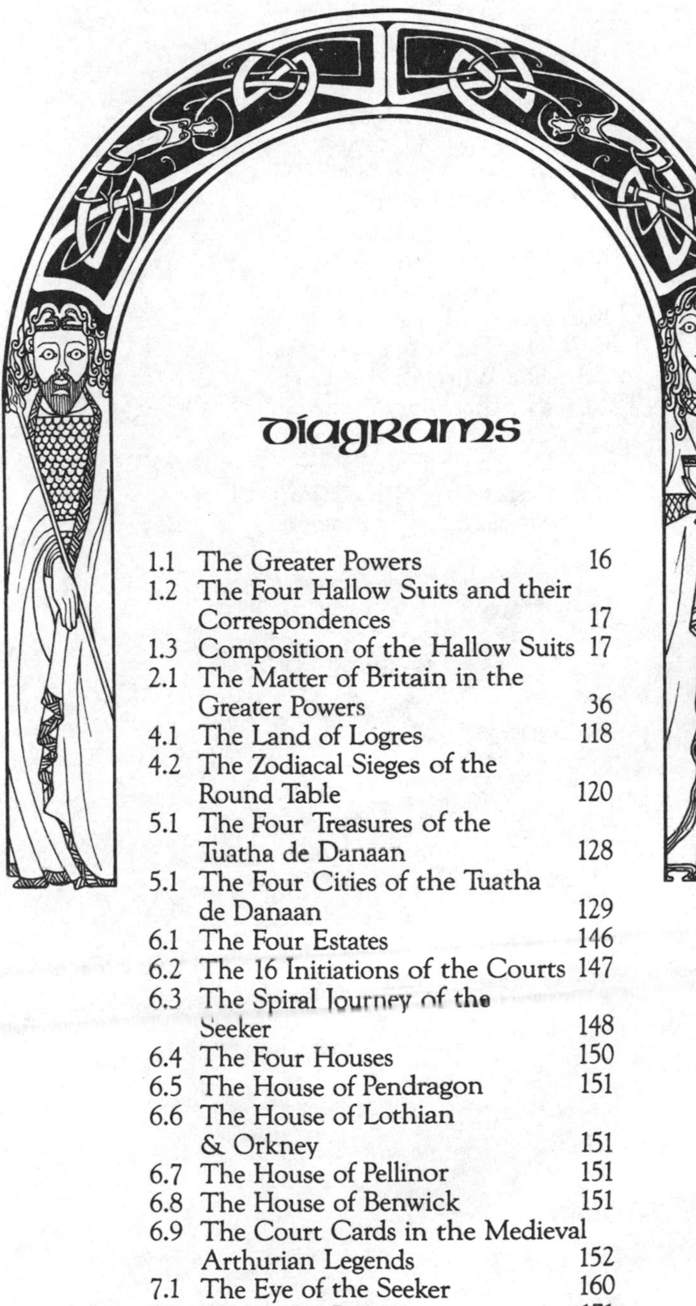

Diagrams

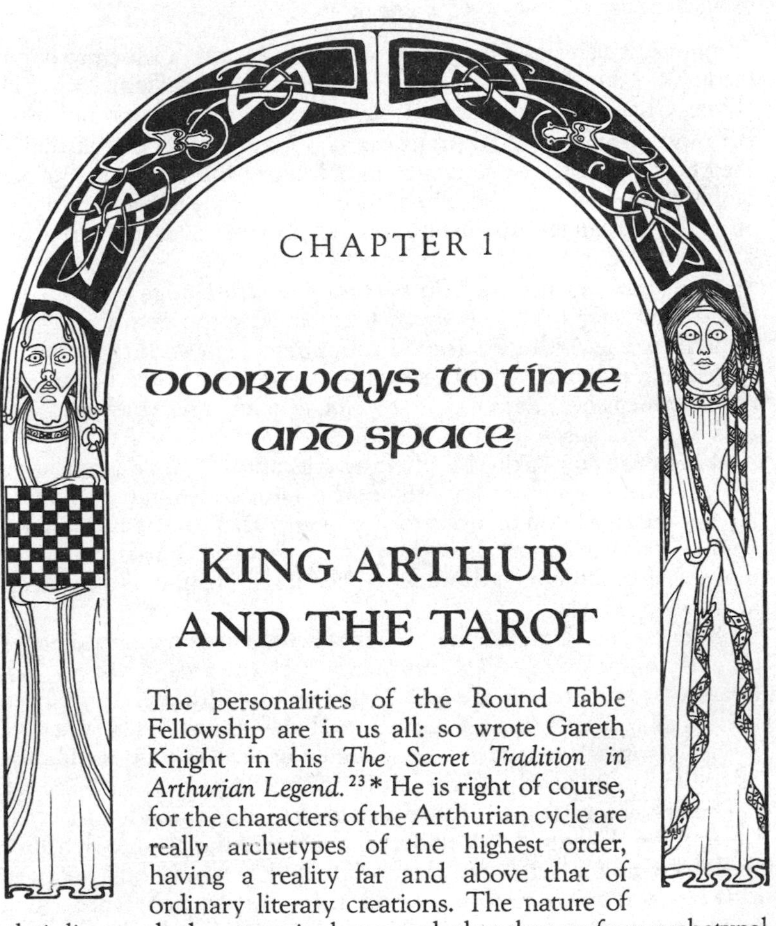

CHAPTER 1

Doorways to Time and Space

KING ARTHUR AND THE TAROT

The personalities of the Round Table Fellowship are in us all: so wrote Gareth Knight in his *The Secret Tradition in Arthurian Legend.*[23]* He is right of course, for the characters of the Arthurian cycle are really archetypes of the highest order, having a reality far and above that of ordinary literary creations. The nature of their lives and adventures is always such that they perform archetypal actions. This is their mythic function, for they perform essential roles on behalf of the rest of humanity and this makes them suitable for esoteric work, for here such archetypal forces are codified and aligned with natural and inner world patterns.

The use of a literary creation with an esoteric system such as the Tarot may seem extraordinary. Indeed, if the Arthurian legends *were* solely literary inventions we could not have created the *Arthurian Tarot*. It is because the stories about King Arthur and his court arise from much earlier levels — from the mythic and oral traditions of Britain — that we are able to trace the archetypal threads which keep the mythic web in shape.

The mythology of the Arthurian world is a cumulative one, drawing

*All reference numbers are keyed to the Bibliography (pp.295–98).

on native British tradition, Romano-British history, Celtic myth and medieval elaboration, with, latterly, additions from Tennyson, T.H. White, Charles Williams and numerous modern poets and novelists. For most people, the Arthurian world is permanently established in the Middle Ages by the conventions of Malory. But this formalization of the legends, while perhaps helping to preserve the Matter of Britain, as the Arthurian legends are known, has also obscured them in many ways.

It has been our task to help restore the mythic links between the earlier and later traditions so that in this way the mythic patterns underlying the Arthurian legend could provide us with the basis for the *Arthurian Tarot*. What began as a corpus of stories to be enjoyed by everyone is here depicted as the *Hallowquest*: a series of doorways into time and space.

That we are able to do this offers a verification, if not a vindication of the archetypal nature not only of the Tarot system but also of the Arthurian mythos. The universality of the Tarot needs no proving; neither for that matter does the power of the Arthurian stories to move, and to illuminate those who encounter them, in a universally acknowledged way.

Of course the Tarot, like the Matter of Britain itself has traded under more than one guise. It is more than a pack of cards, far more than a game, far more than a method of divination. Although it has been used as all three, its original use was probably as a pictorial system of magical images, designed to be meditated upon and then realized by its utilization in ritual and inner-dimensional work.

The first Tarot decks which we possess date from no earlier than the late fourteenth century, but this does not mean that prior to that time there were none. Just as the Arthurian mythos was in oral tradition long before it was transcribed, so too the symbolic archetypes which go to form the Tarot were in circulation. Although there is no scope in this book to give a history of the Tarot, the reader will find a number of titles in the bibliography beginning on p.295 which will supply numerous theories.

We have purposely chosen to distance the *Hallowquest* from the standard symbolisms of traditional packs, although the reader will find many similarities and overlaps. Orthodox Tarot packs have acquired a massive set of correspondences upon which their interpretive symbolism rests. While such highly syncretic correspondences may be welcomed by the Qabalist and magician, they are not necessarily those which derive from the Arthurian world.

The cards which form the *Hallowquest* are the result of long meditation. Nothing has been depicted because it seemed aesthetically pleasing or intellectually correct. We have gone back to the proto-Celtic roots of the mythos, drawing upon deeper Otherworldly and timeless qualities to produce the cards of the Greater Powers; while the land of Britain itself has been our inspiration in creating the cards of the Lesser Powers.

The symbolism which governs the whole pack is that of the Hallows themselves — the Sword, the Spear, the Grail and the Stone, which are emblematic of the elements of Air, Fire, Water and Earth, respectively, as well as being the objects of the *Hallowquest* itself. This fourfold elemental correspondence is not only nearer to the spirit of the Celto-Arthurian mythos, but also central to an understanding of the Tarot.

Those readers who are attached to the medieval format of the Arthurian legends may be disappointed in not finding it depicted here. We hope that there is sufficient fusion between the so-called Dark Age Arthur and his more elaborate flowering as a medieval king, and that readers will persevere with the earlier images and find them rewarding. The Arthurian mythos is like a great tree planted in ancient soil: although everyone sees the branches, it is the roots which channel the earth's nourishment to the leaves and fruit upon it.

The Arthurian legends furnish an exciting and deeply moving symbology in which to operate, for they provide the mythic levels from which its themes and characters draw their life and potency. Without these qualities, the images do not step off the cards into the imagination, and unless they do so, the Tarot is a worthless system.

That the two systems of the Matter of Britain and the Tarot should work reciprocally is itself a wonder, as we discovered as we entered deeper into the hidden worldscape of the *Hallowquest*. There we encountered forces at once personal and universal in their application — as are all great archetypes. The characters and themes of the Arthurian court who came to represent the Greater and Lesser Powers (the Major and Minor Arcanas) stood forth ever more clearly as we worked. Though we knew, or felt we knew them already, as our work proceeded we came to know them more deeply in their essential format.

One effect of working with the *Hallowquest* pack must be to broaden our awareness of the deeper truths implicit in these stories. From this we may be moved to reread or to seek out for the first time, some of the original texts listed at the end of this book. There, to our newly alerted awareness, will be revealed the secrets of the Quest and the Table, the meaning of the Higher Chivalry, the transcendent nature of the Kingly and the Divine. When we move at last, haltingly perhaps, like Lancelot towards the door of the Grail Chapel, what lies within will be more wondrous than we ever imagined. It will change us ultimately, like the Grail itself, that most protean of images, which underwent Five Mysterious Changes. Perhaps also, if we are lucky, we will glimpse the heroes and heroines of the cards standing around us, welcoming us to their ranks, whither we have found our way after a long and wearisome journey.

All this and more may be opened for us as we pass through any of the 78 doorways of the *Hallowquest*. What we do with the knowledge we have gained is for us to decide, but whatever choice we make will most certainly be profound within the inscape of our lives.

GETTING TO KNOW THE HALLOWQUEST PACK

You may already be familiar with the Tarot, or perhaps have never handled a pack before. Whichever is the case, the *Hallowquest* pack will take some time to get used to. But, of course, you will want to use it right away.

Without worrying about the meanings of each card or noticing the ways in which it varies from traditional packs, take the cards out of their box and scan each of the images in a relaxed way. Some will appeal to you straight away, others may repel you, while some may be baffling or unclear. Spread them out around you on the floor; play with them, make up stories by putting one card next to another at random. Each individual card has its mood, quality or feel, and these can be perceived without having to look up the meanings.

In the next few weeks, try to handle the pack as much as possible. This handling will break the printed, laminated cards from the factory into your own personal set of symbols. Let the cards become familiar to your fingers and to your imaginative senses. Some books on the Tarot suggest all manner of arcane ways of making the Tarot special to you; if you want to protect the cards both physically and psychically by wrapping them in silk and placing them in a special box, then by all means do so, but it is not essential. The *Hallowquest* pack is first and foremost a tool for you to use and it is better for becoming the companion of your travels — both inner and outer ones. It is easy enough to create a medicine bag or shaman's pouch in which the cards can be carried about, if that is what appeals to you, but they will be quite as companionable in your pocket or handbag.

If you are going to do any serious work with these cards for yourself or others, you are going to have to learn their ascriptions very thoroughly. This process is an organic one which cannot be rushed. Even the fastest Tarot student is going to find deeper and deeper levels to assimilate.

Learning by rote is very boring: it is the educational equivalent of factory farming. Many of us learned multiplication tables this way, but not with any enthusiasm. The learning process must engage the imagination if it is to be effective. If you have a photographic memory then you might consider it an advantage to be able to 'snap' each card with your remembering eye, but this is not going to help much when you are reading for a querent with a set of complex needs. Single cards may have fixed meanings, but when they interrelate in a spread they modify their effect. Adaptability is the order of the exercise.

To learn the cards you are going to have to interrelate with them yourself. The best method of learning the *Hallowquest* is undoubtedly by meditation, about which you can read more in Chapter 8. Throughout the book you will find many exercises, games, meditations and rituals to help you learn faster. Do not despise these practical exercises for they will bring you into immediate relationship with the archetypes underlying the cards far faster than merely reading what is written down in this book.

As you begin to work with the *Hallowquest* pack you will discover many correlations and meanings, even stories and other realizations arising from your research and use of the cards. The freshness and vitality of these discoveries are often swiftly lost and you may wish to record them in a workbook. Any loose-leaf folder will suffice, enabling you to rearrange and insert pages where and when you like. In this way you will be making the *Arthurian Tarot* your own.

The value of records or notes is much understated in the learning process. By writing down your discoveries immediately when things are going well for you, you will be able to refer to them again on the days when you feel depressed or discouraged. A record or workbook will also give a sense of shape and an idea of your progress.

Decide at the outset what kind of learning programme you want to follow: remember, you can be both systematic *and* creative. You may wish to start meditating or studying one card at a time until you work your way through the pack. In this case you can assign a number of pages in your workbook for each card on which to record your findings.

Study each card, noting down as you go your initial feelings or impressions. Now look up the meanings given to your card. These archetypal symbols are going to represent real life situations for any querents who consult you, so take time to imagine real situations or circumstances which that card might represent. For example, XVIII, the Moon. This card represents the state of inner preparation and the cyclicity of growth. Several images will immediately occur to you: the growth of a child in the womb, just as is depicted in the card. But it might also represent a pregnant woman, the burgeoning of creative ideas, the receptivity for inspiration of all kinds. The cards will not always represent concrete objects or situations, but feelings, concepts or influences.

Whatever part of the pack you decide to work with first, whether it be the Greater or Lesser Powers, be consistent and regular in your approach. You can supplement your learning programme by the practical exercises, which will get your imagination working as well and help you free the knowledge which you are acquiring from the book into practical expression and application.

Getting to know the *Hallowquest* pack is your first task. The only precaution the authors enjoin here is to avoid working with the Tarot before going to bed. This is not due to the supposedly sinister influence of the Tarot, but a common sense measure: such strong images have a way of invading one's dreams, which can lead to an unsettled night in which repetitive images recur. Enjoy working with the cards and finding new ways to see and use them. The methods outlined in this book are only suggestions upon which you can base your own method. It is your task to recreate the Arthurian world and to pursue the *Hallowquest* for yourself.

THE SHAPE OF THE HALLOWQUEST

In order to understand the way the *Arthurian Tarot* works, the following diagrams show the shape of the pack and its correspondences with traditional Tarot systems.

THE GREATER POWERS

No.	*Traditional Title*	*Hallowquest Title*
0	The Fool	The Seeker in the Wasteland
I	The Magician	Merlin
II	The High Priestess	The Lady of the Lake
III	The Empress	Guinevere
IV	The Emperor	Arthur
V	The Hierophant	Taliesin
VI	The Lovers	The White Hart
VII	The Chariot	Prydwen
VIII	Strength	Gawain
IX	The Hermit	The Grail Hermit
X	The Wheel of Fortune	The Round Table
XI	Justice	Sovereignty
XII	The Hanged Man	The Wounded King
XIII	Death	The Washer at the Ford
XIV	Temperance	The Cauldron
XV	The Devil	The Green Knight
XVI	The Tower	The Spiral Tower
XVII	The Star	The Star of Prophecy
XVIII	The Moon	The Moon

No.	Traditional Title	Hallowquest Title
XIX	The Sun	The Sun
XX	The Last Judgement	The Sleeping Lord
XXI	The World	The Flowering of Logres

Fig. 1.1: The Greater Powers

THE LESSER POWERS

The Four Hallow Suits and their Correspondences

Hallowquest Tarot:	Traditional Tarot:	Playing Cards:	Season:	Element:	Colour:
Sword	Swords	Spades	Spring	Air	Yellow
Spear	Wands	Clubs	Summer	Fire	Red
Grail	Cups	Hearts	Autumn	Water	Blue
Stone	Pentacles	Diamonds	Winter	Earth	Green

Fig. 1.2: The Four Hallow Suits and their Correspondences.

The Composition of the Hallow Suits

Aces	=	the four Hallows of Celto-Arthurian tradition: the Sword, the Spear, the Grail and the Stone.
Cards 2–9	=	the landscape of the Hallowquest through which the Seeker journeys.
Card 10	=	one of the four Courts of the Hallows, represented by a castle.
Court Cards	=	the Maiden, Knight, Queen and King of each Hallow castle.

Fig. 1.3: The Composition of the Hallow Suits

REVERSED MEANINGS

You will notice that the *Arthurian Tarot* does not have any reversed meanings given. The reason for this is an esoteric one. Every aspect of life has its dual quality or application. However the archetypal or Otherworldly levels function differently for they are powers in their own right: they are neither good nor evil, beneficial or detrimental in their essence. They just exist. This is why we have called the Major and Minor Arcana 'The Greater and Lesser Powers'.

The reversed or contrary meanings are therefore implicit in each card by virtue of their placement in a spread, and we have left it up to the discernment of the *Hallowquest* user to find these, where they are appropriate.

There is no virtue in attempting to stare at a reversed card which the artist has drafted to be comprehended in an upright position, since the potency and symbolism are thereby lost. If cards turn up in reversed positions when you are reading them, turn them the right way up, considering, as you do so, the implication of that card and its interrelation with the others in more detail. If you are using them for story-telling, myth-making or any of the other creative exercises then do not hesitate to turn them upright and work with them that way.

If you have been used to working with reversed meanings in other packs you may wish to do so with the *Arthurian Tarot*. If you wish to explore the possibility further then you could do no better than refer to Gail Fairfield's *Choice Centred Tarot*,[7] which will give you ideas on how you can adapt the *Hallowquest* pack.

If you are using one card alone, then it is always 'neutral'. When the cards are placed side by side certain combinations automatically call into being a response which will be different, depending on the querent, the reader and the cards chosen. We cannot give set patterns of such combinations because they would be different for everyone. Just as no homeopathic practitioner would prescribe the same remedy to two people suffering from flu but would consider each person's make-up and symptoms — the way they reacted to their illness — so too, no Tarot consultant can interpret the same spread of cards for two different people whose reactions to their own life circumstances varied wildly from each other.

You will find more about divination in Chapters 9 and 10.

TAROT ETHICS

There is a great deal of mystification surrounding symbolic systems such as the Tarot. Some Tarot books — especially those written early on this century — seem to abound in dire warnings, but no satisfactory explanations are given as to why. Some of this caution is a legacy of the time when mystical systems had to go underground in order to survive, for to be in possession of anything to do with the ancient mysteries which preceded Christianity was to be a heretic and an unbeliever. Of course, this was not always the case, since the old mysteries found their exponents among the learned clerics of medieval Europe as often as among the unlettered wise men and women of the countryside.

Because during this time there were few guardians of the ancient mysteries, such teachers as there were issued strict instructions concerning the preservation of their tradition: it had to be secret to be safe. We are fortunate to live in times where such interdicts and proscriptions do not govern our lives, although there are parts of the world, even in the enlightened West, where people are understandably reticent about their beliefs and practices.

However enlightened we imagine our culture to be, the residue of fear and distrust is still with us. Anything 'occult' — literally, 'hidden' — is still considered to be dangerous or possibly devilish. The possession of a Tarot pack may seem no big deal today, but many people are frightened by them, often quite irrationally, or else are credulous in the extreme and capable of believing the Tarot system to be some kind of god in cardboard form.

Because the Tarot has survived almost solely as a divinatory system, there are many strange ideas about its possible powers. We have tried to clarify these in Chapter 9, but throughout the book we have addressed ourselves to the problem of esoteric ethics underlying the Tarot.

We cannot be certain just where and when the Tarot originated but, like the general system of astrology which was part of many cultures, including our own until the introduction of the Copernican universe to science, the Tarot was undoubtedly part of the ancient mysteries which were administered by professional guardians who understood its use and application far better than we can.

Today no such guardians exist and the Tarot is divorced from its esoteric context. Certainly there are a great number of conscientious and ethically aware Tarot readers, but for every one of them there are a hundred others whose integrity leaves a lot to be desired. This is a do-it-yourself era in many ways and, while it is good to learn skills and assimilate wisdom, we must also be aware that, whatever craft we adopt, we should try to learn it as thoroughly and apply it as perfectly as we know how. The amateur musician will not play to the standard of a national orchestra member, but he will strive to play better and practise more. The esoteric arts also need their professionals, and while there are increasing opportunities to study with esotericists who have learned their skills in a hard school and are prepared to teach others, there is nothing like the old mystery schools appearing yet. Until that time, we all have to be aware of our esoteric attitudes and maintain a standard of discernment and integrity in our approach.

You may not have to look over your shoulder for the inquisitor before you take out your Tarot cards, but if you produce your pack at work or at a party then expect to be asked to perform wonders before the eyes of the credulous. This is not the kind of use to which you should subject your Tarot pack for it represents a body of wisdom which should be respected. The new instrument of repression is ridicule. Esoteric things can now be dismissed by mockery, as a glance at the way they are treated by the media, both television and the newspapers, will testify. If someone wants to consult the *Hallowquest* pack, then let him or her come to you privately where there is time and quiet enough to reach the levels which lie waiting for all people who are on the quest for inner knowledge.

THE LANGUAGE OF SYMBOLISM

> *The Tarot is symbolism; it speaks no other language and offers no other signs. Given the true meaning of its emblems, they do become a kind of alphabet which is capable of indefinite combinations and makes true sense in all. On the highest plane it offers a key to the mysteries . . .*

So writes A.E. Waite in his *The Key to the Tarot.* And indeed the Tarot speaks a universal language, for each of its qualities is an archetypal constant. The same is true also of astrology which, whatever one decides to call the planets, their qualities and symbolic ascriptions still give the same messages and meanings. Of course the *Hallowquest* draws on the Arthurian mythos. Once the connection between the medieval and more familiar Arthurian stories with the earlier British ones is recognized, the language of the Tarot works just the same. So although the meanings and correlatives given in this pack may vary from conventional Tarots, the language is symbolically consistent.

The Tarot is a pictorial language, a symbology which has a number of uses, the least of which is fortune-telling. You will find many different ways to utilize the pack in the following pages. It is possible that you never conceived of the Tarot as being anything other than a divinatory system. If you read the chapters on meditation, ritual and story-telling and try some of the exercises, we hope that you will be pleasantly surprised and excited by the potential of the cards.

Symbolic systems are not confined to one kind of people, to men or women only, to esotericists or magicians only. The wisdom they contain extends to all who can respond to their messages and meanings. So while the *Hallowquest* deck draws its inspiration from the cultural mythos of Britain, of which the Arthurian legends are but a part, this does not limit its application to merely one time or place. Since you have purchased this pack, you are undoubtedly interested in the Arthurian world and its deeper levels, but the *Hallowquest* is not reserved solely for Arthurian experts or people born in Britain.

The inner Britain, called Logres in the early texts, is part of the Otherworldly reality which is available to all. Tibet has its Shambhalla, Greece its Hesperides, Britain has its Avalon. These timeless realities are always available, since they are the mystical repositories of wisdom and ancestral lore; they transcend the barriers of race, culture and time. Anyone who has responded to the Arthurian legends, will find the *Hallowquest* usable as a mythic system of understanding. The Arthurian Powers and their totems will lead the *Hallowquest* user to discover these very Otherworldly levels of wisdom for themselves.

It is important when dealing with symbolic languages to understand that they have many levels of application and that, in their pure form, they exist in their own right. Many recent feminist Tarots have attempted to expunge all male images and revise the Tarot solely for a feminist usership, but that seems to us to be imbalanced and to ignore the esoteric levels which are at work within the Tarot. The images which appear in the *Hallowquest* pack sometimes depict men, sometimes women: no amount of special pleading will alter the fact that Arthur is male and Guinevere is female, for instance. However, the application of these two cards is not confined exclusively to men or women respectively.

The images and characters depicted in the *Arthurian Tarot* represent archetypal or Otherwordly powers. It is inappropriate to apply the archetypal roles on a purely human plane, because this confuses symbolic levels. The Arthurian or Greater Powers do not represent either divine or human energies. They may be rightly described as daemons. Daemons are not demons, but the inner guiding agencies which are neither incarnate humans nor non-incarnate gods. They are the inner voices of our dreams, our guardian angel or inner companion spirit. The language they speak is symbolically exact and authoritatively voiced. To expect them to speak of our very mundane concerns is as foolish as to imagine that an angel might advise us financially.

The Greater Powers speak of deeper and more archetypal matters than the payment of bills or the unhappy relationships we may have. When the *Hallowquest* pack is used in divination, the appearance of the Greater Powers signifies a more urgent voice, reminding us that even we mortals have our part to sing in the larger harmony of creation. They urge us to recall that we too are part of the great weaving pattern of the earth's fabric and make us look more closely at the overall pattern which our lives are making. The Lesser Powers speak more plainly and mundanely; they speak about our general direction and the ways in which we both make our path more difficult and how we might make it smoother.

The method of reading the pictorial language of this symbolic system cannot be taught. It is like the language of the birds, the mysterious ability to remember that which we have never consciously known, the ability to pick out of the air the patterns and shapings of a greater reality. This is part of the learning and interpretative process which you will acquire or not, depending on whether you are able to align your willingness to learn with an equal receptivity to understand.

The *Hallowquest* Tarot possesses its own set of teachers in the shape of the Greater Powers: listen to them carefully and you too will learn to speak, read and understand the language of the Otherworld.

CHAPTER 2

the arthurian world

THE MATTER OF BRITAIN

An understanding of the way in which the archetypal and magical aspects of the Arthurian mythos grew and developed is essential to an understanding of the power of the *Hallowquest* images — just as it is essential to understand the way in which the Arthurian legends developed as a continuing tradition, to which each succeeding age has added its own notion of what they are about. Nowadays we would hardly think of rewriting a modern novel in our own words and with significant changes, yet during the Middle Ages it was perfectly natural for the clerics who copied the earlier texts to rewrite and modify them according to their own understanding, putting the characters into contemporary dress and suppressing anything they felt to be pagan, outlandish, or detrimental to Christian morality.

This resulted in the loss, or obscuring, of many elements within the stories, and only in recent times have these begun to be uncovered and reinstated. In the process, much that had seemed obscure has become clear again, and a new shape has begun to emerge from the mass of material gathered together under the general heading of the Matter of Britain. This has resulted in the re-emergence of the mythical Arthur — a far more important figure than either the literary or the historical personality: though both of these in turn are affected by the new approach.

Yet what is still known today by most people, who either read the stories in versions retold from medieval texts, or who perhaps seek out some of the more readily available translations, is a far cry from reality. That reality, which concerns a sixth-century war-leader and his efforts to halt the onset of a savage invader, is another story altogether, and one which is still not often told.

In the same way, the deeper symbolic references remain hard to find within the welter of romantic dressing which has surrounded the Arthurian mythos from the Middle Ages onward. Part of the work of preparing the *Hallowquest* pack has been to rediscover the true power of the images hidden within the oldest texts, as well as in the later medieval versions.

Just how an obscure sixth-century hero, possibly not even of noble descent, came to occupy a place of primary importance in the history and literature of several continents, is part of the mystery. It is a question we have to ask before we can begin to understand the nature of the material itself. Before we can answer it we need to look briefly at what we know, or can surmise, of Arthur's life and times — and then at the way in which the story grew and changed through successive generations until the present.

When the last of the Roman legions left Britain in AD 410 it was only the final stage of a gradual withdrawal brought about by internal strife and the onset of Barbarian incursions along the eastern frontiers of the empire. The Romans left behind a country divided into many small islands of Celtic and Romano-British rule. On the one hand the always restless, warlike tribes in the north and east of the country, began to reassert ancient claims to territories long since lost; on the other, the citizens of the Romanized towns of the south and west strove to preserve the order and civilizing effects of Roman rule.

Matters were further complicated by raiders from Fresia, Jutland and Germany, who attacked all along the coast of Britain from around AD 442 onwards, and the continued attacks of the Picts and Scotti, who after long years of warfare along Hadrian's Wall, began to pour through and down into lowland Britain.

A minor king named Vortigern attempted to gain an advantage over his neighbours by inviting Saxon mercenaries to fight against the Picts. But though at first they were successful — earning Vortigern the position of High King — the Saxon *feoderati* soon began to demand land by way of payment, and when this was refused, invited still more of their number to join them, and threw in their lot with the Picts.

At this point there arose the figure of a Romano-British general named Ambrosius Aurelianus, who seems to have come from a noble family, and may also have fought with the legions in Gaul. At any rate he was an extremely able soldier, and it was he who first attempted to unite the various factions in the country into a single force designed to fight against their common enemies.

To some extent he was successful — enough to ensure himself a place in the history of Britain. But it was his successor who was to carve out a name of such might that it became etched into the soul of the land itself.

This was Arthur, and of his historical presence we know almost nothing. Indeed we cannot even say with any certainty that he existed; only that, if he did not, someone of like stature and abilities did; and that he changed the direction of British history forever.

We do not know when, or where, Arthur was born, though it must have been round about AD 490, possibly in the Midlands or Wales. He seems to have come into his full strength and abilities early, or at least to have risen through the ranks of Ambrosius' army with great speed — where he caught the eye of the general. It is possible also that he was of native stock, though whether of royal blood we cannot say. At any rate he was able to win the support of both the Roman and British factions, and like Ambrosius he had a charismatic ability which made him a natural commander.

During the next five to ten years he fought 12 major battles against the Saxons, culminating in the Battle of Badon Hill (possibly near Bath in Avon) where he inflicted such a crushing defeat that he effectively brought peace to the island for the next 20 years.

Then, somewhere about AD 535 he died, or vanished, possibly at a place which tradition names Camlan, fighting against an opponent who in later versions of the story is either his nephew or his son. But so powerful was the effect of his presence that what had begun as an invasion ended as a semi-peaceful settlement, and what was to become Anglo-Saxon England was born in this time, despite the period of confusion which followed Arthur's departure.[46]

The belief that Arthur was not really dead rapidly grew and took root in the fertile soil of Britain. It was said that he was sleeping beneath some hill in the heart of the land, and that when he was needed he would come forth again to lead his people to victory over an unknown foe. It was the beginning of what was to become the greatest legendary and mythical cycle of stories ever to come out of these islands, and its effects are still being felt today as the ancient mysteries of Britain are slowly restored.

The stories of Arthur and his warriors became part of oral tradition and circulated for several centuries before they were finally written down. During that time they changed radically; they were added to to take on the weight of earlier archetypes. A few fragmentary references still exist which hint at a larger body of material than that which has survived — but this, alas, is lost. The monkish historian Gildas, who may have been a contemporary of Arthur's, wrote an account of the times which totally omits any mention of the hero. But

Gildas believed all the rulers of the day were evil tyrants, and spent most of the book castigating them. His reason for not mentioning Arthur may have been personal — clues exist which imply that Arthur may have executed Gildas' brother for piracy.

Nennius, writing a little later in his *Historia Britonum* (*c.* 900) gives us the only authentic account of Arthur, including the 12 famous battles, that has survived. But even this is ambiguous, and though much work has been done on the text, the identification of the battlefields remains elusive.[53]

It is to the ancient Welsh texts that we must turn for a better picture of the heroic Arthur. In particular the *Mabinogion* and the *Book of Taliesin*, though they were not written down until the Middle Ages, and are both corrupt and difficult to interpret, give us much that is older and clearer.[30, 59]

Taliesin's poetry, though complex and difficult to translate, retains references to Arthur which may well be the earliest we now possess; while one poem, the *Preiddeu Annwn* (*The Spoils of Annwn*) gives an account of a raid on the Otherworld to capture a magical cauldron, which is almost certainly the earliest version of the Quest theme which was later to dominate the cycle.[29]

In all, the figures presented in this material are a far cry from those of later versions. There are no knights in armour, no silken ladies in their gorgeous pavilions, no shining castles — in fact none of the normal trappings of romance. This all came later, in the twelfth century, when a cleric named Geoffrey of Monmouth wrote a book which he called the *Historia Regum Brittaniae* (The History of the Kings of Britain), and gave over more than two-thirds of its pages to Arthur. The story he told was, very roughly, the same as the historical reality, but with significant differences. Arthur had become a medieval king, his warriors medieval knights; Merlin was his prophet and councillor, Guinevere his queen, and he ruled over a kingdom which included Norway, Iceland and most of France.[8]

Geoffrey's book became a bestseller, with hundreds of copies distributed throughout Britain and the continent. Arthurian tales became all the rage and began to appear with extraordinary proliferation all over Europe.[27]

A French writer named Chrétien de Troyes created at least five new texts, including one which introduced the character of Lancelot and told of his illicit love for Arthur's queen. Chrétien brought the Arthurian mythos firmly into the world of Courtly Love and gave women a prominence within the stories which had been lacking before. He also wrought one of the strangest tales in the entire Matter of Britain. It was called the *Conte del Graal* (The Story of the Grail) and it told of a wondrous vessel and a spear which dripped blood. Both these objects were the goal of a quest undertaken by a young knight named Perceval.[4]

In all probability Chrétien drew upon earlier versions of the stories he told, perhaps not even written down, but circulated by wandering singers, or *trouvères*, whose ancestors had migrated from Britain across the channel to Amorica (Brittany) to escape the Saxons, and taken with them not only a vast amount of oral literature, but also some newly-minted tales, already beginning to circulate, of Arthur.

Thus, in circular fashion, these original stories returned to their place of origin, but changed by time and fashion and influenced by European mannerisms. From here on the avalanche had begun: it did not even begin to slacken its pace for another three hundred years.

Chrétien's stories, taken up and elaborated into vast prose cycles mixed with other fragmentary Celtic tales, became all the rage in medieval Europe. His tale of the Grail, left unfinished at his death, was 'continued' by numerous imitators until another cycle, beginning with the crucifixion of Christ and the fate of the cup of the Last Supper (now transformed into the Grail), and ending in Arthur's medieval realm, also came into being.

The mystery at the heart of the Arthurian stories had by now been largely forgotten. The texts told of high adventure and chivalrous encounters between heroes. Only occasionally fragments of the older Celtic stories showed through — the Lady of the Lake brought Lancelot up in a mysterious paradisal realm beneath the water; knights engaged in an adventure met with three women of 15, 30, and 60 years — representing the ancient triple-aspected Goddess.

Certain knights, among them Gawain, Owein, Kay, Perceval and of course Lancelot, had stories devoted to their personal adventures within the setting of Arthur's splendid court at Camelot. The romantic entanglement of Lancelot and Guinevere found a rival in the similar tale of Tristan and Isolt, which drew upon more ancient Celtic sources in the Irish saga of Diarmuid and Grainne.[5,31]

Arthur, Merlin, the Round Table, the quest for the Grail, the splendid dream of Chivalry and its doomed ending in death and destruction, followed by the departure of Arthur for the mysterious island of Avalon to be healed of his wounds — these were the parameters within which the legends flowered, producing some of the finest literature of any age.

And always, behind the facade of the romantic story, lay the deeper, archetypal realm of the mythic Arthur, the undying king who would return when he was needed, whose master, Merlin the wise, had at his command an ancient magic.

Nor was this the end of the story. Thomas Malory's *Le Morte d'Arthur*[31] published in 1485 is generally considered the finest single version of the legends. It was the last true medieval version, but it was by no means the last Arthurian story. Throughout the Renaissance new versions continued to appear, though of lesser quality than before. Spenser's great epic poem *The Faerie Queen* appeared at the height of the Elizabethan period and drew upon all the richness of contemporary allegory — and upon the Arthurian legends.[61] The eighteenth century had less interest in myths, but there were those who began to look again at the reality behind the legends and to speculate about their meaning. Revival Druidism came into being at this time, and drew for its inspiration on such works as the poems of Taliesin.

Then, in the nineteenth century, the Arthurian industry began in earnest. William Morris, Edward Burne-Jones and others of the pre-Raphaelite movement became enamoured of all things medieval — especially the tales of Arthur and his knights. They produced some unforgettable pictures of famous episodes and characters from the romances, many of which began to be translated for the first time into English. Morris himself produced one of the finest editions of Malory, with decorations by Burne-Jones. And Alfred, Lord Tennyson, Poet Laureate and the voice of Victorian England, chose for his greatest work the subject of Arthur. His *Idylls of the King* outsold every other volume of poetry ever written and spawned hundreds of imitators.[74] Tennyson's Arthur was very much a Victorian gentleman who just happened to be dressed in armour rather than a top-hat and frock coat, but he captured the imagination of thousands of people.

Since then, the avalanche has grown to be almost overwhelming, with countless novels, stories, plays, poems and films about Arthur. Writers as varied as John Masefield, T.S. Eliot, John Steinbeck and G.K. Chesterton have taken up the themes; while film directors like John Boorman (*Excalibur*) and Marcel Bresson (*Lancelot du Lac*) have added a significant dimension to the written word.

More recently, there has been a swing towards historical Arthurian fiction, with some brilliant novels by Rosemary Sutcliff,[72] Henry Treece,[76] Mary Stewart[64,65,66] and Marion Zimmer Bradley,[2] bringing the stories firmly into the twentieth century with new and radical interpretations.

In all this welter of material, what is it that has kept the stories fresh and alive and given them an ever-new relevance for successive generations? Of course, they are magnificent stories in their own right; exciting, colourful and full of rich and wonderful characters. But more than this, it is the underlying archetypal quality of these stories which unites the material and causes it to speak directly to us. It is this unity and quality of timeless myth which has enabled the creation of the *Hallowquest* pack, in which two powerful sets of images, Celtic and medieval, each of which in its own way tells a story able to resonate at the deepest level of the human psyche, are brought together. The Arthurian courts, with their elaborate levels of human adventure and inner quests, are the perfect setting for a magical system. Here are characters who represent an entire spectrum of the human condition — love and hatred, strength and weakness, noble aims and deep defects — the elements in fact with which the characters of the Tarot are themselves imbued.

Arthur is the central pivot about which the court revolves. In the pack he is the Emperor, and the courtiers — King, Knight, Magician, Priestess, Hermit and Fool — turn about him in an endless dance of creation.

To work with the Tarot one must first be completely familiar and at ease with the characters and images featured on each card. One must know the Fool (The Seeker, in the *Hallowquest*) the Hermit (the Grail Hermit), the Magician (Merlin) and the Empress (Guinevere) before one can begin to understand the complex relationship which exists between them, and from which the meanings and derivations of the cards arise. In the same way, to work properly with this pack it is necessary to get to know the characters of the Arthurian mythos as well. This means, ultimately, reading as much as possible about them and meditating on the meanings of the cards. Nothing else can really replace this — the most we can do here is provide a breakdown of the central episodes within the Arthurian cycle first in their medieval and then in their Celtic forms, before assessing the archetypal amalgamations of these two overlapping patterns.

THE MEDIEVAL ARTHUR

Beginning then, with the later, more familiar stories, the following are the basic elements, extracted from many texts and placed in a chronology which is implicit within the Arthurian mythos.

1. The Coming of Merlin

Vortigern, fleeing from the Saxons and the British, tries to build a tower in the mountains. But it will not remain standing, and his Druids advise him to find a fatherless child and sacrifice it. Merlin is discovered and brought to Vortigern. He reveals the presence of two dragons, one red and the other white, whose perpetual combat shakes the foundations every night. He then prophesies Vortigern's imminent death, the coming of Arthur and much more. All comes to pass as he has predicted.[8,53]

2. The Magical Conception and Birth of Arthur

Merlin arranges the conception of Arthur by giving Uther Pendragon the semblance of Gorlois of Cornwall so that Uther may lie with Gorlois' wife, Igraine. Meanwhile, Gorlois is slain in battle and Uther becomes king of Britain. When a child is born to Igraine, Merlin claims him to bring him up in secrecy and safety. He names the boy Arthur.[8,31]

3. The Ascension of Arthur to the Throne of Britain

At 15, Arthur comes to London to take part in a tournament. In the churchyard of St Paul's, a stone with an anvil stuck into it appears. Only the rightful king of Britain can pull it out and claim the land, Uther now being dead. By accident, Arthur pulls out the sword and after Merlin has revealed his identity, he is made king of Britain. Soon after, he is gifted with the sacred sword, Excalibur, given to him by the Lady of the Lake.[31]

4. The Coming of Guinevere
At his coronation, Arthur encounters Morgause, his half-sister, with whom he lies in ignorance of her identity. She will later give birth to Mordred, who will be Arthur's nemesis. Meanwhile, Arthur meets Guinevere, the daugher of Leodogrance, and the two are married.

5. The Establishment of the Round Table
At Merlin's instigation, Arthur founds the Fellowship of the Round Table, where knights may come from all over the land and be equal. There are 150 seats and the name of each knight appears magically written in letters of gold when they take their places at the Table.[31]

6. The Dolorous Blow and the Coming of the Wasteland
Balin, a wild knight of the Round Table, finds shelter at the castle of King Pelles. There he slays the king's brother, Garlon, who is able to assume invisibility, striking down other men unfairly. Pelles chases Balin through the castle until they reach a room wherein the Grail and Spear are kept. The Grail is the cup used by Christ at the Last Supper; the Spear is that which pierced his side on the cross. Balin seizes the Spear and strikes Pelles in the thigh, making him impotent. The castle falls in ruins and the land on all sides is made waste.[31]

7. The Coming of Lancelot
Lancelot, who was fostered by the Lady of the Lake, comes to Camelot and takes his place at the Round Table. He soon proves himself unbeatable and stronger than any other knight there. He is given the task of guarding the queen, and soon after falls in love with Guinevere. She returns his love and they begin an affair.[31,80]

8. The Cleansing of Britain
Arthur sends out the knights of the Round Table to cleanse the land of evil and injustice. They are sworn to help and protect women, children and those in distress.

9. The Roman Wars
Arthur receives a demand for tribute from the Emperor of Rome. He refuses and so begin the Roman Wars, in which Arthur carries the battle into Gaul and finally close to Rome itself. There he defeats the Emperor and is crowned as lord over Europe and the East. Lancelot comports himself with particular valour and is recognized as the greatest knight in the world. Arthur divides the empire between his faithful followers and returns to Britain.[8,31]

10. The Departure of Merlin
Merlin meets Nimuë in the Forest of Brocéliande and is besotted with her. Though she is probably a nymph of the wood and well-versed in spellcraft, she persuades Merlin to teach her his magic, including a spell which will give her power over him. She then entombs him beneath a great rock for all time. He is overheard lamenting by Gawain who rides past the stone and takes word of what has happened to Arthur.[31,19]

11. The Coming of the Grail
While the Round Table Fellowship meet at Camelot one Pentecost, they see a vision of the Holy Grail which floats through the hall and out again. Gawain swears to seek it to the ends of the earth and the rest of the Fellowship follow suit.[36,31]

12. The Coming of Galahad
Before the Quest can begin, a strange youth is brought in, dressed in red armour. He successfully pulls a sword from a block of red marble found floating in the river and is announced by a hermit as Galahad, the son of Lancelot. He is the son of Lancelot and Elaine le Blanc. She it was whom he had rescued from a bath of boiling water and after lay with her under enchantment in which he thought she was Guinevere.[31,36]

13. The Quest for the Grail
The Quest now begins and for many years the knights wander the length and breadth of the land. They encounter many strange and wondrous adventures and meet many wise hermits in the forest who tell them the significance of what they have seen. Lancelot comes close to achieving the Grail, but is turned away because of his love for Guinevere. Gawain also nearly succeeds but in the end is too worldly to be successful. The three knights who do penetrate the final mysteries are Galahad, Perceval, known as the 'Perfect Fool', and Bors, the worldly but gentle-hearted knight. These three reach the holy city of Sarras and witness the mysteries of the Grail. The Wasteland is then healed, Galahad dies, Perceval becomes the new Grail guardian, and Bors alone returns to Camelot to tell of the events.[31,36]

14. The Trial of Guinevere
The long Quest has weakened the Round Table and many have died. New blood joins the Fellowship, including Arthur's bastard son, Mordred, the product of his brief amour with his half-sister, Morgause. Evil stalks the land and suspicion, fostered by Mordred, points to Lancelot and Guinevere. Discovered in her chamber, Lancelot escapes while the queen is arraigned for treason and sentenced to be burned at the stake. Lancelot rescues her, but in the fighting accidentally kills Gawain's two younger brothers, Gareth and Gaheris, making Gawain his most bitter opponent.[31]

15. The Wars Against Lancelot
Arthur is forced by Gawain to declare war on Lancelot and, leaving Mordred in charge of the kingdom, crosses to France to besiege him in his castle of Joyous Garde. Gawain and Lancelot fight against each other in several single combats, and Gawain receives a near-fatal wound. Then word comes of Mordred's treachery. He has declared Arthur dead, and made himself king, holding Guinevere prisoner in the Tower of London.[31]

16. The Fall of the Round Table
Arthur hurries back to Britain and wages war against his son. Mordred calls a truce but an adder stings one of Arthur's knights in the foot and the flash of his blade as he kills it is the signal for battle. At the end, all the knights are killed save a handful, among whom are Arthur and Mordred. In a final struggle, Arthur kills Mordred but is himself seriously wounded.[31]

17. The Departure of Arthur
Carried from the field of conflict by Bedivere and Lucan, Arthur bids Bedivere throw Excalibur, his mighty and magical sword, back into the lake from whence it came. After three hesitations, Bedivere does so and a hand catches it, drawing it beneath the waters. When Bedivere returns, he finds that Arthur is gone. Then he sees the king laid on a barge with three veiled and queenly women escorting him. Arthur says that he is going to Avalon to be healed, but that he will return when he is needed. The barge vanishes into the twilight and Bedivere is left alone.[31]

18. The Deaths of Lancelot and Guinevere
The last of the Round Table Fellowship depart to the four corners of the world, some to the Holy Land, some to remote hermit cells in the hills. Lancelot becomes a hermit and Guinevere a nun, but they meet once more before the queen dies. Lancelot soon follows her and they are buried in adjacent graves. With them dies the last of the Arthurian world, but it is still remembered in the land that Arthur will come again.

Within these 18 divisions is contained the whole great symphony of the Arthurian cycle in its medieval form. It has all the shapeliness of a great musical work, and of the purest kind of myth. The Birth, Adventures, Quest and Mysterious Departure of the Hero is recognized in mythologies the world over; if we did not already know that Arthur was an archetypal figure, this alone would inform us of the fact.

THE CELTIC ARTHUR

The archetypal coherence of the Arthurian legend is more apparent in the sub-strata of ancient material which lies behind and beneath the familiar medieval tales. Much of this is Celtic in style and content, and displays a mythic dimension of the highest order. Beneath the shape of the cycle outlined above, is another structure in which elements of the later versions are prefigured. Sometimes the stories have remained virtually unchanged (like the early adventures of Merlin, which still retain their Celtic resonances) while others (such as the story of Lancelot and Guinevere) are shown to have a totally different purpose. This other structure may be outlined as follows.

The headings marked with * indicate where the medieval and Celtic stories overlap, and these passages have not been repeated.

* 1. *The Coming of Merlin*

* 2. *The Magical Conception and Birth of Arthur*

3. *The Wasting of the Land*

There are, in certain places in Britain, sacred wells, and these are guarded by the Damsels of the Wells, who offer hospitality and succour to all travellers. A king named Amangons rapes one of the damsels and carries off her golden cup. His men rape the other damsels and the land becomes barren. In subsequent years, the warriors of Arthur swear vengeance on the kindred of Amangons and seek to find the Court of Joy where the Rich Fisherman and the Grail are hidden.[41]

4. *The Calling of the Companions*

Arthur is brought to the place of king-making by Merlin, who also calls all the greatest warriors to the Island of the Mighty to come and serve the new king. With them, Arthur rids the land of a great serpent and is made Pendragon of all Britain.[78]

5. *Arthur's Marriage to the Land*

Arthur meets Gwenhwyfar, daughter of the giant Ogfran Fawr, and weds her. She is the representative of Sovereignty, the Goddess of the Land, and in marrying her Arthur is also becoming espoused to the land itself.[41]

6. *The Quest for the White Hart*

At the first hosting of the Companions of Arthur, a White Hart enters the feasting hall and several of the knights go in search of it. This is the first test of Arthur's men, and they are successful, though their adventures are fearful. The Hart is another of Sovereignty's disguises and its capture seals the right of Arthur to be King of the Land.[30,41,31,36]

7. *The Departure of Merlin*

Merlin, having grown tired of watching over the kingdom and its king, departs to the Island of Bardsey, where he builds an observatory with

70 windows from which he watches the stars in their courses and prophesies many of the future events of the world.[9,78]

8. The Voyage to Annwn

Arthur and his heroes make a raid upon the Otherworld kingdom of Annwn to steal the Cauldron from its master, Pen Annwn. They sail in Arthur's ship, Prydwen, and Taliesin accompanies them. He makes a song of the voyage in which the refrain, 'Except seven, none return' is repeated. The quest was a Pyrrhic victory, for though the cauldron was achieved, only seven returned to rejoice in its Otherworldly powers.[9,44]

9. The Rape of the Flower Bride

In retaliation for this theft, Pen Annwn persuades Melwas to carry off Arthur's queen, but she is subsequently rescued by her lord. This role of abductor is one which Medrawt (Mordred) may well have shared.[78,41,24,82]

10. The Breaking of the Fellowship

Medrawt returns with an army of Saxon mercenaries and there is a great and terrible battle in which most of the companions are slain, and Arthur himself gravely wounded, though he does succeed in killing Medrawt.[8,78]

11. The Departure of Arthur for Avalon

Feeling his death coming upon him, Arthur is borne by Merlin and Taliesin to the island of Avalon, where the Goddess Morgan and her nine sisters rule. He remains with them to be healed until the day when he shall be restored to fight for Britain's need once more.[9,41]

Parts of this Celtic cycle are speculative, drawn together from fragmentary stories and traditions, yet we have drawn consistently on the earliest traditions relating to Arthur. The Celtic scholar, Jean Markale, in his book *King Arthur, King of Kings*,[34] suggests an alternative schema and puts forward his own theoretical reconstruction of the saga of Arthur. Our own tentative version is provided solely to show the way in which the seeds of the later cycle were always present, perhaps soon after the time of Arthur's Avalonian departure.

In this we see the earlier sub-strata laid bare. Gone are the medieval trappings; what remains is a mythical structure from which the humanizing elements have been purged. Arthur is still a mortal man, as are most of his followers. Their roles, however, are archetypal, adhering closely to patterns laid down in the distant past.

Of Merlin it is hardly necessary to speak, since he so clearly embodies all the characteristics of the Wizard and Wise Man, the shamanic figure who stands behind the king and advises him at the beginning of his career. Even Merlin's own strange fate, imprisoned in a cave or magical bush through the love of an Otherworldly woman, is part of the pattern. It is the destiny of the Otherworldly mage to return to the Inner Realms, and this is most often achieved through the agency of a faery woman. Arthur himself is taken to Avalon by Morgan le Fay and Merlin by Minuë, she whose father is a votary of the Goddess Diana.[19]

This earlier pattern is also retained by the figure of Gawain who began life as a knight of the Goddess and ends it as a boorish, wenching braggart, who has strayed from his archetypal role. Even Lancelot, a latecomer from the literary stable of Chrétien de Troyes, retains certain features of an earlier personality. He is fostered by the Lady of the Lake, trained in secret to become the greatest hero of the Arthurian court, discovers his secret name (he was called Galahad at birth, but this was changed by the Lady of the Lake who foresaw the coming of his son), and achieves success and status at Camelot. But he is flawed, allowing his love of Guinevere to overwhelm him. Madness follows, and the birth of a son who will supersede him.

Theirs is one of the great stories of human passion, aspiration and glorious failure in which the mythical structure has been overlaid by literary accretions. Thus, with much of the medieval Arthuriad, we have to look beneath the surface of courtly romance for the older elements which are still there, only a little way beneath the surface.

The story of *Gawain and the Green Knight*, for instance, has come down to us in its most famous guise as a poem written in the thirteenth century, but its antecedents are demonstrably earlier, stemming from the same sources as that of the Cuchullain story.[22, 51]

We read of Gawain's challenger, the Green Knight, with whom he enters into the Beheading Game. In this story, Gawain is restored to early tradition as Arthur's champion, and the champion of Sovereignty. In the primitive story, the king would rule for a year, at the end of which time another champion would come forward to repeat the Beheading Game challenge until the next successor took the throne.

Behind the many levels of the Green Knight story stands the Goddess, Morgan, who, as Morgan le Fay, is Arthur's most bitter opponent in the later medieval cycle. It is she, as a disguised aspect of the Goddess of Sovereignty, who turns the wheel of the succession which, like the wheel of the seasonal round, has its phases.[41]

At the core of the Celtic cycle is the quest for the sovereignty of the land, which is sought by many challengers. In *Perlesvaus*, we read of the death of a king. It is the custom of that country for a perpetual fire to be kept burning until such time as a new king shall be crowned. In this instance, the crown is offered to Lancelot.[3] The annual kingship theme recurs so often in the Arthurian legends that it is clearly central to the original cycle.

It is almost certain that it was once Arthur himself who undertook the challenge of the sovereignty quest, but instead of relinquishing his position after a year, he sent out other champions in his stead, so that he remained the uncontested king. This explains why much of the medieval cycle is concerned with the demise of the Round Table Fellowship.

It also clarifies much that is unclear in the later cycles where it is evident that Arthur himself once took the role of the Wounded King, rather than his surrogate, King Pelles, who suffers the Dolorous Blow and receives a wound that will only heal when the Grail is achieved. This is all part of the broadening of the original story to accommodate additions made to the original Hallowquest in the later romances.

The emphasis has shifted away from the four Hallows which were the foundation of the Island of the Mighty (Britain), towards the Grail in its Christian form. This has helped conceal the original shape of the Quest, which we must recognize in order that the references in the *Hallowquest* are fully understood. For in choosing to portray certain characters and events on the cards, we have always been mindful of the deeper resonances which establish Arthur and his kindred as every bit as archetypal as the original characters of the Tarot.

As well as the two basic patterns already outlined, we are able to propose a third cycle, closest in its terms of reference to the earlier, Celtic pattern, but keeping in mind also certain of the aspects of the medieval cycle, which have added important factors to our understanding of the whole. For it is important to remember that we are not dealing with frozen tradition. The Arthurian mysteries are still very much with us, still growing and changing; nor are the recent and contemporary developments less valid than those set out in the Middle Ages or earlier.

A more detailed exposition of the meanings of each card will be found in Chapter 3. What follows here is simply a listing of the archetypal myth-structure, derived from both the Celtic and medieval cycles which have gone into the creation of the *Hallowquest* and which take into account the magical dimension found therein.

The Titles of the Cycle	*Tarot Card No:*
1. The Coming of the Perfect Fool	0
2. The Acts of Merlin	I
3. The Lady of the Lake	II
4. The Coming of Guinevere	III
5. The Acts of Arthur	IV
6. The Song of Taliesin	V
7. The Quest for the White Hart	VI
8. The Voyage to Annwn	VII
9. The Coming of Gawain	VIII
10. The Voice of the Grail	IX
11. The Round Table Fellowship	X
12. The Encounter with Sovereignty	XI
13. The Dolorous Blow	XII

The Titles of the Cycle	*Tarot Card No:*
14. The Washer at the Ford	XIII
15. The Power of the Cauldron	XIV
16. The Beheading Game	XV
17. The Ascent of the Spiral Tower	XVI
18. The Vision of the Kingdom	XVII
19. The Salmon of Wisdom	XVIII
20. The Child of Morning	XIX
21. The Sleeping Lord	XX
22. The Flowering of Logres	XXI

Fig: 2:1: The Matter of Britain in the Greater Powers

This schema, which follows the natural sequence of the cards, ascribes a new set of titles to the 22 Greater Powers and gives a glimpse into both the Celtic and medieval realms of Arthur, allowing, in their merging, a completely new cycle to appear. Many of the episodes appear to be out of sequence, but when they are meditated upon this proves not to be the case. They have a cyclicity of their own. This can be experienced for yourself in Chapter 8, in the Seeker's Journey meditation. (p.201.)

THE MYTHIC ARTHUR

More important than either the Celtic or the medieval figures of Arthur is the mythic Arthur. It is he and his cycle of followers who are activated by the inner resonances of the *Hallowquest*.

There is little doubt that Arthur was once a god. Native to these islands he may, as previous writers have suggested, have been a bear god, named Artos, of whose cult fragmentary remains have been cited in both Britain and Scotland. Nineteenth-century writers saw him as a type of solar king, and there is a certain residual quality of this still to be found in, for example, his splendour and guardianship of the Treasures of Britain. For whether we view him as a Celtic chieftain, a Romano-British general or a medieval king, there is, beneath all of these, another figure who was guardian of both the land, to which he was mystically married in its form of Sovereignty, and of the Hallows.

Although he is seen as leading, or as sending forth his representatives to seek the holy objects, there is little doubt that he once held them as rightful Lord of the Land: they are his regalia. The later development comes from a split which occurred some time before the written texts, when the Court of the Hallows, a place sought for by all, became the goal of its one-time protectors.

In the earlier, Celtic texts, the mythic figure of Arthur is more clearly defined. He still plays an active role, rather than a passive one, as in the tale of *Culhwch and Olwen* from the *Mabinogion*, where Arthur and his warriors are listed in a fantastic catalogue of more than 200 names. They assist the young Culhwch in the search for his bride, Olwen, the daughter of the giant, Yspaddaden Pencawr. In the process, a whole constellation of stories were brought in. Arthur leads his warriors in the hunt for the giant boar, Trwch Trwyth, helps rescue the divine child, Mabon, and defeats the nine hags of Gloucester — all described in graphic and often bloodthirsty detail which seems a far cry from the courtly epics of the Middle Ages.

However, it is these stories and others from the chronicles tradition, and the ancient Welsh texts, like *The Four Ancient Books of Wales* or *The Welsh Triads (Trioedd Ynys Prydein)*, which inform and underpin the later stories.[59,78]

Here we read of Arthur's stealing of the sacred pigs belonging to King March (later known as the ill-starred husband in the Tristan and Isolt triangle). Arthur also appears as the leader of a fantastic guerrilla band of semi-immortal heroes in a raid on the Otherworld, already mentioned.

This is all a long way from the ideas of the medieval Arthur, the Once and Future King, with his shining court. Yet even here echoes of his godlike status remain. His mysterious birth, engineered by Merlin, and his equally mysterious departing, bracket a life paved with the signs and symbols of the mythic hero. He is possessed of magical weapons; he has a mantle, ship and chair of magical properties; he is aided by the greatest magician and mystagogue of the age; he cannot die, but must join the ranks of those who sleep beneath the Hollow Hills until recalled to their country's need.

Even in the stars, traditionally the home of the gods and goddesses, there is Telyn Idris or the Harp of Arthur (Lyra) and Arthur's Wain (the Plough or Great Bear). Druidic tradition has named a season of the year — from the Winter Solstice to the Vernal Equinox — Alban Arthan or Arthur's Season, from which we may judge for ourselves the reverence in which he was held.

It is this Arthur, rather than the purely Celtic or medieval figure, who informs the *Hallowquest*. For here is an archetypal figure of immense proportions, capable of containing a whole mythos. Small wonder that the great mythographer, William Blake, said of him that, 'the stories of Arthur are the acts of Albion,' clearly pointing to the way in which the figure of the hero looms large in the mythical history of these lands.

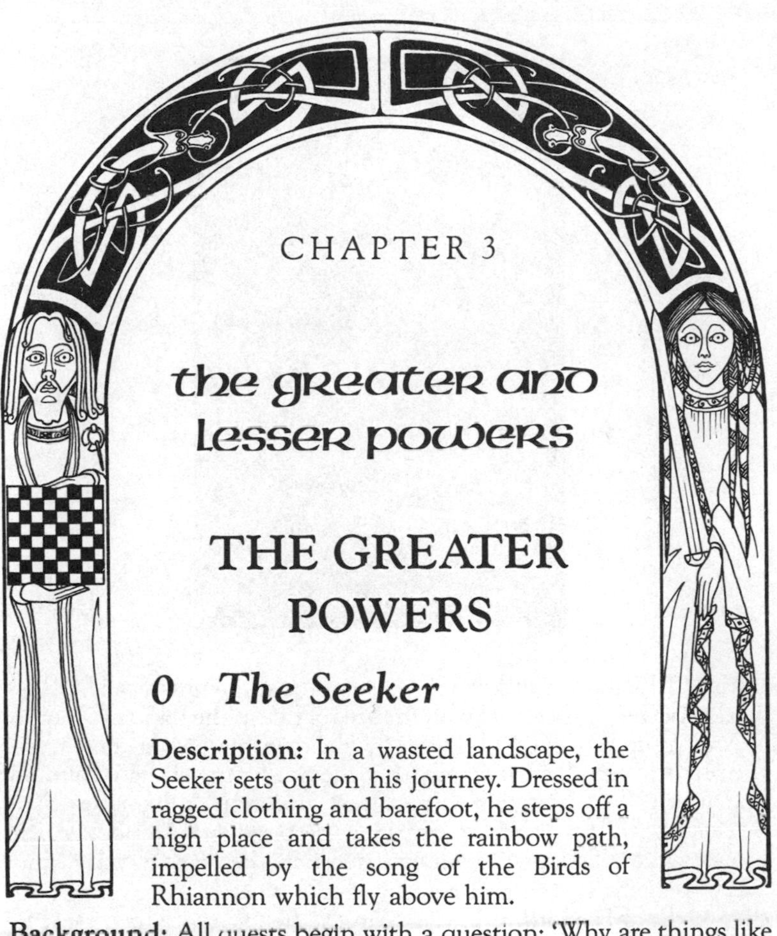

CHAPTER 3

the greater and lesser powers

THE GREATER POWERS

0 *The Seeker*

Description: In a wasted landscape, the Seeker sets out on his journey. Dressed in ragged clothing and barefoot, he steps off a high place and takes the rainbow path, impelled by the song of the Birds of Rhiannon which fly above him.

Background: All quests begin with a question: 'Why are things like this?' This is a variation on the famous Grail question: 'Whom does the Grail serve?' This inquisitiveness is the hallmark of the Seeker, who is not content to let imbalances remain unchallenged. The Hallow seeker is impelled by a deep urgency to know and experience: to find the world's healing and to seek for a personal direction. This path is both journey and goal.

Potentially, every Seeker is the Grail winner — a role which is open to women and men alike. The legends tell of Peredur or Perceval whose desire for experience of the world leads him into becoming one of Arthur's knights and eventually in his being the 'One Who Frees the Waters', as the Grail winner is known. Yet he starts as the Perfect Fool, the one whose divine unwisdom uncouples the chains of time and space.[58,30]

The Seeker's steps upon the quest are directed by his communion with the Otherworldly messengers whose song sounds in his ears. The

Birds of Rhiannon betoken joy, sorrow, and awareness of the Otherworld, for they sing eternally on the Tree of Life in the Land of Promise.

And yet to gain the Otherworldly Hallows, the Seeker must travel the physical world, for it is only that the Seeker travels light, humbly and in a guise which will attract least attention to his quest. The Seeker, like the Fool and the poorman, despised and overlooked, can go everywhere. So it is with our own quest. It is better to travel without everywhere. So it is with our own quest. It is better to travel without the weight of fixed ideas; only so can the free flow of our destiny be unwound. Those who explore the inner worlds cannot retain their preconceived ideas of themselves: dignity and self-esteem must be left at home, for this is a journey which will change us.

The Seeker can ask questions and weigh answers, free to juxtapose whatever ideas come his or her way. And this is the rainbow path, the way of experience upon which the Seeker learns how to heal what is broken, balance what is imbalanced, align what is out of alignment.

Archetypal Meaning: The Seeker represents all who go on a spiritual quest as well as those who seek for the healing of the Wasteland. He is the wise fool who embarks on his quest without a thought for the consequences or those left behind, for this inner journey can only be undertaken singly. His wisdom is to unconsciously follow the path to the Grail and the healing of Logres.

Divinatory Meaning: Childlike trust; divine discontent; carefree enthusiasm; protection; the folly to be wise; optimism; adventure;

spontaneity; youthful energy; longing to find one's heart's desire.

I Merlin

Description: Merlin stands before a stone table on which is laid a map of Britain. The four Hallows, the Sword, the Spear, the Grail and the Stone Chessboard lie upon it. Above his head a red and white dragon intertwine. To his right is the dark, crumbling tower of Vortigern; while to his left is his Otherworldly dwelling with many doors and windows.

Background: The early life of Merlin is often forgotten, but it is of prime importance for understanding his role in the Arthurian cycle. Merlin was born of an earthly mother and an Otherwordly father, thus establishing him as a prime mover and mediator between the two realities of this world and the Otherworld.[70]

In early legend he is called Myrddin Emrys.[53] As a child he was brought before Vortigern, the unworthy King of Britain. Vortigern had attempted to build a tower in which he might take refuge from his enraged subjects, but it fell down three times. His magicians said that it would remain standing only if the blood of a child who had no father was sprinkled on the foundations. But Merlin confounded the magicians and showed that the cause of the tower's collapse was because of the two dragons which warred continuously beneath it. The red one signified the Britons and the white one the Saxons whom Vortigern had settled in Britain.[9]

According to Geoffrey of Monmouth, Merlin prepares the way for the Pendragons, for Arthur and his father, Uther,[8] and although later texts speak of Merlin's imprisonment at the hands of Nimuë or Vivienne, who is said to have enticed him into revealing his magic through love of her, a closer investigation of the earlier texts reveals that Merlin's retirement is a voluntary one. His sister, Gwendydd or Ganieda, builds for him an observatory having 70 doors and windows, from which he may view the heavens.[70] This legend is closely associated with an oral tradition concerning Merlin's guardianship of Britain which is called *Clas Myrddin* or Merlin's Enclosure. Further legend credits Merlin with retiring to Bardsey Island, to a Glass House, in which he keeps the 13 treasures of Britain.[78]

Archetypal Meaning: Merlin is the inner herald of dreams, relaying the messages of the Otherworld in symbolic form. He is also prophet and seer. He enables the manifestation of events which lie in embryo through his mastery over the four elements, although he does not manipulate events. His real magic lies in his balanced mediation of inner and outer worlds.

Divinatory Meaning: The impulse of creation; imaginative insight; mastery through disciplined skill; initiative; self-confidence; perception on all levels; alignment to and free flow with one's life patterns.

II The Lady of the Lake

Description: On the middle of an island in the middle of a lake sits the Lady of the Lake on a throne of reeds. She holds a sword and a

book, while at her feet is a basket. Beside her is a crane.

Background: Throughout the Arthurian legends, Otherworldly women guide and instruct Arthur and his court. During the Middle Ages, these many aspects of the Goddess splintered into numerous maidens, wronged ladies and widows. If we return to the earlier texts we find that rather than a bevy of damsels who need knightly assistance to gain their rights, certain powerful women of great stature appear at crucial times to aid and assist the knights.

The Lady of the Lake stems from a very circuitous lineage of such women, chief of whom is Morgen or Morgan, described as the daughter of *Rex Avallonis* or the king of Avalon, as the sister of Arthur, or as queen of a ninefold sisterhood in her own right.[19,41] It is she who tends Arthur's wounds after the Battle of Camlan and in whose charge he remains, in Otherworldly time, until he is called again.

But the role of healer is not the only one which the Lady of the Lake fulfils. She is also fosterer and initiator into knowledge. Traditionally among the Celtic races, women warriors trained boys in the arts of combat. In all the earlier stories about the Grail winner or champion of the Hallows, the boy is fostered in the Otherworld. Fosterage was a custom prevalent among the Celts, stabilizing the tribe and establishing bonds of love and mutual obligation.

The unknown boyhood of Arthur, which the later texts say was spent in the care of Sir Ector of the Forest Sauvage, may indeed have been with the Lady of the Lake in one of her guises in the lost stories of the oral tradition.[41] It is from her that he gains his sword, Excalibur, and to her island that he is later borne to be healed of his wounds.

Medieval French tradition tells of Lancelot's upbringing with the Lady of the Lake. She raises him in accordance to the code of the Otherworld, as well as in courtesy and combat. She both names and arms him in accordance with the principles of Celtic story wherein the hero has to earn his name by his deeds.[80]

Elements of the Lady of the Lake as fosterer are also apparent in the story of Taliesin. (See p.47.)

Archetypal Meaning: The Lady of the Lake is the primal initiator into Otherworldly knowledge. She is foster-mother, mistress of wisdom and inspirer. She empowers the seeker after truth, and acts as the conscience of the initiate. She may appear in many forms to admonish, guide and instruct. She is the guardian of inner wisdom.

Divinatory Meaning: Esoteric knowledge; enlightenment; inspiration; wisdom; the ability to impart instruction; counsel; psychic healing; learning.

III Guinevere

Description: Guinevere sits spinning in a meadow. A white cow grazes nearby.

Background: Guinevere seems to exist in most people's minds as the faithless wife of Arthur whose guilty love of Lancelot caused the downfall of the Round Table. Such a picture is not consistent with the early figure of Guinevere who, as Gwenhwyfar, is described as 'one of the three, gentle, gold-torqued ladies of Britain',[78] whose integrity upholds the honour of Arthur's court and whose beauty reflects the fertile face of the land.

The accusations of infidelity levelled against Guinevere are without foundation in the early traditions which certainly speak of her abduction by a series of men, including Medrawt (Mordred) and Melwas.[24] It is not until Chrétien de Troyes' *Le Chevalier de la Charrette* in the late twelfth century that we find Lancelot in the role of rescuer, though not yet as the active lover of Guinevere.[4]

Putting the evidence together, we find that Guinevere aligns to an archetype identified as the Flower Bride — the Otherworldly woman, often a representative of the Goddess of Sovereignty — who becomes the consort of a king. Her role is to manifest, in her own person, the harmony between king and land. But if she is not matched on every level by a reciprocal love from her consort then she looks for a champion to challenge the king and remind him of his duties towards his queen and the land which she represents.

She is indeed championed by many knights, including the Grail winner, Peredur (Perceval), and Gereint; they both avenge Guinevere in separate incidents when she is insulted by an unnamed knight, who is possibly of Otherworldly provenance.

Perhaps the clearest key to her original role is found in the Triad which describes her as the Triple Gwenhwyfar — as three women, each of whom was supposed to be the spouse of Arthur. Celtic tradition has a strongly developed sense of triplicity which extends to the aspects of a particular archetype or deity. Guinevere, as the Flower Bride, along with the Lady of the Lake as the foster-mother, and the Washer at the Ford as the Cailleach or hag, make up the composite manifestation of the Goddess of Sovereignty in the Arthurian world.[41]

Archetypal Meaning: Guinevere as the Empress of Logres (the inner Britain) creates the conditions for growth, establishing peace and contentment. She spins a thread of inner concord which is woven into the fabric of the land and its people. She imparts sensitivity to nature and harmonious awareness to all life.

Divinatory Meaning: Energy in creative growth; material and spiritual health; fulfilment; beauty; abundance; fertility; motherhood; health; harmony.

IV Arthur

Description: Arthur sits in a stone chair on a mountain-top. The draco standard flies behind him and Excalibur lies across his knees. A Cornish chough perches near the throne.

Background: The figure of Arthur is a complex one made of many strata of tradition. Most people are familiar with Arthur the medieval king and champion of Christendom, but behind this there lie other, equally valid personas: Dark Age battle lord, Romano-British chieftain or Celtic god-hero. The Arthur of the *Hallowquest* pack is a mixture of all three of these designations.

The primary feature of Arthur's role is his guardianship and defence of the land, which takes us into the realm of mythic reality where the historical sixth-century battle leader is subsumed in a welter of divine and heroic traditions. As William Blake wrote, 'The stories of Arthur are the acts of Albion'. This perhaps explains the curious rippling out of the legends surrounding him, for around Arthur constellate the Greater Powers of the Arthurian world. From being a lone heroic figure he gathers about him an actual as well as a withdrawn court, in which knights, ladies, heroes, gods and goddesses are numbered.

This great panoply of archetypes is not immediately apparent from a cursory reading of medieval Arthurian romances whose complex enlacements cross and recross the original tradition confusingly. In the later romances, Arthur is a figurehead, based squarely upon the model of Christian kingship; he no longer engages in adventures in his own right — these are performed by the knights of his court. He is represented by numerous champions, chief of which is Gawain. Turning to the earlier stories, we find that Arthur leads his army into the underworld of Annwn; he rescues Gwenhwyfar (Guinevere) from her faery abductor; he encounters the Goddess of Sovereignty and takes the empowerment of the Hallows.[41] He is an active, initiating leader whose care is for his people and the land.

The divine or heroic elements within his role are amplified by tradition. Whenever he attempts to depart from his kingly responsibilities within the legends, or to live a life of his own, he comes to grief. Where he fulfils the duties of a king, he is given the support and assistance of the Goddess of Sovereignty. She is his foster-mother who instructs him in wisdom, she brings him to the kingship, she provides him with a wife and eventually receives him to her again in the Isle of Avalon from whence prophecy says he will come again to defend the land once more.

Archetypal Meaning. Arthur is the Emperor of Logres, the Pendragon. He draws together the resources of his land and welds them into a kingdom full of strength and vitality. His creative energy is fuelled by close Otherworld contact through the mediation of Sovereignty (XI).

Divinatory Meaning: Leadership; authoritative energy; the wielding of power for the good of all; will-power; organization; courage; responsible love; fatherhood; dynamism.

V Taliesin

Description: Taliesin sits in a firelit hall. He tells the story of his initiatory transformations to two children who sit at his feet listening intently. The golden links of tradition pass from this hands into theirs.

Background: The legend of the transformations of Gwion Bach into the poet Taliesin is told in the *Hanes Taliesin*.[30] We read how Gwion was set to tend the magical cauldron of Ceridwen. This cauldron of inspiration was intended for the drinking of Afagddu, Ceridwen's son, who was so ill-favoured that his mother wished to compensate for his lack of natural beauty by the gift of wisdom. However, young Gwion's fingers were splashed with liquid from the cauldron and, to cool them, he thrust them into his mouth and so acquired the cauldron's wisdom for himself. Realizing his own danger through his new-won omniscience, Gwion transformed himself into a hare but Ceridwen pursued in the form of a hound; he changed into a fish and she into an otter; he changed into a bird and she into a hawk; lastly, he became a grain of wheat and she scrabbled him up into her crop as a hen. He was reborn of her womb nine months later as the infant Taliesin.[30]

This story is a parable of bardic initiation in which the young poet establishes his essential links with the Otherworld. By means of his totemic associations with the different birds, beasts and fish — each of whom represent a level of knowledge — the poet is able to participate simultaneously in every part of creation in an omniscient way. He knows what has happened in the deep past and what will happen in the times to come.

Although Taliesin is primary chief bard to Elphin in this legend, he is associated closely with Arthur in other texts. According to the ninth-century poem *Preiddeu Annwn*,[44] Taliesin accompanies Arthur on his quest to Annwn; while in Geoffrey of Monmouth's *Vita Merlini*,[9] Taliesin helps Merlin bear Arthur to Avalon to be healed by the Goddess, Morgen.

The greatest repository of lore is to be found within the writings which constitute *The Book of Taliesin*.[59] This takes the form of intricate, gnomic poetry packed with references to myth, legend and magic. The frequent list of 'I have beens . . .' in which the poet refers to events throughout history at which he was present, reflect a mystical understanding of creation seldom found elsewhere.

Taliesin is the guardian of tradition. By means of his insights he is able to impart wisdom by means of song and story so that the youngest child can hear and understand. It is by such means that the mythic impact of the Arthurian Powers has been transmitted to our own century, for the living links of tradition pass into our keeping. While there will always be special guardians, traditional lore is embodied by the people who tell and listen to the stories.

Those who seek earnestly and sincerely for wisdom will encounter Taliesin who, though his real dwelling place is the 'region of the summer stars', is nevertheless ready to aid the seeker and help him or her to contact the living wisdom of the Otherworld.

(Readers wishing to learn more should consult *Taliesin, the Shamanic Mysteries of Britain and Ireland* by John Matthews; Unwin Hyman, 1990.)

Archetypal Meaning: Taliesin is the guardian of tradition. By song and story, by prophecy and far memory, he can instruct and guide the seeker. His is an interpreter as well as a teacher, well able to represent images to the receptive mind and forge connections in the waiting heart.

Divinatory Meaning: Tradition; revelation; inspiration; insight; preservation of heritage; initiation; advice or counsel; transformation of the mundane into the spiritual.

VI The White Hart

Description: In a forest clearing we see Gereint out hunting transfixed at the sight of Enid, who sees the White Hart coming towards them.

Background: The lovers depicted here are Gereint and Enid. Their story appears in the *Mabinogion*[30] as well as in Chrétien de Troyes' *Erec and Enid*[4] Gereint is a knight of Arthur's court who seeks to avenge an insult done to Guinevere by Edern ap Nudd. He pursues Edern with neither arms nor armour, but is given these by Earl Yniwl, who has been dispossessed by Edern. The only way Gereint can avenge the

VI the white hart

insult to Guinevere is to fight Edern at the Sparrowhawk contest — a tournament in which a kestrel is awarded to the knight who successfully overcomes all challengers. The contest rules state that each combatant must fight for his lady's honour, and Gereint has no lady. He asks to champion Enid, Yniwl's daughter. He beats Edern, wins the sparrowhawk and wins Enid as his wife.

The hunting of the White Hart — a ritual hunt which is the preserve of the Pendragons only — takes place in Gereint's absence. Arthur himself captures the beast and cuts off its head; the custom is that the head should be awarded to the fairest lady, but Guinevere delays the disposal of the head until Gereint returns with Enid. Guinevere takes Enid under her protection and prepares her for marriage to Gereint. The head of the White Hart is then awarded to Enid.

The testing of Gereint and Enid's love in the ensuing story is very much as a result of the foregoing incident. The appearance of the White Hart in Celto-Arthurian literature usually heralds a change in the order of things, for it is a messenger of the Goddess of Sovereignty whose Otherworldly influence leads the lovers in this story into further testing and many severe trials of their affection.

Gereint's rather superficial affection for Enid is deepened, while her unworldly idealism is assimilated into a more practical manifestation of love. The White Hart represents the call of the Otherworld to compassion and commitment to the spiritual quest. The attainment of its head is a royal or initiatic task which only king, champion or lover can undertake.

For a fuller breakdown of this story see *Arthur and the Sovereignty of Britain.*[41]

Archetypal Meaning: The White Hart is the Otherworldly messenger into spiritual adventure and the purity of love. Those who hunt it are drawn deeper into themselves and made aware of the pure power of love to overcome all obstacles. It also represents the silver chain of sexual desire which is between men and women, but it also enhances that desire into love that is strong as death.

Divinatory Meaning: Love, both sexual and spiritual; the vision of inner beauty; emotional ties; trust; the marriage of minds and hearts; platonic friendship; fulfilment of desire.

VII Prydwen

Description: Arthur's ship, Prydwen, sails into the entrance of the Underworld, Annwn. From the mast-head flies the White Boar standard.

Background: One of the earliest British poems, *Preiddeu Annwn*[29] or *The Spoils of Annwn* tells of Arthur's journey to the Underworld to win the Hallows of Britain, specifically the cauldron of Pen Annwn. He sails on his ship, Prydwen, with three companies of men. The poem tells of the arduous journey in which they pass the seven caers or towers of the Underworld, taking with them the cauldron of plenty. It relates the releasing of the youth who is held prisoner there, who is a type of Mabon, the divine youth of Celto-Arthurian legend. (See p.69.) Prydwen returns to Britain, but only seven of Arthur's company return to speak of their adventures.

This refrain 'except seven, none return,' is a feature of another exploit to do with a cauldron in which the legendary Bran the Blessed goes to Ireland to rescue his sister, Branwen, from ill-treatment at the hands of her husband, Matholwch, the Irish king. In the ensuing battle, the Irish reanimate their dead warriors in the miraculous cauldron of rebirth; they out-number the British so badly that only seven return from that adventure. Legend says that Taliesin was one of each of the two companies of seven.[30]

This almost forgotten incident in Arthur's career once formed part of a greater cycle of stories in which Arthur was the prime hero; the voyage in Prydwen is Arthur's *immram* or Otherworldly journey, comparable with the Irish *immrama* of Maelduine and Bran mac Febal.[16] The raid on Annwn is closely associated with another story in which Arthur pursues the giant boar Twrch Trwyth, between whose ears are certain Otherworldly treasures. In this story he also voyages on Prydwen, to Ireland — which we can see as analogous to the Underworld — and does battle with the boar in person, sustaining many grievous injuries as well as a considerable loss of men.[44]

The overlays between the voyage of Arthur and that of Bran suggest a closer mythical association. There is a Triad which tells how Bran's head was buried at the White Mount (the Tower of London) in order to act as a Palladium against invasion. The ravens which are kept at the present day Tower are a reminder of this (Bran means raven). But the Triad goes on to relate how Arthur, wishing to have no other defence but his own, disinterred the head. We perceive here a gleam of an earlier tradition in which Arthur's voyage to Annwn was to win the Treasures of Britain, the Hallows themselves, from the hands of Pen Annwn, the Lord of the Underworld — a role perhaps fulfilled by Bran himself.

Archetypal Meaning: Prydwen represents the Otherworldly journey which is undertaken by all seekers, so that the inner life becomes the basis for a sound outer life. In this card, faith in one's abilities and the true strength of one's determination are tested to the utmost. By the balancing of hard work with periods of contemplative insight, victory is gained.

Divinatory Meaning: Victory; self-confidence; self-discipline; the harnessing of abilities towards a great purpose; tests and trials; achievement; travel; determination; courage.

VIII Gawain

Description: Under the midday sun, Gawain stands armed, ready for combat, at a ford near a pass. Above him a hawk hovers.

Background: Gawain or Gwalchmai, as he appears in the earliest stories, is the prime champion of Arthur who is his uncle as well as his king. Later tradition robs Gawain of much of his courageous integrity, making him a boorish lout. However, earlier tradition establishes him as the most courteous knight of Arthur's court, one who is most involved with the championship of the land.[51]

This is evident from his close association with the Goddess, whose many representatives he encounters. Chief among these is Lady Ragnell who, in the medieval story of *Gawain and Ragnell*,[8] appears as the Loathly Lady whom Gawain has to marry in order to save Arthur from a terrible foe. (See p.165.) It is Gawain and not Arthur who in this story kisses the hideous representative of Sovereignty; Ragnell then assumes her real guise of a beautiful woman. Although we have only the medieval evidence of this story, we know from Irish parallels that the Goddess of Sovereignty's champions establish a pattern of behaviour which is emulated by Gawain.[51]

Gawain's championship of Arthur's kingdom may be interestingly envisioned in the light of Celtic kingship customs which established a *tanaiste* or likely successor during a king's lifetime. In this way, the tribe had a nominated successor in the event of the king's sudden death. The *tanaiste*'s duties entailed keeping a close eye on his future inheritance. As Arthur's nephew, Gawain has a double right to this role, since he is the son of Arthur's sister — she is called Morgause in the later texts, but the earlier ones call her Anna,[8] Gwyar[41] or Morcades.[51] The Celtic royal bloodline descended through the mother's side, since the royal woman of a clan was her tribe's sovereignty.

Gawain is perhaps best known for his exploits within the medieval story of *Sir Gawain and the Green Knight*,[18] in which he successfully combats the Green Knight in a contest which demands both physical strength and inner resourcefulness. (See p.63.) Traditionally, Gawain's strength increases up to midday when it starts to wane. This is perhaps reflected in his original name — Gwalchmai — or Hawk of May.

Archetypal Meaning: Gawain represents the balanced strength of the initiate who is both physically healthy and spiritually whole. In him the polarities of life are resolved and balanced: male and female, strength and compassion, severity and mercy. He is the knightly extension of Arthur (IV) himself, fulfilling the will of the King and loyal to the Goddess of Sovereignty in the land of Logres.

Divinatory Meaning: Self-discipline; enduring strength; balanced exercise of one's abilities; health of mind, body and spirit; moral certitude, without self-righteousness; courage to accept challenges; fortitude.

IX The Grail Hermit

Description: A forest clearing in which the Grail Hermit has his dwelling. He sits outside his bothy, writing in his book. His flowering staff grows nearby, while on an engraved menhir a dove roosts.

IX the grail hermit

Background: The Grail tradition in Arthurian legend springs from two sources: from the native stories about the cauldron and various regenerative vessels, and from the apocryphal stories which grew up from the amalgamation of pagan and Christian traditions.

In both of these, a kingly hermit plays a central part. Medieval legend, drawing upon traditions about Bran the Blessed and the sacred wounding of the king, portrayed Brons as the Grail guardian.[45] Christian tradition supplied Joseph of Arimathea and the lineage of hermits who spring from his family. Venerable tradition states that Joseph brought the infant Christ to Britain on one of his trading voyages. Similar legends relate that the relics of Christ were brought by Joseph to Glastonbury, where he founded the first church.

These relics have been variously described as the two cruets which contained the blood and water from the side of Christ, or, alternatively, the Cup of the Last Supper. Both traditions merged, and in the fullness of time they were grafted onto the indigenous Grail legends.

The Grail hermits of Arthurian legend fulfil a necessary task in the quest, admonishing the lazy, explaining the significance of the wonders which are encountered and providing welcome rest and shelter from the rigours of the search.

The seamless garment of tradition has wrought the twin realities of the pagan and Christian visions into a dynamic and potent mythos. For while the Celtic cauldron is the object of individual kings and heroes, all people are included within the dispensation of the Christian Grail — the finding of which does not necessitate being of a royal or holy lineage. The combined Grail tradition is open to all people of good will and intent, who are invited to go and search for the life-giving cup. The old kingly sacrifice is transmuted into a once and for all time redemptive sacrifice by the Son of Light, who, by his incarnation as a human being, brings all peoples within his own bloodline, by virtue of the Blessed Virgin's own humanity which he himself assumes in order to die and so overcome death.

This mystery is at the heart of the Grail legends and is implicit within the mythos of the Celtic god, Mabon — whose name was sometimes interchangeable with that of Christ in British tradition. The Grail Hermit frequently features as the co-fosterer, with the Lady of the Lake, of the Grail winner.

Archetypal Meaning: The Grail Hermit represents the keeper and transmitter of esoteric lore. Neither Druid nor priest, as hermit he mediates the functions of both. His book is opened to all who go on quests. It warns them of the dangers and terrors which await them, but it also comforts and sustains those who lose their way on the path of spiritual renewal. His dove goes on before to guide seekers, while his staff steadies their failing steps.

Divinatory Meaning: Guidance; spiritual truth; illumination;

wisdom; counsel — especially from an older or wiser person. Introspection; a necessary space for reassessment; inner companionship; maturity; the voice of conscience or one's guardian angel/spirit.

X The Round Table

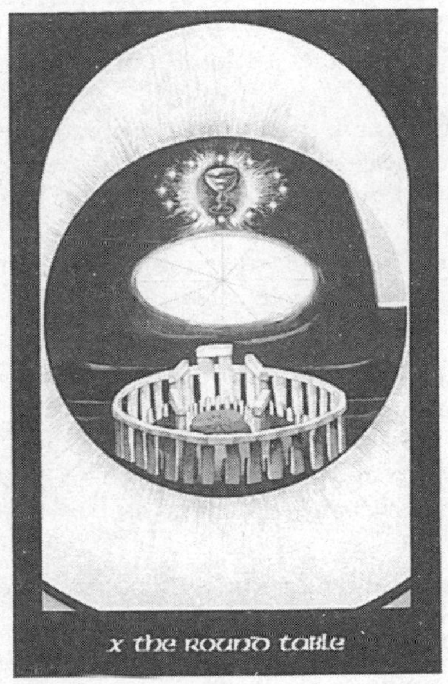

Description: We see through the pupil of a hawk's eye a great plain on which is a henge of great stones, within this is a circle of swords. Above the henge is the Round Table. Above the Round Table is a circle of stars within which is a crystal cup.

Background: The Fellowship of the Round Table is at the heart of the medieval Arthurian legends. It inspired many historical orders of chivalry, contributing to the civilization of Europe during the Middle Ages, though, as with Fellowship described by Malory and others, these were not always consistent with the ideals of Christian compassion. The concept of a round table at which knights sit to relate their deeds and to regulate the laws of the land by their personal vigilance and action has descended into modern times where many social and welfare organizations have adopted it as their symbol.

The Round Table signifies a place of meeting and council and is a microcosm of the land itself where its representatives sit. Whatever is planned, discussed and experienced at the Table is manifested throughout the land.

The first meeting places and assembly points were probably the stone circles, such as Stonehenge, which Geoffrey of Monmouth says was magically transported by Merlin from Ireland as a memorial for Uther Pendragon.[8] Such legends are not without foundation, for we know that such megalithic monuments were indeed the focus of seasonal assembly. It is Merlin also who speaks of the making of the Round Table after the fashion of earlier tables, including the Table of the Last Supper, within the *Didot Perceval.*[58] He speaks there also of a third table which was made by Joseph of Arimathea — the Table of the Grail.

We see here these three tables superimposed one above the other. The stone circle of ancient sacred assembly, the Round Table of the medieval Arthurian legend, and the starry circle which is the gathering point for the disincarnate archetypes who mediate the powers of the Grail. When all three tables are aligned, then all levels of life are likewise harmonized with the cosmic laws governing our world.

Archetypal Meaning: The Round Table represents the stability of eternal laws which manifest in every age and cycle; to earthly perception these laws seem to be changeable and unpredictable, yet they follow certain cosmic patterns. Those who sit at the Round Table are subject to these laws and adapt themselves continuously to their manifestation.

Divinatory Meaning: Evolution; cyclic change; sequential patterns which result from any action; adaptation; incarnation or manifestation of a project; the passing of a concept, project or relationship to another phase; cosmic law or karma.

XI Sovereignty

Description: The Goddess of Sovereignty sits beside a spring. In her hands is the four-sided cup of truth. At her feet is an ermine.

Background: We have already heard much about Sovereignty in the backgrounds of the other Arthurian Powers. She is the epicentre about which the Arthurian legends revolve, for she is the Goddess of the Land and whatever affects the land causes changes in her. For this reason she is very difficult to discern among the later texts, for in her many guises she is scattered throughout the Matter of Britain.

She is called Sovereignty because this gift of royalty lies in her gift. All candidates for kingship must encounter her and accept her challenge. Usually she takes the form of a Cailleach or hag who demands a kiss from the hero; if he kisses her without revulsion, she will turn into her maiden aspect, often becoming his Flower Bride. (See p.42.) She will only accept the worthiest candidate to be king: he must be truthful, compassionate, just, courageous, and loyal to the land and its peoples. She will not accept anyone who is a self-serving

individual given to lies and prevarication, just as she will not accept a blemished man — one who is physically imperfect.

Arthur encounters her in many forms, but usually within the persons of Guinevere, Morgan, Morcades and the Lady of the Lake. We lack the main stories of his encounters because these have become attached to his champions, Gawain, Perceval and others.

It is within the Grail legends that Sovereignty can be clearly seen as the Grail Maiden, who bears the regenerative cup; she appears also as the Queen of the Hallows in *Peredur*;[30] while, in her aspect of hag, she appears as the Grail Messenger or Hideous Damsel whose admonitory guidance brings the Grail winner to his goal.

In Celtic tradition, the Goddess of Sovereignty gives three drinks from her cup, purveying the white milk of fostering, the red drink of lordship and the dark drink of forgetfulness. These she offers successively in her aspects as Foster-Mother, Consort and Renewer.[41]

The four-sided cup of truth held by Sovereignty here is that of truth and justice: if three falsehoods are said over it it will shatter in pieces; but if three truths are said over it, it will reunite.

Archetypal Meaning: Sovereignty represents the inherent unity of the King and the land. She also stands for just and truthful dealings among all peoples. Whoever does not uphold the laws and customs of the land in their true spirit, is responsible for eroding the influence of the Goddess of Sovereignty. Like the earth itself, she must be respected.

Divinatory Meaning: Justice; equity; rightful rule; vindication of integrity; perception of motives; fair exchange; honest relationships; good measure; balanced reaction.

XII The Wounded King

Description: In a forest clearing hung with banners, the Wounded King lies on a bed. By his side is a hound; at his feet is a stone.

Background: The Wounded King appears in the Grail legends as its disempowered guardian. His unhealing wounds keep him in continual suffering and he is unable to be healed until the Grail winner has achieved the redemptive vessel. Most people are familiar with this figure from Wagner's opera *Parzifal* where he is called the Fisher King. Wagner drew from Wolfram von Eschenbach's reworking of the French Grail romances[79] which in turn derive from British oral traditions.

The wounds of the King are reflected in the Wasteland which his kingdom has become: only the Grail can heal them both. It appears in the Wounded King's hall as a redemptive vision, usually as part of the procession of the Hallows which are borne in after the meal. But the Grail cannot do its work unless a worthy champion comes and asks the Grail question: 'What does this signify?' or 'Whom does the Grail serve?'

The asking of this question demonstrates that the seeker is aware of the wounds of the king and the wasting of the land, and truly desires to heal them both. It is only so that the Grail quest is activated.

But why is the King wounded in the first place? This question takes us into the deep mythos of the land. The medieval romances speak of the Dolorous Blow, by which Balin wounds King Pelles with the Lance of Longinus, thus causing the Wasteland.[31] But this is but one side of the story. We may cite Celtic kingship customs whereby a blemished or maimed king was forced to abdicate in favour of a more worthy candidate from the tribe. It was felt that an imperfect ruler could not worthily represent his people, for the king had to reflect the fertility of the land in his own person: a maimed king meant a barren land.

Mythically, we can see that the guardianship of the Hallows is itself a formidable task which the king can only maintain if he co-operates with the Otherworld. This relationship between the worlds is symbolized by his mystical marriage to the land, to the Goddess of Sovereignty herself. His vows of kingship to the people are in effect his marriage vows to Sovereignty, from whom he holds the Hallows in trust. If he breaks his binding oath, imbalances appear in his kingdom. The medieval romances show how clearly this is reflected in the career of Arthur himself who virtually becomes a Wounded King because of his disempowerment: Guinevere gives her affections to Lancelot and so the kingdom's unity is shattered.

The Grail winner is potentially the new king, for he quests for the Hallows and, by his achievement of the Grail, he is able to heal the Wounded King. His Grail quest has brought him into relationship with the Otherworld, with Sovereignty and, ultimately, with the guardianship of the land. So although the Wounded King is healed, he does not remain the guardian of the Hallows: the Grail winner continues to maintain this role.

The origins of the Wounded King's sacrifice are deeply rooted in a prehistoric tradition by which the tribe's leader dies for his people. One such ruler is Bran the Blessed who, in Celtic tradition, is beheaded by his followers who then bury the head to repel invasion. Bran descended into medieval Grail tradition as Brons, the Fisher King — a title which arises from the confusion between the two similar French words *pécheur* (sinner) and *pêcheur* (fisher).

The Wounded King depicted here derives from the folk carol, *The Corpus Christi Carol*, where the wounds of the king are related to the redemptive sacrifice of Christ in a perfect fusion of ancient and Christian tradition.

Archetypal Meaning: The Wounded King represents the redemptive sacrifice of the Grail mysteries. His sufferings bring wisdom and insight, not only for himself but for his people. His is a willing sacrifice, not a gratuitous holocaust of blood. It is enjoined upon all seekers to ask the Grail question in whatever situation they find themselves: 'What is this about?' 'How may I remedy this?' The answer to these questions is the service of the Grail. There are many answers.

Divinatory Meaning: Wisdom gained through hardship and experience; spiritual insight; commitment to inner principles; the pain and misunderstanding caused by this commitment to others not so dedicated; metanoia — a changing of one's life; inner healing; meditation; purification; the stripping away of inessentials; self-sacrifice.

XIII The Washer at the Ford

Description: At a ford by night, the Washer at the Ford washes bloody linen. A raven perches upon a boundary stone, while in the distance hounds bay under a gibbous moon.

Background: The Washer at the Ford is one of the oldest figures of death in Celtic tradition. Those who see her washing out bloody linen are normally warriors whose vision of her presages their pending death in battle.

The north-west European tradition is at variance with Classical tradition in depicting a woman as the archetype of death, but this is the dark face of the Goddess who, though she gives birth to all creation, gathers it all back at the end of time. The Valkyries of Norse legend, the choosers of the slain, are not so very different from the threefold Goddess, the Morrighan, who, under her personas of Badh, Macha and Nemainn, pick the battlefield clean in the form of ravens. Breton tradition also has its *Lavendiers de la Nuit* — women who haunt streams at midnight, washing linen.[19] The woman ('the Nightmare-Life-in-Death') who dices with death in Coleridge's *The Rime of the*

Ancient Mariner draws on this very same tradition.

The Washer at the Ford is one of the aspects of Morgan, who inherits the mythos attached to the Morrighan. Geoffrey of Monmouth describes her as 'Morgen, a Goddess, who receives Arthur into her island realm of Avalon, there to heal him of his wounds.'[9] Later texts make Morgan a mortal woman but a powerful enchanter, bent on bringing Arthur to his ruin: this development shows a fusion of early traditions and results in a character who is indeed aligned to the Morrighan of Irish myth.

Elsewhere, in oral Welsh tradition, she is called Modron, the Great Mother. It is she who is encountered by Urien of Rheged at the Ford of Barking; by him she conceives twin children, Owain and Morfydd. (This Owain features in *The Dream of Rhonabwy* and other romances of the *Mabinogion* both as Arthur's champion and his opponent.) Urien does not die in this story, for his encounter with Modron results in a birth, not a death.[41] Modron is the mother of Mabon (see p.69) and her search for him is comparable to Ceridwen's pursuit of Taliesin (see p.47): both women depict the archtype of the Goddess as initiator.

The Washer at the Ford is essentially a challenging figure, yet she is also known as the Dark Woman of Knowledge in tradition because she is a teacher who initiates us into knowledge of ourselves.

Archetypal Meaning: The Washer at the Ford is the shape-changer, challenging and inviting all who approach her to change. She represents renewal, changing that which is static into that which is vital. Her katabolic action destroys outworn ideas, leaving room for fresh growth. Hers is a positive destruction, a clearing away of old growths.

Divinatory Meaning: The elimination of outworn ideas, stale relationships and static customs; fallowness; sexual union; ecstasy; the disruption of old patterns; renewal; ruthless yet compassionate action.

XIV The Cauldron

Description: In an underworld cavern hangs the cauldron of rebirth, tended by three women: a maiden, a woman and a crone. The carvings behind them depict ancient kings, including Pen Annwn, the Lord of the Underworld. Near the cauldron an adder darts.

Background: The cauldron is the main object of Arthur's descent into Annwn on the ship Prydwen. The poem *Preiddeu Annwn*[29] tells that the cauldron owned by Pen Annwn is cooled by the breath of nine maidens. This card depicts three figures tending the cauldron, for the ninefold sisterhood referred to in the poem are really aspects of the Goddess who frequently appears under three guises.[41] Such a sisterhood are under the aegis of Morgen in the *Vita Merlini*,[9] where they

are said to be in possession of the arts and sciences. Morgen herself is a healer in this text, and various parallel texts speak of her ability with the admixture and brewing of herbal remedies for the care of Arthur's wounds.

We are already familiar with the story of Taliesin and Ceridwen's cauldron which is one of knowledge and inspiration (see p.47), as well as with the cauldron of rebirth which Bran the Blessed owns. (See p.138.) The cauldron which Arthur seeks is said to be one which will not boil the food of a coward. This vessel clearly reflects the Celtic custom of apportioning special cuts of meat for warriors, poets, kings etc., all of which were laid down by law. Some aspect of all three cauldrons is apparent in the vessel of the Grail itself, for it gives knowledge of the Otherworld, it renews the Wasteland and heals the Wounded King, and it gives the food which everyone desires, according to various sources.[31]

The chains by which the cauldron hangs in this card connect the three worlds: the Underworld, here represented by the ancient kings, the ancestral heroes who have descended to seek the wisdom of the cauldron; the Earth, which seeks the empowerment of the cauldron; and the Otherworld, represented by the sisterhood tending the cauldron. Both ancestral kings and maidens oversee the regenerative forces of the cauldron; they are the Sons of Knowledge and Daughters of Memory within Celtic tradition — a concept also known as the interrelation of the sibyls and prophets in later Christian tradition.[38]

Archetypal Meaning: The Cauldron represents the regeneration of all orders of creation in the land of Logres. There is no loss, only changing and transmutation in this life beyond life. It is the source of spiritual empowerment to the initiate who goes beyond the gates of death in the search for the Grail.

Divinatory Meaning: Regeneration; fusion; recombination of resources or potentials; tempering outer circumstance by inner values; blending or merging with a new idea; polarized living; correct balancing of one's personality.

XV The Green Knight

Description: The Green Knight stands in the entrance of a hall. The winter snow swirls in with him. He carries a great axe and is dressed in evergreen leaves. A wren sits by the door.

Background: The famous entrance of the Green Knight into Arthur's Christmas court is recorded in the fourteenth-century text, *Sir Gawain and the Green Knight*,[18] but the story has much earlier analogues. The Green Knight bursts into the hall bringing a winter game or challenge called the Beheading Game. He offers his axe to any challenger, kneeling so that his head can be cut off: in return the challenger must also kneel and offer his head to the axe. No one imagines that the return blow will ever be struck, and only Gawain takes up the challenge. After he has cut off the Green Knight's head, the Green Knight rises and demands that Gawain meet him a year hence and offer his head to the Beheading Game. Gawain eventually meets his opponent, after sojourning at the house of Sir Bertilak, at the Green Chapel. He kneels for the blow, but is only nicked on the neck with the blade of the axe, since he was tempted by Bertilak's wife into accepting magical assistance of a green garter against his opponent. It transpires that the Green Knight is none other than his host, Sir Bertilak. Arthur decrees thereafter that Gawain shall employ the green garter as his emblem, in token of his challenge.

The prime forerunner of this story is told in the Ulster cycle where Cuchulainn is similarly challenged by a terrible giant who is Cu Roi mac Daire, King of Munster, in disguise. In this version, three warriors take up the giant's challenge, but only Cuchulainn is brave enough to face the return blow and it is he who is accorded praise as the Champion of Ulster and given the hero's portion of the feast.[5] The fact that we have both early and later versions of the same story means that we can observe the nature of Gawain's role as Champion of Britain.

The medieval story explains away the mystery of the Green Knight by making him an ordinary knight, Sir Bertilak, who has been placed under enchantment by Morgan le Fay. In the earlier version, we see that Cu Roi mac Daire is a powerful Otherworldly figure in his own right, well able to test and try the warriors of Ulster. He has been identified as an instrument of the Goddess of Sovereignty, and so the part of Morgan in the later story also becomes clear: for Morgan is herself a manifestation of the Goddess in her aspect of Cailleach or Dark Woman of Knowledge. Behind both the Green Knight and Morgan we can discern a pair of archetypes: the Lord and Lady of the Wheel, who stand as guardians and challengers within the Spiral Tower.[41]

The Beheading Game incorporates an ancient tradition concerning the King of Winter and the King of Summer, sometimes polarized as the kings of the Otherworld and of Britain. Gawain's earlier name, Gwalchami, Hawk of May, indicates that he is the candidate for the King of Summer or Britain. Tradition also makes him stronger as the sun reaches midday. The Green Knight, attired in midwinter evergreen, is the King of Winter or the Otherworld, and he stands for the old year which cedes place to the new year, in the person of Gawain. The wren which roosts at the Green Knight's feet is symbolic of the sacrificial bird. It is still processed in parts of Ireland in a folk custom enacted by the Wren Boys who sing:

The wren, the wren, the king of all birds,
On St Stephen's day was lost in the furze.
Although he is little, his portion is great . . .[54]

Archetypal Meaning: The Green Knight represents the challenger whom all seekers meet on their quest. He answers questions and gives advice, but he also sets riddles and puzzles. Those who think that they know everything he leads astray and torments. His greatest desire is to be bested by a worthy opponent.

Divinatory Meaning: Challenge; obstacles which must be overcome; ignorance; self-limitation; inflexibility; unconscious fears realized; stagnation; incisive change; creative possibilities.

XVI The Spiral Tower

Description: Upon a high tor, a tower is struck by lightning, masonry falls to the ground. But while the physical tower is shattered, a spiral tower of crystal remains. About the tor, the signs of the zodiac glow within the land. An owl flies upwards.

Background: Throughout the search for the Grail, the questers encounter many dangers and tests. Only one seeker is destined to find the regenerating vessel in each age, although it is a quest which all seekers are directed to follow individually. The Grail finder in the Arthurian legends is Perceval or Peredur in the earliest texts. Later tradition gives this task to Galahad, Lancelot's son; his two companions are Perceval and Bors.[31]

The Grail is only achieved by the worthiest quester, just as Sovereignty only accepts the worthiest candidate for the kingship of the land. When it is achieved, the Grail passes out of manifestation as a symbolic cup and becomes imprinted physically in the life of the land and its peoples.

This cycle of change is seldom appreciated, being viewed as a catastrophic alteration of the patterns of time and space. This is apparent in the later Arthurian cycle where the achieving of the Grail heralds the breaking of the Round Table Fellowship. But though the Round Table knights meet no more, the concept of the fellowship remains etched in the land itself.

The Grail is withdrawn in order that its influence shall become operative and remain so. The Grail winner also becomes withdrawn or dead to the world, in some sense. Sometimes his physical body seems to die, as Galahad does at Sarras upon looking in the Grail itself.[31] In other traditions, it is Perceval who wins the Grail; he remains in the Otherworld or on the borders of this world and the other, in order to mediate between the land and its peoples, becoming the new Grail King. In reality the Grail winner lives a life beyond life. His physical body is the vehicle for earthly existence only. By his achievement he or she is changed, transfigured to partake of both existences, mediating the regenerative influence of the Grail to all seekers.

Glastonbury has traditionally been associated with the Grail and Arthur, almost from the beginning of the tradition. It is a special place of pilgrimage which veils a deeper reality. The physical contours of the land are aligned to inner potencies that can be contacted at different times of the year. It is perhaps for this reason that it has been called 'this holiest earth'. There is no physical earth zodiac at Glastonbury: this is a transcendent reality mediated by the Grail guardian whose point of contact is the Tor itself: a locus which is mystical and actual at once.[32] The shattering of the Round Table on earth sees its reformation in the Otherworld. The Spiral Tower is the place of initiation within Celtic tradition. Each individual has a different experience therein. But only a poet like Taliesin is enabled to speak, however obscurely, about what one finds there.

Archetypal Meaning: The Spiral Tower represents the inner hostel of all seekers, where spiritual nourishment is given and deep instruction imparted. Within Logres, it functions as the spiral pathway to the Glass Caer of a new existence. Within its confines the current Grail guardian of the epoch will be found.

Divinatory Meaning: Reversal of energies; withdrawal of old customs, phases and concepts; shocking change; liberation from outworn concepts; humility; the realization of limitations; natural forces at work; a curative illness, e.g. one which expels poisons from the body; loss of cosy security; transfiguration, self-awareness.

XVII The Star

Description: A hill-fort at night. Two watchmen, one asleep, are witness to the dragon-shaped comet which rushes across the sky,

xvii the star

breaking through the constellation of Great Bear. From its mouth stream two rays of light. A cockerel proclaims the hope which is to come, although it is not yet dawn.

Background: In his *History of the Kings of Britain*, Geoffrey of Monmouth writes about a meteor in dragon shape which appeared over Logres. Uther called Merlin to interpret this omen. Merlin immediately announced the death of Ambrosius Aurelianus, and urged Uther to become King of Britain. The dragon was interpreted as being Uther himself and the two rays which came from the dragon's mouth signified his son, Arthur, whose dominion would be great, and Uther's daughter, Anna, whose sons and grandsons would be kings of Britain. Uther immediately ordered the making of two golden dragons, one which he gave to the cathedral of Winchester and one which he carried into battle.[8]

The dragon-star then heralds the coming of the Pendragons, and the golden dragon which Uther has made is the draco standard which is carried into battle as a sign of hope and victory.

Throughout the history of Logres, the hope of the people is ever renewed as the tides of time ebb and flow. At the conclusion of Arthur's reign, when all seems in despair, hope rises of a new coming which is both resurrection and a new birth at once. When all seems dark, the duty of the seeker is to look ever for signs of renewal, to be vigilant at all times, to encourage the down-hearted and strengthen the doubtful.

Just as the land of Logres was in disarray before the coming of the

Pendragons, so all times of crisis need their inspiration and rallying point. Here the vulnerability of the land finds a new protector, announced by a heavenly sign. As the Grail guardian is withdrawn into the Spiral Tower, so a new cycle is imminent.

In every land, in every time, there are guardians who were once seekers. Like Merlin, they read the signs of the times and wait in order to help the influence of the Otherworld to manifest. In every land and every time, individuals whose vocation is to bring great change or greater cohesion are being born. The precession of the equinoxes which brings us into the New Age, reveals many such people, and they are our hope.

Archetypal Meaning: The Star of Prophecy represents the springs of hope in the land of Logres. The seeker is bidden to be watchful and faithful in his or her service, ready to sublimate his or her energies to all manifestations of justice, truth and integrity.

Divinatory Meaning: Hope; renewal; the beginning of a new cycle; inspiration; faith born of desire and trust; love of another's good; refreshment; the raising of popular consciousness.

XVIII The Moon

Description: Under a full moon stand two dark towers. The moon encloses an embryonic child, curled as though in the womb. Striving to leap the weir is a solitary salmon.

Background: There is always a period of waiting before the Pendragon or the Grail winner show themselves to the people. In the case of Arthur, he is taken from his parents, Igraine and Uther, by Merlin to a place of fosterage where he will learn the skills which he will need when he is king. Perceval is raised in the seclusion of a forest, in ignorance of arms and knighthood, by his mother.[4] Galahad is raised in a monastery.[31] Lancelot is fostered by the Lady of the Lake and taught the skills of war as well as the courtly manners of a noble youth. Nothing can hasten this necessary process of preparation any more than a child in the womb can be born before the time is right.

The coming of Arthur and the Grail champions stand in the long tradition of the Wondrous Youth who is destined to reappear after a period of devastation of despair. Within Celtic tradition this youth is called Mabon, the son of Modron. These names mean, respectively, Son and Mother, and they represent archetypes which can be identified and reapplied to many of the figures within the Arthurian tradition.

Mabon's story survives fragmentedly in *Culhwch and Olwen* in the *Mabinogion*,[30] where he becomes the object of a quest by Culhwch, a youth who is set many impossible tasks in order to win his chosen bride, Olwen, the giant's daughter. Arthur and his court assist Culhwch in accomplishing his tasks.

Culhwch is told to find Mabon, a mysterious character who was taken 'from between his mother and the wall when he was three nights old and no-one knows whether he is alive or dead'. By questing through the levels of time, each represented by a totemic bird, beast or fish, Culhwch and his companions are enabled to find the Salmon, the oldest of the animals in Celtic tradition — who takes them to Mabon's place of imprisonment. There he is liberated, no longer a baby, but a vigorous youth who is both harpist and hunter. Mabon further assists Culhwch achieve his tasks.[44]

In this fragmentary mystery story, Mabon's imprisonment is not necessarily an unwilling one. Just as the Grail passes out of manifestation into a withdrawn state, so too do certain archetypes wait for the right moment before manifesting again. Mabon's imprisonment is hinted at in the *Preiddeu Annwn*[9] where he is described as a youth bound with golden fetters — a hostage to the Otherworld who awaits from the beginning of time for a chance to manifest.

Mabon's story is clearly paralleled by that of Taliesin who, as Gwion Bach, was transformed as an initiate poet-seer into many forms, including the salmon who, as the oldest of animals, taught him all wisdom. He suffered 'three periods in the prison of Arianrhod': a reference to the Spiral or Glass Caer of initiation. Lastly he was born of Ceridwen, his instructor in wisdom.

Mabon is the son of his mother, the Goddess Modron, but his father is not mentioned in any tradition. This aligns him with Merlin who is likewise 'a child without a father'.

Archetypal Meaning: The Moon represents the inner destiny of the One Who Will Come, be he or she monarch, hero, poet, seer or champion of truth. The potentiality of Logres strives to be born in this card, but it remains latent until the times and tides are right for it to manifest.

Divinatory Meaning: Clear visualization; generation; cyclic patterns of growth; fertility and increase; fluctuation; dreams and visions; introspection; necessary preparation; fallowness; the seasonal round; the tides of time.

XIX The Sun

Description: Under the midday sun rides a naked youth upon a white mare. On his back is a harp; in his hand a spear.

Background: In the card of the Moon, we saw the embryonic child growing in the womb of the Goddess. In this card, Mabon emerges into the world, ready to set out on his quest. As stated in the previous entry, Mabon's role is an archetypal one which can be applied to more than one of the Arthurian heroes. The youthful hero whose innocence and worthiness shine from him usually comes into a world torn by war and confusion. In his aspect of innocent youth, the hero brings a new perspective and the wisdom of his mother.

Mabon's mother, Modron, is here represented by the white mare on which he rides. The White Mare was emblematic of the sovereignty of the Goddess, frequently appearing as a chalk hill figure or on Celtic coins. (The same image may be found on Arthur's throne in card IV.) The White Mare was how the Celtic Goddess, Epona, was represented. She, Macha and Rhiannon share a common symbology.[44]

Throughout Celtic tradition, we read of youthful heroes who vindicate their mothers in some way or else they become champions of their land. Usually their mothers are disgraced or sent into slavery. In order to preserve the life of their sons, these women send their children into fosterage where they obtain the necessary empowerment to return and overthrow an oppressive king or stepfather.

Arthur's career begins when he successfully pulls the sword from the stone. This is not the same sword as Excalibur in later legend, for that is gifted him by the Lady of the Lake and is one of the Hallows. The ability to pull the sword from the stone is a sovereignty-bestowing act and Arthur becomes king, bringing his youthful might to restore the kingdom.

The archetype of Mabon derives from the Romano-British god, Maponus, who was very popular among the legionaries along Hadrian's Wall, as well as among the tribes of the north. The Romans incorporated many Classical features into this archetype, chief of which are those of Apollo. Whether earlier, Druidic teachings had already made this connection cannot be proved, but the overlay is certainly there. Mabon, like Apollo, is both harpist and hunter. In both roles, the God is searchingly direct: he meets injustice either by the challenge of his judgement, represented by his harp — for he is judge, poet and Druid — or else by force of arms.

In Arthurian tradition, we find the twofold role is represented by different sorts of men: the knights, such as Perceval, Gawain and Kay, exercise their chivalric skills in defence of their land; the poet-seers, such as Taliesin and Merlin, bring the clarity of their prophetic and poetic insight so that injustice is brought out and exposed publicly. It is only Arthur himself and Mabon who still combine both roles within them.

Archetypal Meaning: The Sun represents the outer or revealed destiny of the One Who Will Come, be he or she monarch, poet, seer, hero or champion of truth. The Sun conquers by innocence, revealing falsehood by its shining beams and gladdening the earth with its warmth.

Divinatory Meaning: Innocence; purity; enthusiasm; warmth; a loving heart; joy; freedom; enlightenment; wholeness; health; intolerance of shadows in any aspect of life; clarity; directness; true vocation realized.

XX The Sleeping Lord

Description: The gigantic figure of the Sleeping Lord lies as a hill, incorporated into the land itself. On his thigh stands the youthful hero blowing a horn. All about the landscape, people of many kinds, ages and eras rise out of their tombs and barrows. They look upwards to a great eagle which flies overhead.

Background: Consistent within Arthurian tradition is the assertion that Arthur will come again. Many hills and sites have been associated with this legend, and stories have been told about daring individuals who entered the Hollow Hills to discover Arthur and his court asleep therein. Usually the finder is given the opportunity to summon Arthur from sleep by blowing a horn, drawing the sword from its scabbard, or cutting the baldric which lies near the king. But though he is tempted to do so, the finder usually returns to his own world without doing this, because Arthur may only be awakened in the time of Britain's greatest need.

The medieval poet, Lydgate, wrote of Arthur:

He is King crouned in Fairie,
With Sceptre and sword and with his regally
Shall resort as Lord and Soveraigne
Out of Fairie and reigne in Britaine;
And repaire again the Round Table.
By prophesy Merlin set the date

Among princes King incomparable,
His seat again to Caerlion to translate,
The Parchas sustren sponne so his fate,
His epitaph recordeth so certaine,
Here lieth King Arthur that shall raigne again.[30]

The undying legend of Arthur is like this very same story of regeneration and perpetual defence of the land, a role which has been applied to many military leaders, monarchs and heroes who throughout the history of Britain have attracted similar legends.

The sleep of the Pendragon beneath the land or in Avalon is very like the burial of Bran the Blessed's head under the White Mount: both kings are Palladiums of their country. And yet no one character can be expected to remain in this condition forever. New guardians and protectors continually emerge: they are born, they fulfil their vocations and they pass again into the renewal of the Otherworld. Within the context of the inner sovereignty of the land, a cycle which has been identified as the Succession of the Pendragons is discernible.[44] This is not a familial or necessarily royal lineage, but an initiatic one which is open to all seekers.

The return of Arthur is a prophesied event which can happen at the changing of the tides of time, at the turning of the aeons. It can happen, has happened and will happen within the circles of eternity. Time is not what we have understood it to be and the ways of regeneration are wonderful and mysterious to us.

Archetypal Meaning: The Sleeping Lord represents abiding promise of renewal. He indicates the apocatastasis — the point where creation is drawn back to its origins and remade. When Arthur or any salvific figure comes again, the times are understood to be at their end and their beginning. Those who partake of the mysteries are liberated from time into an unknown existence governed by the Dwellers in Avalon.

Divinatory Meaning: Renewal; resurrection; recapitulation of events or ideas; prophetic vision; ending or beginning; forgiveness; adjustment; recovery of that which has been lost sight of; impulse to change one's life.

XXI The Flowering of Logres

Description: In a burgeoning landscape, the Seeker dances with two children. The rainbow scarf which is held in their hands swirls out to border the scene. Beyond and around it is the starry firmament in which the liberated and active Hallows of the land, the Sword, Spear, Grail and Stone, are illuminated.

Background: The restoration of the Wasteland is the hope and goal of the Seeker. This can be achieved by the quest for the Hallows and by their skilful wielding in the world. When the land is restored, the

xxi the flowering of logres

Wounded King is healed, a new Grail guardian is appointed and Sovereignty assumes her beautiful guise as the Maiden Goddess.

This search for the Hallows happens at many levels of existence: their finding correspondingly has many ripples throughout creation. All peoples, animals and growing things are brought into contact with the deep springs which well up as a result of the empowered Hallows.

The Seeker in card XXI is a different person from the quester who set out in card 0. He has undergone a severe and testing journey. The two children with whom he dances in joyful celebration are the same two who appeared in card V, listening to Taliesin's story. These archetypal children are the twin innocents whose dwelling is the terrestial paradise. Within the Grail texts, they appear to Perceval and guide him on his journey.[58] The links of tradition lie in their hands, ready to pass on to other seekers in other ages. The rainbow road upon which the Seeker set out has become a woven scarf which encompasses the world.

The Hallowquest is not a selfish or individual regeneration, for the healing of one person; one's alignment with one's spiritual source, is also the partial healing of the land. The healing of one land is a partial healing of the world. There is still a great deal of work to be done. May your own quest be fruitful!

Archetypal Meaning: The Flowering of Logres represents the restoration of fertility on all levels. The moment of renewal announces a timeless joy throughout the hearts of all orders of creation: rocks, plants, animals and people. The quest is over for one cycle. There will be other seekers and other quests.

Divinatory Meaning: Restoration; culmination; triumph; attainment; perfection; rapture; spiritual healing; creative growth; the new aeon.

THE LESSER POWERS

The following section gives descriptions and divinatory meanings for the Lesser Powers. The backgrounds which accompany these cards suggest ways in which each card can be further explored. They are not essential to an understanding of the *Hallowquest* Tarot, although they may act as useful information and further reading if you wish to use the cards for story-telling or if you employ the Three Worlds Spread (see p.236). Some of the stories referred to here are to be found in fuller form within this book, but due to lack of space the reader is referred to the bibliography. The stories are drawn from the widest possible frame of reference, including both the early British and later French romances.

Swords: Air, Spring

Sword Hallow

Description: Out of a dark underground chamber arises hot steam. The Sword of Light rises up in scintillating brilliance.

Background: The ancient Glaive or Sword of Light which is wielded by the hero in Celtic folk story is the prototype of this Hallow, as is the Sword of Nuadu in Irish tradition. (See p.130.)

Meaning: Incisive energy; the dispelling of illusions; conquest; championship; strength and power; love of truth and justice; the power of the mind; rational deduction or perception; light in dark places.

Sword Two

Description: Under a hazy sun is a steep wooded valley with a path running through it. On either side of the path two swords are stuck into the earth. An adder darts from the grass.

Background: The Battle of Camlan, sometimes called the last battle within the Arthurian legends, is suggested in this card; the two swords represent the armies of Arthur and Mordred drawn up in truce. An adder moving in the grass caused a man to draw his sword to slay it, and so battle was provoked.[41]

Meaning: Amnesty or temporary peace; indecision; compromise; suspension of deeply held beliefs or opinions; hesitation; analysis of the situation is required before action.

Sword Three

Description: A gorge in mountainous country with a broken bridge. A sword falls into the gorge.

Background: When Peredur or Perceval left his mother, she died of sorrow. But this was as a direct result of her possessiveness, which caused her to raise her son in ignorance of weapons and the way of knighthood in the seclusion of the forest. Perceval would have been unable and unprepared to achieve the Grail had he stayed at home.[4]

Meaning: Sorrow, separation; deep disappointment; loss. The possession of the thoughts by jealousy; brooding upon personal slights. It is necessary to analyse one's receptivity to the tide of events and acknowledge one's responsibility for others' pain.

Sword Four

Description: A sword lies on the altar within a chapel or hermitage.

Background: Although Perceval learns skill at arms from his uncle, his education is incomplete until he learns from his other, hermit uncle, the ways of the spirit. Traditionally, novice knights laid their swords on the altar before taking their final chivalric vows.

Meaning: Respite; hermetic seclusion; meditation; self-exile or retreat; convalescence; rest; replenishment of spirit; solitude; it is time to reassess one's powers and limitations in quiet seclusion.

Sword Five

Description: Heathland swept by war and destruction. Beside a burning house, a broken sword lies.

Background: Throughout the Arthurian legends, we encounter many criminal knights, none more so than Sir Bruce Sans Pitié, whose cruelty and devious methods make him an enemy to be feared. He is finally overcome by Lancelot, but not before he has caused widespread suffering and destruction.[31]

Meaning: Defeat; slander; cowardice; unethical behaviour; divisive means; thwarted plans; sloppy or malicious thinking causes things to go awry.

Sword Six

Description: A quiet sunny river winds through a willow copse. A sword stands in the barge which is moored nearby.

Background: After the many trials and difficulties of the Grail knights, a ship appears mysteriously to bear Galahad, Bors, Perceval and Dindraine further upon their quest.[36]

Meaning: Success after trouble; safety and protection; a journey; new perspectives; difficulties and blockages are cleared as a result of perceptive thought.

Sword Seven

Description: A river in full flood. A stone floats in the waters with a sword stuck into it.

Background: When Galahad first comes to Arthur's court, he is

summoned to the Adventure of the Stone. This consists of a floating red stone in which a sword is stuck. Many of Arthur's knights are totally unable to pull it forth, but Galahad succeeds, thus emulating Arthur, who came to the throne by pulling a sword from a stone.[31]

Meaning: Unstable effort; little progress; plans fail as a result of confused thinking. Self-deceit; passivity; over-defensiveness; the need for proper conceptualization.

Sword Eight

Description: In a brown marsh, a sword stands solitary.

Background: Gereint's stubborn attempt to prove himself a man of prowess in Enid's eyes leads him into many fruitless adventures in which he is wounded. His own pride forbids him to ask Arthur's help and he exiles himself from court in a further series of mad adventures.[30]

Meaning: Restriction; one's bounden duty; fear of what others say; bigoted opinions; intolerance; imprisonment; illness; thought is in bondage; the time for out-worn thought patterns is over.

Sword Nine

Description: Night. Under a waning moon is a palisaded fence with severed heads upon its spikes. In a ditch lies a sword.

SWORD EIGHT

SWORD NINE

Background: The culmination of Gereint's self-determined quest for knightly accolade leads him to the court of Owain where the Enchanted Games are held. This challenge consists of entering a magical enclosure, surrounded by a palisaded fence on which the heads of former challengers are staked.[30]

Meaning: Suffering; grave doubts; guilt; premonitions and nightmares; cruelty; despair; depression; inability to take personal responsibility for one's path; the need for a disciplined life-style and commitment to logical thought.

Sword Ten

Description: A fortified lake dwelling is reached only by a narrow stone bridge. On the near bank stands a sword, while over the bridge a hawk hovers in the rain.

Background: When Guinevere is abducted by Meleagrance and held captive in his castle, Lancelot comes to the rescue. The only means of entry is by means of a perilously narrow sword bridge over which Lancelot crawls in order to rescue the queen.[4]

Meaning: Life and death decision; the final solution dictated by ruthless logic. Pain; affliction; total oppression; masochism. The need for extreme daring and resolution. The acknowledgement and confrontation of karmic debts.

Sword Maiden

Description: Under a tree sits the Sword Maiden embroidering a scabbard. She has cut off her own hair to make a plaited belt for the sword.

Background: Dindraine, Perceval's sister, is part of the Grail quest. She cuts off her hair in order to weave a belt for the sword which Galahad shall carry.[36]

Meaning: She quickly grasps ideas and materializes them. Perceptive and discerning, she is vigilant in the cause of truth and justice. She cuts through difficulties by taking the way of self-sacrifice.

Sword Knight

Description: At dawn, the Sword Knight rides on a dun horse, raising his sword to the distant tower.

Background: It is Llwch Lleawc or Lleminawc the Irishman who, in the *Preiddeu Annwn* wields the Sword of Light and enables Arthur to steal the cauldron of Pen Annwn. This character's name and attributes are reflected in the person of the later Lancelot.[44]

Meaning: He is incisive and fearless, prompt to defend the weak and swift to halt injustice. He asserts the idea of right with skill and courage. He is the upholder of the Sword of Light.

Sword Queen

Description: The Sword Queen sits on a fallen tree burnishing a sword.

Background: The Black Maiden who admonishes Perceval for not persevering in his quest and for not asking the all-important Grail

question well represents the Sword Queen. In *Peredur*, part of her role is fulfilled by one of the Nine Witches of Gloucester who train Peredur in arms, after the fashion of Celtic warrior women.[30]

Meaning: She is intelligent and self-reliant, speaking her mind and not suffering fools gladly. As the defender of the unprotected, she is assiduous and fair-minded. She imparts a sense of justice to all who encounter her.

Sword King

Description: The Sword King sits enthroned with his sword, on the mound of justice.

Background: The medieval romances made Arthur the paragon of justice and law-giving. The Round Table Fellowship was founded in the spirit of justice for all and for protection of the weak. From it Arthur dispensed the laws that made his kingdom great.[31]

Meaning: He is the giver of justice, a wise counsellor whose analytical judgements cut right to the heart of the matter. His severity is tempered by impartiality and he shows how self-analysis and love of truth may govern one's life.

Spears: Fire, Summer

Spear Hallow

Description: From deep cracks in the earth, sheets of fire flame up. The Spear which both heals and wounds rises up with great force and power.

Background: The Spear which heals and wounds is the prime implement which both causes and heals the Wasteland, depending upon who wields it. When it is touched to the Wounded King's wounds, health enters both king and land.[79] (See p.58.)

Meaning: Creativity; the beginning of a project; innovation; purpose; birth; the faculty of intuition; inspiration; energy; challenge; the healing of all that is corrupt.

Spear Two

Description: On a hillside overlooking a network of fields is a sparrowhawk on a perch. A spear stands beside the path which leads into the valley.

Background: In order to avenge Guinevere, Gereint pursues the knight who insulted her. He enters the Sparrowhawk Contest in which he overcomes the knight and wins the game.[30]

Meaning: Choice; control; mastery; the skilled organization of resources leads to achievement of desire; intuitive synthesis; dynamic drive.

Spear Three

Description: The path leads between the trees in a beechwood. A spear points the way.

Background: During the Quest the knights often met with guidance

through the vast entanglement of the Forests of Adventure. Sometimes this took the form of a hermit figure, sometimes of two naked children sitting in a tree and indicating the way.[58]

Meaning: Established strength; controlled intention; intuitive understanding gives an expansive outlook and resulting opportunities; scrupulous responsibility; enterprising initiative.

Spear Four

Description: The path leads from distant woods, branching off at a settlement. Beside the path stands a garlanded spear.

Background: After Gereint succeeded in the Enchanted Games, the Joy of the Court was celebrated. This relates closely to the central mystery of the *Hallowquest.*[41]

Meaning: Completion of an enterprise; a time of festival and celebration; enjoyment of the fruits of one's labours; harmonious conclusion; acknowledgement of intuitive strength.

Spear Five

Description: Against a setting sun are crossed spears against a monolith.

Background: The combat of Balin and Balan is the most grievous in the whole of Arthurian literature, since they are brothers and they kill each other, unknowingly. Balin's sword is set by Merlin in a floating stone which Galahad later draws to prove his right to sit at the Round Table.[31]

Meaning: Contention and strife; salutary struggle; competitiveness;

dictatorial attitudes cause obstruction; the need to distinguish between rightful intuition and unassuaged desires.

Spear Six

Description: Beside a winding river is a ceremonial mound on which sticks a spear with a standard of victory upon it.

Background: At the beginning of his reign Arthur successfully defeated 11 kings who were opposed to his rule. He then went on to conquer Scandinavia and Gaul, approaching the very gates of Rome itself.[8]

Meaning: Victory; advancement realized through steady growth; pride in achievement; recognition; intuitive self-confidence; ceremonial honours.

Spear Seven

Description: At the entrance to a stone fort, a spear stands, defensively.

Background: The historical figure of Arthur successfully united the Romano-British forces to defeat the invading Saxons, thus turning conquest into settlement and earning himself an honoured place in history.[46]

Meaning: Courageous ability; success despite opposition; tenacity and persistence upheld by strong intuition; defence of strongly-held beliefs.

Spear Eight

Description: A mountain river in spate takes a spear downstream.

Background: Tristan and Isolt frequently saved themselves from capture by King Mark by the expedient of twigs floating downriver on which were carved secret signs as a means of warning.[31]

Meaning: Swiftness; expediency; hasty perpetration of intuitions; prophetic insight; speedy progress and rapid growth; communication.

Spear Nine

Description: A turbulent sea crashes against high, jagged cliffs, on which a spear stands.

Background: Woken from sleep Arthur spied a strange ship in which was the body of a dead knight. He learned from the letter in the knight's hand of the mysterious events surrounding the Grail.[3]

Meaning: Enduring strength; great reserves; dedication to intuitive purpose; obstinacy; defensiveness; the wisdom to prepare against adversity.

Spear Ten

Description: The path leads down into a valley and climbs to a distant hill-fort. Beside the path stands the spear. Two ravens guard the way.

Background: Corbin or Corbinec was the home of the Grail King, Pelles. He was wounded in both thighs and unable to walk, and awaited the coming of the Grail winner to heal him.[31]

Meaning: Responsibility; excessive burdens; over-expansion of

spear nine

spear ten

resources; resolution by test of fire; crisis brings restoration; the need to delegate to others or the readjustment of power in order that the intuitive faculties can operate.

Spear Maiden

spear maiden

Description: The Spear Maiden runs with her spear raised. On her right wrist is a hawk.

Background: Lunet or Linnet is the resourceful maiden who guides Owain or Gareth to help her mistress. She gives Owain a ring of invisibility and helps him avoid capture.[4,30]

Meaning: She is a resourceful and enthusiastic messenger, faithful and loyal, if uninhibited and forthright; she shows the way through impossible situations by her daring, often by disguise or shape-shifting.

Spear Knight

Description: Under the midday sun, the Spear Knight rides full pelt on a roan horse, with spear raised.

Background: Bedwyr is one of Arthur's chief warrior companions in the early texts. It is said of his spear that the head of the shaft would leave the lance and draw blood from the wind before returning to its shaft again. He aids Culhwch in many adventures.[30]

Meaning: He is an energetic and impetuous champion. His inspired companionship leads into exciting adventures; but he is fearless of the unknown and his hasty decisions are often risky.

Spear Queen

Description: The Spear Queen offers her spear, kneeling in front of a number of grave mounds. The spear drips with blood.

Background: The Lady of the Fountain's husband is killed by Owain in a magical contest of arms. Afterwards, Owain marries the Lady with Lunet's encouragement and help, and so the Lady's lands are held against her enemies once more. But before she can be persuaded to take Owain, she mourns her husband grievously.[30]

Meaning: She is deeply attuned to the needs of the land and has suffered in its service; her grief is well hidden and she is generous and friendly to all; she imparts a deep commitment to the healing of the earth.

Spear King

Description: At a forge, the Spear King tests the keenness of his spear's point.

Background: Perceval's uncle, as part of his initiatory training, demands that he sever an iron staple which immediately renews itself after each blow.[4]

Meaning: He is honest and passionate, committed to his intuitive understanding of the land, even to the point of sacrifice; he teaches the ways of healing by his wisdom; he is the upholder of the Spear which both heals and wounds.

Grails: Water, Autumn

Grail Hallow

Description: Out of the living rock, a swift underground stream rushes in a great fall. The Grail appears in refulgent light.

Background: The Grail is prefigured in many proto-Celtic stories of cauldrons and enchanted vessels. It gives fulfilment, fertility and joy. [52] (See p.136.)

Meaning: Fertility; abundance; nurture; spiritual joy; healing; gladness; the emotional faculty; restoration after barrenness.

Grail Two

Description: In autumn elm woods, two doves drink from an earthenware dish.

Background: The dove is one of the prime totems of the Grail. It appears on the head-dress of the Grail messenger, Kundrie. When the Grail knights see this, they rejoice for they recognize that the achieving of the Grail is not far off. [79]

Meaning: Love; harmony; partnership; co-operation; concord; emotional reciprocation.

Grail Three

Description: In an apple orchard, a table is set with harvest fare.
Background: One of the prime functions of the Grail is to provide

plenty to all who set forth on the Quest. At Camelot, when the Grail first appeared to Arthur and his men, each person received the food he most desired. This can, of course, also mean spiritual fare.[31]

Meaning: Abundance; solace; fulfilment; fortunate conclusion; the power to communicate joy and gladness; generosity of spirit.

Grail Four

Description: Near a standing lake of stagnant water, a cup lies overturned in brambles.

Background: It was said of Arthur's kingdom that there were no chalices in all of the land. It was for this reason that many of the knights undertook the Quest for the Grail.[3]

Meaning: Dissatisfaction; lethargy; accidie; stagnation of the spirit; boredom; the need to establish emotional maturity.

Grail Five

Description: A ship with the Grail on its sail makes little headway against swelling seas and heavy mist.

Background: The mysterious Ship of Solomon bore Lancelot to a meeting with his son Galahad. This was a time of great bitterness and disillusion for Lancelot, who learned that he could never achieve the Grail.

Meaning: Disillusion; disappointment; vain regret; the ability to

learn from mistakes and assess one's limitations; broken agreements or promises.

Grail Six

Description: In a sacred grove of alders, a holy stream rises from a green mound, flowing into a stone basin.

Background: Gawain has his greatest adventure at such a mound, the home of the fearsome Green Knight. From this he learned much and was reconnected with his own past.[18,51]

Meaning: Rediscovery of one's roots; ancestral memories; the pleasure of remembered links; a sense of tradition and continuance; atavism; karmic recall.

Grail Seven

Description: In the waters of a lake, a fortress is reflected as a faery howe. A cup of silver stands upon the near bank.

Background: When Perceval fails to ask the Grail question, he retires to bed in the Grail castle, but wakes to find the place deserted.[58] Similarly, when Galahad goes to the Castle of Maidens, he is tested. When he refuses to aid the maidens of that place, he discovers that they are not mortal women but enchantments.[31]

Meaning: Self-deception; illusion; an over-active imagination; unrealistic fantasies; the glamour of esoteric practices; the need for emotional discipline.

Grail Eight

Description: Two candles burn on the altar of a chapel while an eight-

sided chalice of wine spills upon the floor.

Background: Lancelot reached the very door of the Grail chapel, only to be turned away, blinded and admonished for daring to come so close to the holy object while still living so much in the world.[31]

Meaning: Discontinuance of plans; withdrawal of energies and desire; self-pity; movement away from old beliefs and values; an over-fearful heart; the need to evaluate things from a more universal standpoint.

Grail Nine

Description: Under a starlit sky, a cauldron hangs over a fire.

Background: According to tradition, the Grail provided the food that everyone desired. This stems from the earlier Celtic cauldron stories in which each person at court was accorded a particular cut of the meat boiling within the cauldron.[57]

Meaning: Satisfaction; one's heart's desire; security; physical pleasure; emotional contentment.

Grail Ten

Description: By the seashore, the path leads to a broch. Nearby stands the Grail.

Background: After long and weary search the successful Grail

winners arrived at Sarras, the holy place from which all the mysteries of the Grail stemmed. Here they found perfect peace and the contentment of fulfilment.[36]

Meaning: Wholeness; perfection of contentment; fellowship and family; the holiness of the home; peace and happiness; the completion of desire shared by others.

Grail Maiden

Description: Beside a spring, the Grail Maiden stands holding an earthenware vessel.

Background: The Grail Maiden guides all who go in search of the vessel, offering them to drink. Not all recognize the meaning of this gesture, as witness the acts of King Amangons and his men, who raped and despoiled the Damsels of the Wells.[41]

Meaning: She is tender and willing; imaginative and loving, she shows the way to fulfil the deepest desires, often through dreams and visions; she exemplifies the way of service.

Grail Knight

Description: The Grail Knight rides upon a white horse through autumn woodlands playing his harp. The Grail appears to him in a beam of sunlight.

Background: The Grail Knight, no matter what his name or origin, always pursues the path to his goal with single-minded truth. An innocent in the ways of the world he is sometimes called 'The Perfect Fool', though his behaviour is never quite what it seems.

Meaning: He is a meditative and poetic champion, often unconventional; his fertile dreams invite fellow travellers to unexplored regions of the quest; he is incorruptible and dedicated.

Grail Queen

Description: Before a rough-hewn doorway in a cliff wall stands the Grail Queen. She pours out a cup, and five streams of wine flow out from it.

Background: In Celtic tradition, the Well of Knowledge had five streams which flowed from it, each one representing one of the senses by which knowledge is acquired. The ways to the Grail are many, but each leads to the truth of knowledge.[5]

Meaning: She is intuitive and sympathetic, her compassionate nature embraces all; she imparts the gifts of love to all who encounter her; the depth of her emotion marks her as the upholder of the Grail.

Grail King

Description: Under a mighty oak tree sits the Grail King, holding an earthenware cup. From the tree hangs a golden bowl from golden chains. Near the stream which flows round the tree is a green stone.

Background: When the Grail Knight meets the Grail guardian, he is challenged. Owain encounters such a guardian and throws water upon the green stone nearby which provokes their combat.[30] The golden bowl which hangs from chains is a frequent feature in the Grail legends, and represents the archetypal vessel of quest, by which the world is healed of its divisions.[3]

Meaning: His generosity is proverbial; his creative counselling shows the seeker the way to negotiate the confusions of the quest, for he is the guardian of the hidden mysteries.

Stones: Earth, Winter

Stone Hallow

Description: In the earth of an underground cavern the *gwyddbwyll* board glows with power.

Background: The *gwyddbwyll* (literally, 'wood-cunning') board was one of the prime treasures of the Island of Britain. Whoever possessed it or played upon it was likewise part of the archetypal movements within the land itself. (See p.140.)

Meaning: Wisdom; spiritual treasures; consolidation and establishment; attainment; fulfilment; prosperity; the faculty of sensation or instinct; mother-wit.

Stone Two

Description: A river splits into two in a snowy valley. A standing stone is on the left-hand bank.

Background: Palomides, the Saracen knight, having fallen in love with Isolt, spent years in fruitless endeavour to win her from Tristan. He finally becomes a Christian in her honour, but still failed to win her and chose instead to pursue the Questing Beast.[31]

Meaning: Fluctuation; integrity and scrupulosity cause tardy begin-

stone two

ning to projects; over-prudence; the ability to keep several things in the air; careful choice; instinctive weighing up of values.

Stone Three

stone three

Description: A standing stone stands near ploughed fields. On a distant hill is a chalk figure.

Background: The smith was honoured above all men by the Celtic peoples. As well as a craftsman he was often a magician as well.[38]

Meaning: Construction; craftsmanship; professional mastery; practical skills; creative instinct; good organization and skill bring honour and reward.

Stone Four

Description: Beneath a striated hill, a great treasure, including a gaming board, is revealed.

Background: The Thirteen Treasures of Britain are those empowering objects of the land. Whoever holds them is ruler of the land, and hence many of the Hallows descend into modern usage as the regalia of the monarch.[78,41]

Meaning: Earthly power; conscientious ambition; material gain; possessiveness; selfishness; spiritual miserliness; time to be generous with others.

Stone Five

Description: In a barren country, a standing stone is seen through a blizzard.

Background: There were times on the quest when the very elements

seemed to oppose the seekers. They travelled through lands that were often barren and desolate, by roads long forgotten, where habitations were few and far between.

Meaning: Adversity; insecurity; strain; barren prospects; loneliness; destitution; loss of home or means; the need for a firm instinctive grounding before undertaking a project.

Stone Six

Description: At night, a great fire burns in the middle of a stone circle.

Background: From the time they were built, the stone circles of Britain were symbols of power and might. Apart from their religious significance they were also used for more secular purposes, when poets and story-tellers gathered to continue the great tradition.

Meaning: Material success; good fortune shared; generosity; charity; patronage; gifts; the exchange of matter with spirit; the Great Work.

Stone Seven

Description: A great wall stretching across northern hills. It is broken. Nearby stands a symbol stone.

Background: After his unsuccessful attempt at the quest Lancelot returned to seek again the love of Guinevere. Spurned by her for a

time, he went mad, roaming about through the wilderness until he was found and brought back to sanity by Elaine le Blanc.[31]

Meaning: Fruitless speculation; anxiety over efforts; lack of fulfilment; fear of failure; the need to live one day at a time and allow events to unfold.

Stone Eight

Description: In a stonemason's yard at sunset, a nearly completed stone carving awaits the mason's chisel.

Background: Before becoming a knight every neophyte underwent a rigorous period of training. Those who went on the Quest, like Perceval, sometimes required additional training before they were fully shaped for their task.[4]

Meaning: Prudence; patient application; discriminating service to a craft; better results through gaining professional skills; apprenticeship; methodical work; detailed preparation.

Stone Nine

Description: In an evergreen clearing stands an ancient stone, marking a place of sanctuary for all wild things, many of whom gather about it.

Background: When Owain sets out on his quest for adventure, he encounters the Wild Herdsman: around him gather all the animals of the forest, for he is their guardian.[30]

Meaning: Accomplishment; enjoyment of solitary pursuits; love of nature; aesthetic pleasure derived from one's goods; relaxation and

leisure; ease; fulfilment of physical sensation.

Stone Ten

Description: In a snowy landscape stands a fortress. Two magpies fly with the *gwyddbwyll* board.

Background: The Chessboard Castle is always a place of testing. Those who come there often find a game of chess under way in which the pieces move by themselves.[58]

Meaning: Tradition; wealth; ancestry; inheritance; property; establishment and permanence; enduring prosperity; the treasures of tradition; ancestral lore.

Stone Maiden

Description: The Stone Maiden walks across the snow bearing the head of a man on a platter. Blood falls into the snow. Over a standing stone a raven hovers.

Background: In the early versions of the Grail story, Peredur sees a mysterious procession, in which a maiden bears a man's severed head in a dish of blood. Later on, his quest deepens when he has a vision upon seeing the blood of a duck lying in the snow with a raven feeding from it.[30]

Meaning: She is a wise and discerning student of the mysteries; capable and supremely practical, she listens to the voice of the earth; she is the upholder of the Stone Hallow.

Stone Knight

Description: The Stone Knight rides a brown horse through a mountain pass at sunset. On his arm is the checkered shield.

stone knight

Background: Bors, Lancelot's brother, is a man with little dynamism, but with a great deal of determination upon the Grail quest. Closest to the average Grail seeker in many ways, he has a deep understanding of human nature.

Meaning: He is a responsible and trustworthy companion; his patient and methodical approach may make him seem rather dull yet he is stubbornly committed to the quest.

Stone Queen

Description: The Stone Queen sits at the window of her castle. Outside, it is snowing. A blackbird perches on her hand. She holds a mirror up to the scene. A *gwyddbwyll* board is set ready for play nearby.

Background: The Queen of the Chessboard Castle is none other than the Goddess of Sovereignty's representative. Her *gwyddbwyll* board is lost by Peredur, who subsequently strives to recover it and win back the queen's patronage. The board represents the land itself.[30, 41]

Meaning: She is noble and practical; she understands the relationship of all life to the land; she imparts a sense of nurture and security to all who encounter her.

Stone King

Description: The Stone King sits before a trilithon of stone, with a

hound at his feet. On his breast is the checkered emblem of the Stone Hallow.

Background: Bran is the most enduring figure of the inner traditions of the Cauldron and the Grail. A figure of might and power in the early Welsh tales, he is later known as Brons, the Rich Fisherman and brother to Joseph of Arimathea.[45]

Meaning: He is the guardian of traditional lore; by his steady and enduring wisdom, he sustains the land; he teaches patience and responsibility upon the path.

Card Backs

Description: The Goddess of Sovereignty appears on the back of each card, surrounded by the protective rainbow of light, with the four Caers or towers of the Hallow suits and the four Hallows themselves.

Background: Each land has its own tutulary Goddess and its own empowering symbols.

Meaning: When every land of our planet realizes its intrinsic identity, and seeks to manifest its hidden treasures harmoniously, the Goddess of the Earth will once more be empowered and our whole planet protected from those who would do it harm.

CHAPTER 4

images of the quest

THE LAND OF LOGRES

It was C.S. Lewis in his novel *That Hideous Strength* who spoke of Logres as 'the Inner Britain'.* All countries have their 'inner' or essential nature. Within Celtic tradition, the Otherworld is a reality in which this inner country is manifest. It is not the same as the physical land itself, but an archetypal expression of the land. Into this Otherworldly landscape go the seekers and questers. Within it they seek for the Four Hallows which are active within the land, expressive of its essential nature.

Figure 4.1 shows the land of Logres, the inner Britain — or indeed, any inner country — as though it were a chessboard or a terrestial tarotscope. One of the Thirteen Treasures of the Island of Britain[78] is the *gwyddbwyll* board — a form of gaming board. There is much traditional lore surrounding this treasure and its appearance in the many myths and stories of Britain denotes its central importance as one of the Four Hallows. The *gwyddbwyll* board has been proved to be emblematic of the land itself.[41] Kings fight over it, heroes encounter its mysterious action as its pieces play against each other, the Goddess

* The word *Lloegr* (Logres) is still used today by Welsh-speakers to indicate England. Throughout we employ Logres to denote the 'Inner Britain' or, indeed, the inner resonance of any land.

of Sovereignty herself clearly has charge over it.

The board itself is a mystical representation of the land.

EAST SOUTH

THE SWORD COURT OF

COURT OF THE SPEAR

XXI 0

K	*M*	*7*	*3*					*5*	*9*	*Q*	*K*
Q	*Kt*	*6*	*2*					*4*	*8*	*Kt*	*M*
9	*8*				*XVIII*	*VII*				*6*	*7*
5	*4*		*10*	*XIV*			*XI*	*10*		*2*	*3*
			X	*II*			*IV*	*XV*			
		VI							*XIX*		
		XVII							*VIII*		
			XIII	*I*			*III*	*XII*			
3	*2*		*10*	*IX*			*XVI*	*10*		*4*	*5*
7	*6*				*V*	*XX*				*8*	*9*
M	*Kt*	*8*	*4*					*2*	*6*	*Kt*	*Q*
K	*Q*	*9*	*5*					*3*	*7*	*M*	*K*

COURT OF THE GRAIL

THE STONE COURT OF

NORTH WEST

Fig. 4.1: The Land of Logres
At the centre of the land lie the Four Hallows of Britain. At the four corners of the land are the Four Hallow Courts. At each of the cardinal points are the Four Inner Guardians of Logres: Merlin, North, guarding the Stone; the Lady of the Lake, East, guarding the Sword; Arthur, South, guarding the Spear; Guinevere, West, guarding the Grail. About them are gathered the Greater Powers, while in the four corners of the land are the Lesser Powers.

Within this chapter and the three which follow it, we will be exploring in more detail the complex relationships of the cards in the *Hallowquest* pack to each other. This chapter will be looking at the nature of the quest in relation to the 'landscape cards' of the *Arthurian Tarot*: that is, the cards numbered 2–9.

These cards are substantially different from those of other Tarots since they are neither pip cards — cards which represent only emblematic patterns of their suit — nor are they scenes in which characters perform some action or other. Each of the landscape cards depicts only a scene in which land features, weather, time of day, season of the year etc. as well as the Hallow of each suit appearing to represent the qualities of each card.

Through such landscape as this we are introduced to an archetypal world, one which is inhabited by the Greater Powers and by the Court cards. Somewhere within this landscape are to be found the Four Hallows. By skilful use of these cards, you will be enabled to make your own quests and inner journeys. The reason why no one appears in any of these cards will become very obvious to you as you work with them. They are for *you* to enter.

On p.125 you will find an exercise to help you begin your journeying. But to recap on the significance of each of the suits here is a reminder:

Sword	*Spear*	*Grail*	*Stone*
Air	Fire	Water	Earth
Spring	Summer	Autumn	Winter

THE ROUND TABLE

The sacred centre of Arthur's kingdom was the Round Table. It was from here that the knights of Arthur's court went on quests, raying out through the land and bringing the influence of the Round Table Fellowship to all. At the Round Table, news of adventures was heard, rumours of imbalanced forces were reported and momentous decisions were made.

The right to sit at the Round Table was one that had to be earned. Many medieval texts speak of the making of a knight: his preparation, vigil, dubbing and ceremonial induction into the rights and usages of knighthood. Manuscripts of the Arthurian stories show the Round Table, each *siege* or seat inscribed with its occupant's name. Apart from the *siege perilous* in which only the destined Grail winner might sit, each seat had its designated knight.

The circularity of the Round Table, at which all were equal *in potentia*, together with the fact that earlier sources number the knights as 12 has led many esoteric writers to equate it with the wheel of the Zodiac.[77] This seems a very obvious parallel, since the Fellowship of the Round Table represented all kinds and conditions of people, just as the full circle of the Zodiac gives the fullest range of personality and inner potential.

Figure 4.2 shows The Zodiacal Sieges of the Round Table, expressed in terms of the Lesser Powers. The original Round Table showed individual knights seated round it: this diagram shows the landscape represented about it instead. It is as though each knight brought his own locality to the Table, where its many features and possibilities are assembled. The diagram essentially shows the unity of the land of Logres (or indeed, of any country in the world).

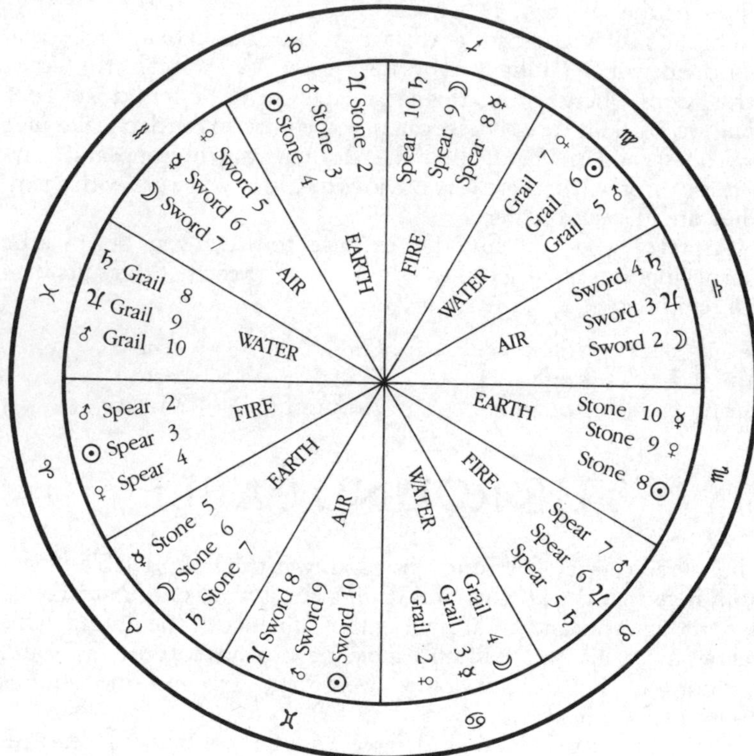

Fig. 4.2: The Zodiacal Sieges of the Round Table

For this diagram we have followed the Golden Dawn teaching on the *decans*:

> *This was an astrological scheme developed by Ptolemy in ancient Egypt. The Zodiac, a flat disc (360°), is divided into 36 sections of 10° each. Thus, each of the twelve houses of the Zodiac has three Decans, and each Decan is a minor card of the Tarot. These same divisions are days of the year, so that each individual may be assigned one of the Minor cards on the basis of birth date.* [81]

Thus, each of us, according to our birth date, may be assigned a place at the Round Table. This can become the basis of our own quest, for we each start out with our given Lesser Power — our intrinsic potential which we enhance, change or co-operate with. M.B. Hashrouck's excellent book, *Tarot and Astrology*,[20] gives an astrological breakdown of these decans of the Tarot zodiac in full detail.

The key to each of the decans is as follows:

March 21–30	Spear Two
March 31–April 10	Spear Three
April 11–20	Spear Four
April 21–30	Stone Five
May 1–10	Stone Six
May 11–20	Stone Seven
May 21–31	Sword Eight
June 1–10	Sword Nine
June 11–20	Sword Ten
June 21–July 1	Grail Two
July 2–11	Grail Three
July 12–21	Grail Four
July 22–August 1	Spear Five
August 2–11	Spear Six
August 12–22	Spear Seven
August 23–September 1	Stone Eight
September 2–11	Stone Nine
September 12–22	Stone Ten
September 23–October 2	Sword Two
October 3–12	Sword Three
October 13–22	Sword Four
October 23–November 1	Grail Five
November 2–12	Grail Six
November 13–22	Grail Seven
November 23–December 2	Spear Eight
December 3–12	Spear Nine
December 13–21	Spear Ten
December 22–30	Stone Two
December 31–January 9	Stone Three
January 10–19	Stone Four
January 20–29	Sword Five
January 30–February 8	Sword Six
February 9–18	Sword Seven
February 19–28	Grail Eight
March 1–10	Grail Nine
March 11–20	Grail Ten

If your birthday falls on 29 February, you should decide by studying both the Grail 8 and 9, which best represents your personality and abilities.

THE QUEST

One of the earliest, if not *the* earliest, accounts of the quest comes from an obscure Welsh poem attributed to the sixth-century bard Taliesin, but not actually written down until the ninth century. The *Preiddeu Annwn* (*Spoils of Annwn*) tells how Arthur leads a band of heroes in a raid on the Otherworld kingdom to steal the cauldron of the lord of Annwn. Warmed by the breath of nine maidens, with pearls around its rim, this cauldron would not boil the food of a coward, and may well possess the gift of life — since if a man were put into it he came forth alive, though bereft of speech, since no one may speak of things seen beyond the door of death.

The raid is far from easy. The heroes must pass through seven grim castles: Caer Ochren, Caer Sidi, Caer Vandwy, Caer Goludd, Caer Rigor, Caer Veddwit, and Caer Pedryfan, and in each of these are guardians who must be encountered and overcome. The poem is ambiguous as to the outcome of the raid, but the refrain which runs through each verse, 'Except seven, none returned . . .' suggests that if Arthur brought back the Cauldron it was hard won.[9]

This is only one of several such miraculous vessels described in Celtic mythology. The Cauldron of Gwrnach the Giant, the 'Hamper' of Gwyddno Garanhir, the Cauldron of Ceridwen, all share attributes which become familiar in the later Grail romances: the ability to provide food of the heart's desire, the gift of vision or prophecy, and perhaps, eternal life.

It may be that these vessels, which on the one hand reflect the cauldrons kept boiling, in hall and house, for weeks on end full of rich broth and fine meat, also represent an ancient form of scrying, in which the stars, reflected in water, were once read to give answers to the deep questions of birth, death and mortality.

These are the earliest resonances of what was to become, in the hands of the medieval *trouvères*, a rich and wondrous tapestry of tales in which the Round Table knights pursued their own quest for perfection through the endless magical forests of Logres.

Certainly the theme of the Quest is the most important single thread in the tapestry. In the later romances, from the moment when the Grail first appears at Camelot, nothing is ever quite the same. Every one of the knights swears he will not rest until he has seen the Grail again and plumbed its mysteries. In effect only three, Galahad, son of Sir Lancelot, Perceval of Wales, the Wise Fool, and Bors de Ganis, the stubbornly gentle and generous hearted, will find their way to the Holy City of Sarras and there behold the deepest mysteries of their goal. For the rest, Lancelot's great heart will bring him close but not close enough, and Gawain, the first to make the vow to seek the Grail, will stumble again and again into proximity with the mystery — each time failing to ask the right question that will set events in motion and bring about the completion of the Quest.

Arthur himself does not take part in these events, almost certainly because he himself is wounded, like the Grail King, with a wound that will not heal until the destined one comes to achieve the sacred mystery. Arthur's wound, as with all the Grail Kings, is connected to the state of the land over which he rules. This is said to be waste and unproductive, without growth, and until its lord is healed so it will remain.

The knights themselves seem unaware of this, being motivated more by curiosity than anything when they first set out. The Quest itself educates them, by direct experience. Again and again we read how one or other undergoes some dread adventure, and how afterwards they meet with one of the legion of wandering hermits who throng the pages of the later Arthuriads, and whose prime function it is to explain the mystical symbolism of the events which have just occurred.

This was, of course, an excellent way of putting across the theological teachings which had by then become an integral part of the stories. The Quest knights themselves seem like blank pages on which are written the inner meanings of the search.

Thus the Quest becomes a paradigm of the struggle between sex and sanctity, the former represented by worldly men like Lancelot and Gawain; the latter by Galahad and Bors, who lived in but were not of the world. Perceval, the third successful quester, seems to fall somewhere between the two, his innocence or 'foolishness' protecting him from either extreme.

At times the texts seem almost to become a battle ground for the opposing forces of the Christian clerics who copied many of the finest manuscripts, and the Troubadours and *trouvères* who purveyed the art of Courtly Love in defiance of the Church's laws. In their efforts to define just what it was the seekers were actually looking for, some commentators have seen this as, more deeply, representing an affirmative and negative way — those in search of the Grail rejecting the world and its way, while those in love with all created things, fallen or unfallen, were lead to seek the Vessel as a symbol of the Divine Feminine in Nature and humanity.

But there are many reasons for the quest, then as now. Those who seek the Grail do so out of a deep-seated need for wholeness, whether in so doing they choose to deny the world of form or affirm its every aspect.

Essentially these reasons fall into two categories: the personal and the cosmic. Neither, of course, is the sole and only valid reason. The Grail is, first and foremost, a vessel of healing, whether it be human sickness or cosmic suffering. As in all esoteric work, a time may come when the seeker is offered the opportunity to serve — to align oneself with the higher powers whose task it is to carry out the designs of the First Cause.

Not all who are so called take up the task; many who do so, fail. We may think of Lancelot who, having reached the door to the Grail chapel and beheld the mysteries taking place within, attempts to enter, for the most altruistic of reasons, (he sees the celebrant staggering under the weight of a wounded man) only to be turned away, struck down by a fiery breath which leaves him blinded for days after.

It is not always enough to desire that one be allowed to serve; sometimes rejection is a gift from which the seeker may learn an important lesson.

Commitment is still nine-tenths of the law. The mystery at the heart of the Quest is the *question*: 'Whom does Grail serve?' The answer is 'all men', and in embarking upon the search ourselves we would do well to remember it. For through the quest we become servants of creation, and our efforts, however poor or faint-hearted, however seemingly unsuccessful, are part of a greater work than perhaps we know of — a work which follows the contours of time and space itself, as our desires and hopes flow forth into the Greater World.

Earlier than this, in the Celtic antecedents of the quest, motivation was different. Then, it was more a question of personal glory that sent the heroes in quest of the cauldron. In *Peredur,*[30] the Welsh version of the story which, though written down after Chrétien's *Conte del Graal*, actually contains much earlier material, the reason for Peredur's quest is vengeance. Instead of the glowing glory of the Grail, he is shown a great dish on which is a head floating in blood. This gruesome object is the head of his cousin — motivation for a vendetta against his killer. Yet even here, the deeper mythic elements obtrude; Peredur's search brings him in contact with beings of the Otherworld, and his incidental adventures hark back to the same themes; Wasteland and cure; the mysterious procession of the elements which lead to deeper things.[30]

So too, in the Celtic sources, attention is focused not only on the vessel, but also on three other objects: the Sword, the Spear, and the Stone. We shall be looking at these in more detail in the next chapter, for each represents a facet of the *Hallowquest* which, taken altogether, make up the whole.

THE INNER COUNTRY

Whether we are dealing with the Celtic or the medieval aspects of the Quest, one aspect is common to both: the landscape. On all quests, one finds along the way clues, deceptions, guides, marsh-lights, mazelike paths, obstacles, signposts, steep hills and narrow valleys. These things are also landscapes of the mind, the heart and the soul. We are all familiar with the inscapes conjured up by the biblical expressions: 'Valley of the Dry Bones', 'Hills of Stones' or 'Valley of the Shadow' etc.

Landscapes can and often do represent states of being, places upon the path, degrees of happiness, contentment or despair. A large factor in our relationship with landscapes, both inner and outer, is the weather. A dark dismal day with rain falling steadily, the kind of day in which one never puts out the light, requires far greater effort to sustain oneself than a bright day in Spring or a snowy morning when everything looks clean and newly washed.

The landscapes of the Quest are no different, except that they are subtler; the bright morning may hide the dark noon, the straight road does not always lead most directly to where one wishes to go, or to the *real* castle of the Grail. The greater the importance of the goal, the harder will be the path and the easiest way may lead to the place where the anti-Grail forces hold sway, or to the home of the wild and untamed magic of the cauldron.

We may journey by land or sea, over hills or through valleys; we may need to climb mountains, or scale sheer cliffs, swim rivers or wade through cataracts; tread quaking marshes or plod down roads iron-shod with ice. Will the fields on either side be filled with standing corn or scarlet poppies? Will the fences that line the path be decked out with human heads? Will the sea-crossing be rough or smooth? We cannot always know, any more than we can tell what lies around the next corner of the maze in real life, whom or what we will encounter, whether they (or it) will be friendly or fierce. This is part of the adventure, which we accept when we undertake the Quest; and it is the nature of the Quest to be endlessly unexpected.

So, in traversing the multi-dimensional world of the *Hallowquest* we should be prepared to begin in Spring and pass at once to Winter, then retreat to Summer and so back to Spring again. Or we may, having been on a path or road winding between hills, find that we must take ship on a restless sea (Spear 9) in order to arrive at a wood (Spear 3), or cross a terrible Wasteland (Sword 5) to a place of broken stones (Stone 7) or a strange Otherworldly broch where the mysteries of the Grail are even now taking place (Grail 10).

The journey exists to teach us, and we will learn more about ourselves and our lives from following it (for assuredly it will lead us rather than allowing us to impose our wills upon it) than by striving to attain the castle or the court, or the Chapel in the Green, by simply willing ourselves to be there. All routes lead to the places of the Hallows, the Courts of Joy, or the Castle of the Grail; the route we take each time is partly of our own formulation, partly the working out of the Quest itself, as it shapes us and helps us to find our way through the maze of being.

To try this out, the following exercise will open some of the many dimensions of the Quest. Separate the Lesser Powers from the rest of the pack. Choose 10 cards at random, laying them face upwards in a pattern of your choosing. This is your proposed route, your pilgrimage, your Quest. Now select one card from the Greater Powers or the Court cards to represent yourself. You may wish to choose the Seeker who stands for the Fool, but pick any card you feel best represents you.

Now look at the cards you first drew. What kind of landscape do they suggest? Are there many sudden changes involved — say, from land to sea, season to season, mountain side to sunny meadow? Begin anywhere and follow the path shown in the cards in conscious meditation. This can be done with a little practice; it is akin to day-dreaming. Let your imagination work as though you were creating a story or the scenario for a meditation. You may like to write down your itinerary and, in your own time, consider how this relates to your life or magical activities. Finally, ask yourself where the journey seems to lead — does it end at all, or simply lead away from the scenes on the cards into another dimension? Use the ideas gained in this way to form the basis of further meditation, allowing the images that rise spontaneously to take you deeper into the lands of the *Hallowquest*. This can take as long or as short a time as you wish, but remember not to overdo things.

Your journey may be the beginning of a much greater one, which may last a long time, but do not worry if you get nothing spectacular. Your first attempts may seem to mean little, but do not be surprised if you find the images cropping up again in your dreamlife, or even in real areas of countryside in which, around the next corner, may lie a scene not unlike that on which you have been working. In this way, gradually, you will begin to familiarize yourself with the landscape of the *Hallowquest* and you may begin to add more of the Greater Powers into your explorations. Each card has a lesson to teach or helpful advice to give you. The moment you first open the *Hallowquest* pack, you step into a deeper realm of wonder and exploration. Good fortune attend your travels!

CHAPTER 5

the hallows in celto-arthurian tradition

THE ELEMENTS IN WESTERN TRADITION

Throughout the history of the Western Esoteric Tradition, the elements are used as the basis for training and practice in ritual work. The qualities of Air, Fire, Water and Earth represent an eternal quaternity of values which is reflected within the *Hallowquest* pack in the suits of Swords, Spears, Grails and Stones.

It was the Greek philosopher, Empedocles of Akragas, who in 430 BC formally identified these elements as the determining basis of creation. A century later, Aristotle added a fifth, aether, which was 'the element of the heavens'. The subsequent divorce of science from philosophical and magical thought, where ancient cosmology departed from rationalist science, has led to the development of the Periodic Table, in which as many as 105 further elements and chemicals have been identified as the substance of the earth and its atmosphere.[1] The original four elements are now almost solely the province of the esoteric practitioner, the astrologer and the Tarot reader.

The system of four elements was of course much older than Empedocles' theory. Shamans and magicians have long constellated the elements to each of the four cardinal points in performing their rituals, for each of the four directions has its guiding quality, its power or god, as well as a mass of symbolism relating to it which varies from place to place according to the inner cosmology of a people.

The system which is used in this book is derived from the north-west European native tradition — a system which was largely followed by the mainstream magical traditions of the Middle Ages and the magical revival of the nineteenth century. These definitions are not finite either to this or any other tradition. The native peoples of Tibet, North America and Australia, for example, each have their own correspondences associated with each quarter. Each are correct, according to their lights. In working with the Four Hallows of the British tradition, certain natural alignments and correspondences of each element emerge which seem orderly and natural, and these have been followed in this book.

W.B. Yeats was perhaps the first to utilize the native mythologies of the British Isles. His dream was to found a magical order which worked on these lines and, though he was a member of the Golden Dawn, he did not see his wish fulfilled in his lifetime.[56] It was he who made the association between the Hallows of the Tuatha de Danaan and the Tarot aces, which Jessie Weston later popularized in her *From Ritual to Romance.*[83] As a Golden Dawn initiate, Yeats made his magical implements: the cup, sword, pentacle and wand — the traditional regalia of the magician which was emblematic of the four elements and of the four directions — to draw upon. And it was doubtless so that he was able better to understand the Hallows of the Tuatha de Danaan, which form the archetypal basis for the teaching of the Four Hallows in Western tradition.

There has been much scholarly debate about the emblems which are borne in the Grail procession, but there is little doubt that these derive, partially, from earlier Irish and British archetypes.

Earth
North
The Lia Faíl

Water
West
The Cauldron of the Dagda

Air
East
The Sword of Nuadu

Fire
South
Spear of Lugh

Fig. 5.1: The Four Treasures of the Tuatha de Danaan

These treasures were each brought from one of four cities, where its bearer was instructed in wisdom by an Otherworldly teacher:

Treasure	*City*	*Name of Teacher*
The Sword of Nuadu	Findias	Uscias
The Spear of Lugh	Gorias	Esras
The Cauldron of the Dagda	Murias	Semias
The Lia Faíl	Falias	Morfessa

Fig. 5.2: The Four Cities of the Tuatha de Danaan

These fourfold treasures represent the empowerment of the gods of the Tuatha de Danaan — the Tribe of Danu, the Great Goddess. They were, according to the *Book of Invasions*,[5] gods of great power and skill, knowing every art and occult science. The mysterious four cities from which they came are located in the Otherworld, and their instructors in wisdom are clearly the original guardians of the Four Treasures.

This information concerning the inner guardianship of the Hallows is valuable, since the early British tradition frequently lacks specific cosmological or mythological references: these are provided in later tradition within the Arthurian cycle and the related Grail corpus.

Within this book, the reconstruction of the British mysteries from the elemental powers and native mythologies becomes closer to fulfilment. But to bring this about, we need to have a firm grasp of our inner spiritual dimension.

INNER COSMOLOGIES

The overwhelming esoteric correspondences, which have been heaped upon the Tarot in absurd profusion, have been avoided here in order to give prominence to the stories underlying each card, but a strong sense of the four elements will stand the reader in good stead. As R.J. Stewart and W.G. Gray have taught,[69,67,12] the establishment of an inner cosmology is of prime importance, and this is built up from the personal experience of each individual. As mortal human beings, we live our lives in contact with the four elements of ancient cosmology: they are our basis, our common ground, if you like. Like the horoscope we are each born under, the inner elements and constellating powers may be worked with, ignored, or enhanced. The Hallows, as representatives of the four elements, are no exception.

Within each of us, one or other elemental quality will be supreme in our make-up. This can be established from a close study of one's birth chart. The remaining elements need to be brought into alignment and balance with our being, and that is the measure of magical work. For we are all magicians, striving to balance the elements of life within our own sphere of influence: to be sensitive to our own needs and imbalances, as well as those around us. We start with ourselves, not to be selfish, but in order to prepare ourselves for the *Hallowquest*.

The achievement of the *Hallowquest* is the healing of the world, by which it is brought into alignment with the Otherword and the Underworld.

The Otherworld and the Underworld of British tradition have no contemporary cosmological equivalent in our society. They are not to be confused with the Christian heaven and hell and are perhaps nearer in quality to certain Classical modes, though the Underworld we speak of here has no twittering ghosts and grey gloom. Rather it is the place of ancestral wisdom, the Great Below from where the accumulated wealth of memory, which underlies our entire existence as created beings is quarried. The Otherworld, on the other hand, corresponds to the Blessed Islands of Celtic tradition, for it is the abode of the gods and the ever-living ones who are no longer mortal, but initiates of the Spiral Tower. It is the Great Above, and with the Great Below and the four elements, it comprises the basic cosmology which surrounds the *Hallowquest*. It is a robust, subtle and transformative cosmology in which the everyday world we live in has an integral part.

In order to show the antiquity of the traditions surrounding each of the Hallows, there follows a full breakdown of the appearances of each emblematic treasure in Celto-Arthurian tradition. Space does not allow us to retell all the stories associated with the Hallows, but the reader is encouraged to follow up the bibliographical references and read them for him- or herself.

SWORD

The function of the Sword within the *Hallowquest* is that of dispeller of illusions. It cuts through obstacles, whether material or spiritual, and brings light to dark places. Like the cutting winds of March it blows, dispelling Winter and bringing the renewal of Spring to the world.

Nearly all swords within Celto-Arthurian tradition draw upon the archetype of the Glaive or Sword of Light, a weapon which can still be found in Celtic folk tales.[6] It is normally wielded by the young hero and has extraordinary qualities, as we shall see below. But perhaps the earliest archetype in Celtic tradition is the Sword of Nuadu.

'From Findias was brought the sword of Nuadu; none used to escape who was wounded by it.'[5]

Within Arthurian tradition we are fortunate in possessing an early poem which may show the connections between the Irish and British myths. In the ninth-century Welsh poem, the *Preiddeu Annwn*,[9] we read that the sword of Llwch Lleminawc flashed before the cauldron of Annwn — the treasure which Arthur went there in his ship Prydwen to obtain. In a parallel version of this story, occuring in

Culhwch and Olwen, it further says that the sword Llwch the Irishman used was Caledfwlch — the old British name for Excalibur.[30]

It has been proved that Llwch Lleminawc and Lugh Lamfada (of the Long Arm) are one and the same person; later tradition has made an Irish god into Arthur's ally. From the internal evidence of many texts, it is evident that Llwch or Lugh passed down into Arthurian tradition as Lancelot, Arthur's best friend and chief knight of the Round Table. Lancelot still retains Lugh's prowess in battle and becomes the British king's champion just as Lugh champions the failing Nuadu, even inheriting his famous sword. A further mythic parallel may be drawn with Cuchulainn, the great hero of the Irish Red Branch cycle of stories. He also had a sword which produced irreparable damage, as well as a fearsome spear, which will be discussed below.

Probably the best example from British tradition concerning the feats of the young hero comes in *Culhwch and Olwen* where Culhwch is challenged to fulfil many impossible tasks, including the taking of a magical sword from Gwrnach, a giant. He is helped in this task by Cai (Kay) and Bedwyr (Bedevere), who both exert their cunning and trick their way into Gwrnach's hall as burnishers of swords. The young and nameless son of Custennin, who accompanies these seasoned warriors of Arthur's court, performs an astounding feat of great daring, by penetrating the three gates of Gwrnach's castle and coming to the inmost courtyard unscathed. It is thus that the boy gains his name — Goreu (the Best). He is destined to become the wielder of the Sword of Light which, until now, was guarded by Gwrnach. With it, Goreu later beheads his father's oppressor, the giant Yspaddeden Pencawr, thus releasing the land from a great tyranny.

The Sword is, then, a weapon for the young hero to win and wield. Its brightness and cleanness of blade are sometimes supplemented by its ability to 'sing' in battle as it cleaves the air. The Sword, like the other Hallows, is a dangerous implement to wield. It empowers its bearer with superhuman stature and ability and may not be wielded unworthily. It is a weapon which a young man must first measure up to.

In the story of *Peredur*, Peredur (the early name for Perceval), comes to the court of his first uncle where he is asked to engage in a combat with club and shield: he is well able to win the engagement. At his second uncle's house, however, he is asked to take up a sword and with it cut in two an iron column. He succeeds at first, but in so doing, the sword breaks in pieces. He is then told to reunite the blade and try again. Again, the column and blade break in two. But on the third attempt he is unable to make either column or sword whole again. His second uncle tells him that he has only two-thirds of his strength yet, but that he will be the best sword fighter in the kingdom.[30] Peredur has to fulfil many adventures until he is worthy of wielding the sword, each task becoming his practice until he completes the Grail Quest.

A similar story is also told of Gawain, who in *Le Conte del Graal* of Chrétien de Troyes, especially the *First Continuation*,[4] the hero undergoes several tests involving a mystical sword which is either broken and must be restored, or which is restored but will break again at a crucial moment. The idea here seems to be that the seeker should not trust overly to the strength of the blade, but depend rather on his personal abilities and intent. There are clear traces that Gawain, who was once himself a Grail winner, once had a fully-fledged Quest for the Sword, and that its finding was his own form of empowerment in the Quest.[51]

In *Perlesvaus*, one of the most intricate of the Grail texts, it is Gawain who goes on a quest for the sword which beheaded John the Baptist. This sword bleeds at midday — the hour at which the Saint was beheaded; when it is drawn, it flashes with emerald fire and becomes green. This whole episode overlays many traditions about the Grail and its original appearance as a vessel with a man's head in it. (See p.142.) Gawain wins the sword by overcoming a giant who has carried off a pagan king's son. Although the boy is dead by the time Gawain arrives, he is still given the sword as a reward. The dead boy is then ceremonially cut up and his body distributed to the people, all of whom eat a piece. The pagan king is then baptized after this curious salvific ritual which restores his people to health. Although Gawain is not able to succeed in winning the Grail in this text, he is nevertheless a prime instigator of the quest, being the first to ride out in search of it. The fact that he obtains the sword which beheaded the Baptist is significant, since there is a well-evolved tradition concerning Gawain's association with midday and midsummer. (See p.64.) Another, equally important tradition makes Gawain the recipient of Excalibur, which he holds in trust for Arthur for a time.[3]

The Quest for the Holy Grail[36] tells of a sword — that of the Strange Hangings. This was the weapon of King David which Solomon's wife sets in the Ship of Solomon which is built by her and sent down the ages where it is found by the Grail knights, Bors, Perceval and Galahad. The sword is found on the ship, set about with dire warnings:

> *I am a marvel to behold and apprehend, for none was ever able to grip me, however big his hand, nor ever shall, save one alone; and he shall pass in excellence all who preceded and shall follow him.*[36]

It further warns that whosoever draws it, unless he is the best knight, shall suffer injury or death. (A feature which we recall from the Sword of Nuadu.) Perceval's sister, Dindraine, who is with them, relates its history and tells them that this sword's unworthy unsheathing was the cause of the Wasteland. The scabbard tells that a maiden who is a king's daughter and a virgin, shall remake the belt with her own hair. She shall call the sword by its true name. (See p.82 Sword Maiden.)

Dindraine then tells the story of Nasciens who had a vision of the sword. He lusted for it more than any other weapon, but when he drew it, it broke in half. King Mordrains was able to reunite it, saying that it had broken because of Nascien's sin and presumption. She further tells of another unworthy unsheathing by King Parian who is transfixed by a flying lance between his thighs. Dindraine then affixes a new belt made from her hair and names the sword: 'The Sword of the Strange Hangings', and calls the scabbard, 'Memory of Blood', since part of the scabbard was made of the Tree of Life which turned from green to red at Abel's murder. All the knights and Dindraine urge Galahad to gird on the sword, 'which has been more impatiently desired in the kingdom of Logres than was Our Lord Himself by His apostles.'[36] Galahad's mighty sword is, then, symbolic of the ending of the Wasteland. Its lineage is crowded with mystic meanings; its function is to cut through evil custom and restore the land's fertility, along with the faith of the people.

The Sword is one of the Hallows most associated with Arthur himself. He gains his throne and is recognized as king by his action of pulling the sword from the stone. Alternative traditions have also given him another sword, Excalibur, which is given to him by the Lady of the Lake. Both stories merely reinforce the tradition that the Sword is the proper empowerment for the young hero who is in the springtime of his days. We are given a portrait of Arthur's sword in *The Dream of Rhonabwy*: it is imprinted with two dragons which shoot forth fire when the blade is drawn from the scabbard, and is so bright that men cannot bear to gaze upon it. This is clearly a depiction of the Hallow of the Sword in the hands of a master who has won to his full strength. The Hallow of the Sword is thus the proper empowerment for the person beginning his or her spiritual quest. It is given into the hands of those who will grow in strength and wisdom, and into their role as protectors of the land against all manner of injustice and tribulation.

SPEAR

The function of the Spear within the *Hallowquest* is that of challenger. It pierces that which is inwardly corrupt and allows its healing rays to pass within. Like the penetrating beams of the Summer sun, it can both warm and sear. The Spear has a double action, like the rest of the Hallows. It is sometimes called, 'the Spear which Heals and Wounds'.

In Irish tradition, Lugh's spear is an instrument of victory. Lugh's nickname, Lamfada or Long-Arm, is derived from his ability to hit his target. With the spear, he pierces the baleful eye of Balor, the Fomorian giant.

'From Gorias was brought the spear that Lugh had; no battle was maintained against him who had it in his hand.'[5]

Within folk tradition, the Spear has become the pillar of combat — a stone or wooden column which the hero has to strike in order to issue his challenge to the powers set against him.[6] Dexterity with the Spear was a feature of the Celtic warrior, as we can see from Bedwyr's prowess in *Culhwch and Olwen*, where the head of his lance can leave its shaft, draw blood from the wind and return to the shaft again. By the time Arthurian stories were being transcribed in the Middle Ages, the jousting lance had replaced the warrior's lance, becoming less of a ritual but more of a chivalric implement of challenge.

This feature of challenge is retained both within Celtic tradition and the Grail cycle where the Spear becomes very much associated with the wounding and healing of the king and the land.

Two early stories establish this archetypal pattern. The Irish story of *Mac Datho's Pig*, tells how Cet mac Matach cast spears against numerous opponents; one of these, Celtechar mac Uthecair, was wounded through the groin, so that he was unable afterwards to father children.[33] This wounding is analogous to that of the Wounded King. According to Celtic customs of kingship, a blemished or maimed man could not become or remain king, since he was considered incapable of maintaining his mystical marriage with the Sovereignty of the Land.

Features of this understanding can be found within the story of *Branwen, Daughter of Llyr*,[30] wherein Bran the Blessed raised the men of Britain to avenge the disgrace of his sister, Branwen, married to the king of Ireland and, though she had borne him a son, had been cast off to serve in the kitches. Bran had earlier salved the wounded honour of the Irish king, whom Bran's brother had insulted, by giving him the cauldron of rebirth. Although a truce was prepared, Bran's brother, Efnissien, cast Branwen's child into the fire and so caused strife to break out once more. During this affray, Bran was wounded in the foot with a poisonous spear. This unhealing wound was so grievous, that Bran bid his men behead him and bear his head to the White Mount (The Tower of London), where they were to bury it as a Palladium against invasion. Before they reach their destination, they sojourn in the Otherworldly confines of Gwales and Harlech. There Bran speaks with them and the company are sustained for 80 years, until one of the company opens a forbidden door and they feel the weight of mortality return to them.

Bran's head is a deep image relating to the Stone Hallow, where it will be spoken of further. But it will be seen that Bran's wounding serves as the earliest analogue of the Dolorous Blow — the unfortunate wounding which causes the Wasteland. (See below.) Bran himself is the prototype of the Wounded or Fisher King, where his name, in later legend, becomes Bron or Brons.

Both these stories reveal the essential role of the Spear in the subsequent Grail legends: it renders impotent the one it strikes, simultaneously wasting his land and casting him into a state of suspended animation in which he can be neither healed nor die.

Celtic legend also shows the Spear to be an instrument of revenge and retribution. When Lugh's father is wounded by the spears of the Sons of Tuirenn, and then killed by them, Lugh sets impossible tasks for them. This includes the finding of a poisonous spear called Aredbair which has to be kept in a cauldron of water in case its incandescent powers should accidentally set the city on fire. It is during their quest that the Sons of Tuirenn are themselves slain by a spear.[4]

The most famous spear owned by a hero is the *Gae Bolg* of Cuchulainn. This was said to roar loudly before it was about to be used in battle. Once it went into the body of an enemy it could not be pulled forth again without causing the death of the warrior. It is, like the spear of Lugh, a weapon of ultimate invincibility.

In British tradition, Llew, Lugh's Welsh counterpart, is killed by a magical spear; he is restored to life by Gwydion and returns the tempered spear which slew him into the breast of his enemy, Gronw.[30]

The cross-fertilization of the Grail tradition by Christianity has given us yet another analogue of the sacred Spear — the Lance of Longinus — the pilum of the centurion who pierced the side of Christ. Contrary to popular thought, this is not an act of violence but one of mercy, since the soldiers thought that Jesus was already dead, they forbore breaking his legs — an act which usually resulted in the death of the crucified victim since he could not thus raise himself properly to breathe and would soon expire. Instead, Longinus thrusts his lance into Christ's side to ensure that he was truly dead and from the wound flowed water and blood which, according to some traditions, Joseph of Arimathea caught in two cruets and which he bore to Europe. This apocryphal tradition lodged deeply in the later Arthurian texts.

While some Grail legends do not speak of the Wounded King's original maiming, others are more specific. Chief among these is Wolfram von Eschenbach's *Parzival*, which tells how Amfortas, the Wounded King of this text, was maimed because of a sexual misdemeanour in his youth. Wolfram nicely balances this tradition by making Klingsor a eunuch in his story, so that Amfortas has his dark opponent — a man who has castrated himself in order to gain esoteric knowledge. Both men are thus sexually disempowered and held in polarized stalemate until the coming of Parzival (Perceval) who actually utilizes the Spear to heal Amfortas of his wounds.[79]

But the central story about the Dolorous Blow is given in Malory where we read about the adventures of Balin and Balan, two brothers. Balin lodges at the castle of King Pellam where he is suddenly attacked by the invisible knight, Garlon. Balin slays him, not realizing that Garlon is Pellam's brother. Pellam then turns on his guest and, in search of a weapon, Balin enters a private room and, finding a spear within, picks it up and wounds the king with it. Thus Balin strikes the Dolorous Blow, for the spear is none other than the Lance of Longinus which Pellam reverently guarded in his castle. He becomes the Wounded King and is destined only to be healed by the Grail winner, Galahad. The land is likewise laid to waste, in fulfilment of the ancient laws of Celtic kingship which tie the life of the king to that of the land: the malaise of one is inflicted automatically upon the other.

The Hallow of the Spear is thus to be handled only with care and by one who has the discernment to strike at the heart of all problems, laying them open to healing. It is the proper empowerment for the one who has acquired experience of the world upon the quest and who is mature enough to become an instrument for divine intervention. Sometimes this role is effected in a seemingly destructive manner, but the destruction of old systems which incubate their own problems is an action analogous to a surgeon cutting into healthy tissue in order to cut out the diseased matter within the body.

GRAIL

The function of the Grail in the *Hallowquest* is that of healing and plenty. The contents of the Grail never fail to satisfy or heal. Like the plenty of Autumn, the Grail dispenses its bounty and gives new life to the land.

The Grail winner is often called 'He Who Frees the Waters' — a title most suitable for the bearer of this Hallow. The Wasteland becomes a dry, barren place, with neither water to fructify its fields nor produce to bring to its tables. The people of that land are in extreme want.

As we have seen from the preceding examples, the Grail Hallow stems from two streams of tradition: from the miraculous cauldrons of Celtic tradition on the one hand, and from the cup of the Last Supper on the other. The fusion of these concepts gives us a singular vessel which many seekers still go on quests to find. When seeking the energies which underlie these Hallows, we must always bear in mind the legends which accompany their history and symbolic development, for these give us the clues which we seek.

There is a wealth of cauldrons in Celtic tradition.

'From Murias was brought the cauldron of the Dagda; no one came from it unsatisfied.'[5]

Irish tradition tells of many other cauldrons with similar functions. It was to obtain the cauldron of Diwrnach the Irishman that Arthur sailed in Prydwen, according to *Culhwch and Olwen*: that cauldron would not boil the meat of a coward and is closely associated with the giving of the best cut of meat to the most valorous hero. (A tradition which has spawned a good many stories of heroic competitions including that of Cuchulainn and Gawain in the Beheading Game.)[51]

Sometimes the cauldron is a vessel of healing. In the *Second Battle of Mag Tuiread*, the well of Slaine is prepared for the revival of the spent Tuatha de Danaan warriors.[5] This kind of vessel descended into Celtic folk tradition as the cauldron of venom and the cauldron of cure, into both of which the young hero is plunged in turn after his labours in order to harden him for future endeavours and to restore him to full strength. Whoever has been plunged into the cauldron of cure is not scathed by the cauldron of venom but given increased resistance.[6]

Celtic tradition shows how the vessel is also one of supreme truth. Cormac, called 'the Irish Solomon' for the wisdom of his judgements, was given an Otherworldly cup by the god Manannan mac Lir. It had the property that whenever three lies were told over it, it broke in pieces. When three truths were spoken over it, it would reunite.[5] (A feature which we encountered with the Sword Hallow).

It is truth of the heart which Tristan and Isolt discover when they drink from the *hanap* administered by Brangwen: into it she mixed the love-potion intended for the wedding night of Isolt with the aged King Mark. The destiny of the lovers is to be ever afterwards in love with each other through eternity.

The vessel is sometimes one of transformation. In Irish legend, Etain is incarnated in her mother's womb when she flies into a cup, having been previously enchanted into the shape of a fly. She is destined to be reborn in many generations and bear the same name — Etain — even though she is occasionally disincarnate from human flesh and transformed into animal shapes. Her husband and lover, Midir, searches for her down the ages.

The transformation which the vessel gives is sometimes the promoter of knowledge. It is through the cauldron of knowledge that little Gwion becomes Taliesin. His fingers are splashed by the liquor from Ceridwen's brew of knowledge and Gwion acquires all knowledge as he thrusts his burning fingers into his mouth to cool them. He flees in many shapes from Ceridwen in her fury, eventually becoming the humblest grain of wheat, and is reborn of her body nine months after she swallows up the grain in her shape of a hen.[30]

The pattern of the cauldron as vessel of knowledge stems from a common Celtic legend concerning the Well of Nine Hazels, over which nine hazel trees drop their nuts. The water absorbs them and five streams issue from the well to water the world of humankind. Whoever drinks of the well, or eats of the nuts, or of the salmon which swims in its waters, will be likewise made wise and become that wisdom's guardian.

This is an ancient Celtic teaching of the initiation into knowledge, where the new seeker eventually becomes the teacher responsible for manifesting and instructing others. This responsibility is a major factor within the Grail legends, as we shall see. It is part of the established pattern that the Grail winner should become the new Grail guardian and so enable the old guardian — the Wounded King — to pass on to his destined place of contemplative peace and renewal.

We come finally to the cauldrons and vessels of plenty which precede the medieval Grail manifestations. This simple and basic property of the Grail is frequently overlooked in the present day quest, which gives material as well as spiritual gifts. We have already heard of the cauldron of Diwrnach, which Arthur sought. British tradition speaks also of the hamper of Gwyddno Garanhir into which food for one can be put and food for a hundred taken out again. The medieval Grail texts did not entirely lose this feature: in Robert de Boron's *Josephe d'Arimathie*, Brons catches a fish which is laid on the table along with the holy vessel, and every worthy person's heart is filled with ineffable delight. Malory's *Morte d'Arthur* is even more specific:

> *Then began every knight to behold other, and either saw other, by their seeming, fairer than ever they saw afore . . . And there was all the hall fulfilled with good odours, and every knight had such meets* (sic) *and drinks as he best loved in this world. Each place was furnished in its wake with the food its occupants desired.*[31]

Pivotal to the fusion of pagan and Christian Grail motifs is the cauldron of rebirth, which features so prominently in the story of *Branwen, Daughter of Llyr.*[30] We have already spoken a little about Bran's sacrificial beheading. The cauldron of this story originally came from an Irish lake and was the property of a titanic couple who spawned warriors at the rate of one every month and a half. Bran gave them shelter and they gave him the cauldron. Its chief property is that dead men can be put into it and revived, but they emerge speechless. This is because they may speak about what lies beyond death: they have only died once, not, like the initiate who dies twice — once in reality and once to the world. (The poets who undergo 'the second death' are gifted with inspired speech which the uninitiated cannot understand anyway!)

Bran gives the cauldron to Matholwch, king of Ireland, in compensation for Efnissien's insult to the Irish, whose horses he mutilates. But this proves to be a chancy gift, since in the resultant war, it is used to revive dead Irish warriors who are therefore better able to best the British. To break its power, Efnissien steps into the cauldron as a living man: the cauldron breaks in two and Efnissien dies. (Yet another breaking in pieces.)

It is only in the Grail texts that the cauldron becomes a cup. Bran's cauldron and the sacrifices which surround it, so basic to the fertility of the land and the health of its people, are a native version of the later redemptive quality of the Cup of the Last Supper. Combined with the Eucharistic function of that vessel is the nature of the Cup of the Agony in the Garden, which Christ prays might pass from him. The cup which heals is also one which must be drained to the very last dregs of life. These two notions are so closely caught up within the Grail traditions of the healing and redemptive vessels, that no one can now unbind them.

The Grail which appears to Arthur and his knights as they sit at the Round Table at Pentecost, manifests at an important point in the King's career. The kingdom is at peace; law and order reign. The Arthurian kingdom is peaceful but dangerously unvitalized, almost stagnating in its own powerful purpose. The Grail shatters that illusion and causes the fragmentation of the Round Table Fellowship, the death of many knights on quest and the real spiritual dispersal of the Round Table energy.

The quest and struggle of the knights shatters the wordly order, but brings something more wonderful into being: it is a deep creative change without which the realm of Arthur becomes yet another mighty king's domain, growing fat at the expense of its inner aspirations.

The Grail is a powerful healer and cleanser, as we see from the later texts. Those who look on it or seek to touch it unworthily find it excoriates and scours rather than heals or cleanses — rather like the cauldrons of venom and cure which both harden and heal the warrior. Lancelot is blinded temporarily when he seeks to enter the chapel where the Grail is being used to celebrate mass; the hermit staggers under the weight of the Grail's goodness and Lancelot attempts to step forward and aid him but, though he is the best knight by deeds of arms in Arthur's court, he is not a fully spiritual man, and is struck by the light of the Grail instead.

This dual action is experienced by Galahad, Lancelot's son. He looks within the Grail as his reward for achieving it: he shortly afterwards expires in the City of Sarras. No one can look at God face to face and live as a mortal. The Grail changes its finders until they can no longer be earthly people content to live materially: they become citizens of the heavenly kingdom, according to the later legends.

The Hallow of the Grail is the cup of culmination and completion. It is the proper empowerment for the mature spirit who has drunk of its wisdom and come to another shore of reality. It is so that the seeker becomes the finder and thereafter, the guardian of the Grail. In many of the texts we read not of Galahad's nirvanic passing away at Sarras, but of Perceval's continued commitment to the Grail and those who seek it. After he has achieved the Grail and restored both Wasteland and Wounded King, he becomes the Grail king for another set of seekers. It is to this duty of love and compassion that the Grail winner is called.

The third of the most famous trio of Grail winners, Bors de Ganis, is the only one who returns to the world of men. He does so both in order that others should know of the events which have passed on the quest (and is thus the type of all teachers who go into the inner realms and return to tell what they have seen), and because his place is in the world, drawing back the things of the spiritual world into the temporal.

STONE

The function of the Stone in the *Hallowquest* is that of preserver of knowledge and guardian of tradition. In the Stone we find consolidation and establishment. Like the frozen darkness of Winter earth, it abides, keeping the secrets of new growth locked up until the appropriate time.

Like the Grail which can appear in various shapes as cup, well or cauldron, so too the Stone has an infinite variety of manifestation: it can be a stone chair, a head in a dish, a *gwyddbwyll* or *fidhchell* board (Welsh or Irish gaming boards similar to a chess-board), or sometimes just as a stone. There is a mystery in which all the Hallows are included within the Grail itself. See *The Grail Seeker's Companion.*[45]

It is as inauguration stone or chair that we see the Stone first of all:

'From Falias was brought the Stone of Fal which Lugh had in Tara; that is what used to scream under every king who took the sovereignty of Ireland.'[5]

This stone represents the prophetic earth itself and will not tolerate an unworthy sovereign. It is the stone of the Goddess of Sovereignty, the Lady of the Land, who is the holy earth. Many such inauguration or king-making stones survive to this day and would have marked points of tribal assembly in the same way that the plain of Tara — the royal meeting place for the High Kings of Ireland — had the Lia Faíl in its centre.

The screaming stone descends directly into the Grail legends as the Siege Perilous (the Perilous Seat). This is the place at the Round Table which is always left vacant because it is the designated seat for the Grail winner. When Perceval comes to Arthur's court, he sits in the Siege Perilous, despite the pleadings of his fellow knights. It screams and splits under him because he is not yet ready to win the Grail. A disembodied voice cries out that Perceval has performed the rashest act in the entire history of the Round Table and that the Fisher King will never be healed of his wounds, nor the land restored to fertility, nor the seat reunited at the Round Table, until a knight from its company shall have accomplished the quest of the Grail. He will have to ask the Grail question and then these enchantments shall cease.[58]

In Robert de Boron's *Josephe d'Arimathie*, Moys, one of Joseph's followers, sits at the first Round Table and is swallowed up into the abyss because he is unworthy. This fate, says the disembodied voice to Perceval, might well have befallen him had it not been for his family's connection with the Grail.

Arthur himself is inaugurated as King of Britain through the mystery of the Stone and Sword Hallows. His task is to pull the Sword from the Stone: an action which cannot be performed by any save the rightful king. Although many strong and worthy knights make the attempt, it is only for the youthful Arthur that the Stone will allow the Sword to be drawn forth.[31] Again the stone, acting as the prophetic earth, the augury of Sovereignty, comes into play. Galahad himself performs a similar action later on in the later Arthurian cycle where only he is able to draw a sword out of a floating stone, in token that he is the worthy and destined Grail winner.[31]

Within Grail literature, the Stone Hallow makes its frequent appearance as a severed head: a fact which has disquieted many scholars who have read into this atavistic survivals of pagan cults. The mystery surrounding this appearance of the head is more profound and is basically aligned with the king-making mysteries of inauguration. When a king steps upon the inauguration stone, he makes certain vows to Sovereignty — to the land itself; he promises to maintain its laws and privileges, to nurture its people as his family and to hand over his responsibilities to one more worthy, should he become incapable of maintaining these vows.

Throughout Celto-Arthurian tradition there are numerous instances of challenge and sacrificial or symbolic beheading. The Celts, though revering the head as the seat of the soul and intellect, did not actually worship it, as has been recently supposed. The head, even of an enemy, was full of power and this might be used for the good of the tribe.

In Irish legend, we read of Lugh's combat with his monstrous grandfather, Balor, whom he eventually beheads. Balor instructs Lugh to set the severed head on his own shoulders in order to be empowered with all knowledge, but Lugh, knowing his wily grandfather, puts it down upon a rock. Blood from the head falls upon the stone, causing it to fragment into thousands of pieces, and the head sinks into the earth, 'three times deeper than Loch Foyle — the deepest lake in the world up to that time.'[6] The liquor which splashed Balor in the eye when he spied upon the preparation of a Druid's cauldron of knowledge in his youth, was envenomed and this, apart from blinding him, has the effect of poisoning his blood also so that it becomes a method of killing his enemy, even after his death. Here, the old king (Balor) is overcome by his young grandson (Lugh).

This challenge and beheading feature is in the Irish story of *Bricriu's Feast*. In this story the Ulster champions are at odds as to which is the best warrior: to him alone shall the champion's portion of meat be apportioned. Loegaire, Conall and Cuchulainn each claim it, and tests are set to see which is indeed the worthiest.

A club-carrying giant comes into the hall and challenges them each to a game which no man has ever dared play with him before: this is to challenge any man to behead the giant in return for which the giant will be allowed to behead the challenger. Each warrior pledges to perform the first part of the game, but all mysteriously melt away when the giant returns the next night to claim his return blow. Only Cuchulainn kneels and, in the full view of the court, offers his neck to be hacked. The giant reveals that he is none other than the King of Munster, Cu Roi mac Daire; and Cuchulainn is accorded the champion's portion. Readers will recall that this is indeed the prototype story from which *Sir Gawain and the Green Knight* derives.

This story is deeply concerned with the challenge of the old order by a new hero and is unusual because the challenge is issued by the old king, not the young champion. Both the giant of *Bricriu's Feast* and the Green Knight of the medieval story are more than mortal men, yet these stories are directly aligned with the Stone Hallow and the mysteries of Sovereignty. Superficially, the struggle between the combatants can be seen as a combat between the Spring King and the Winter King, but if we look deeper we will see that the old champion actually allows the young champion a space in which to gain wisdom and show his true worthiness.

The Stone Hallow as a head is perhaps best instanced by the story of Bran. *Branwen, Daughter of Llyr* is the story which acts as the mortar between the pagan and Christian concepts of this Hallow. As we have already read in this chapter, Bran willingly sacrifices himself, commanding that his head should be cut off. He already suffers an unhealing wound and will doubtless die, but he allows an opportunity for his seven remaining followers to grow in wisdom. Before bearing his head to its allotted resting place, his followers are sustained in a timeless dimension of the Otherworld while the Head of Bran speaks to them. The context does not imply idle conversation between Bran and his men, rather a deep instruction in wisdom. When this instruction has been given, one of their number is overcome with curiosity to see what lies behind the door of the hall and the timelessness is shattered. Linear time begins to run again, the men are subject to mortality and its cares. But during the 87 years of their sojourn, each has learned enough to govern the remnant of Britain which is left. The Head of Bran is buried at the White Mount, where it continues to rule, only after another manner.

The sacrifice of Bran may help us to come to that most bizarre part of the Grail procession in which the Hallows are borne into the hall where the Grail candidate sits feasting with the Wounded King. Two maidens come bearing the dish in which a man's head is placed, surrounded by blood.[4,30] As they pass by, a piteous wailing is heard, which we may see as sorrow for the kingly sacrifice and grief for the unhealing wound of the Fisher King and for the wasting of the land.

At this point, it is the duty of the Grail seeker to ask the Grail question. This is sometimes a formal question: 'Whom does the Grail serve?' But, in the context of most of the versions, the implied question is, 'What is happening? Why are things like this?' Since every knight fails to ask the question at this point in the story in any of the Grail texts, thus shortening a long quest, we are never told what might suddenly happen or what the answer might be.

We can speculate at this point that the Head in the Dish would give the Grail seeker the initiatic instruction in the form of a 'Grail answer'. We know that the Wounded King and the Wasteland would be simultaneously healed. We may speculate that the Head in the Dish would pass into the place appointed for the guardians of wisdom. But what actually ensues are the further adventures of the Grail seeker who is given the opportunity for deepening his wisdom; he passes to a different concluding sequence of events which nonetheless brings about the restoration of all things, just as though he had asked the Grail question in the first place.

The difference is that, by means of his adventures, he is a person of far greater experience and resourcefulness. His failure to ask the Grail question has led him deeper into the unravelling of the quest, and fitted him to be a worthy Grail winner.

The Christian analogues of this tradition are clearly mirrored in apocryphal texts such as the *Golden Legend*. This tells the story of the death of Adam. Seth, who bore out of paradise some seeds of the Tree of Life, placed these in his dead father's mouth, and from that place sprouted the tree which was to provide the wood of the cross. This symbolic story provides us with much material for meditation. The Garden of Paradise is overlaid by the Garden of Gethsemane: the holy earth of origination has become the land of sorrow — the Wasteland. The skull of the first Adam becomes the seed-bed of a new Tree of Life, whereon the second Adam, Christ, is crucified upon the Hill of the Skull. There is sorrow, but there is also joy of redemption beyond the sacrifice.

Further apocryphal Christian tradition is woven into the Grail legends. It is said, in *Perlesvaus*, that the Grail has five changes which should not be spoken about.[3] There is a tradition concerning the Fall of Lucifer in which the Emerald Stone, signifying ancient knowledge, fell from Lucifer's crown when he disobeyed his Creator. As the stone fell, it became gradually impacted in matter, changing its shape from stone to sword, to spear, to Grail-shaped cup.

In *Parzival*, the Grail itself is an emerald stone or *achmardi*, and those who spend even a few moments in its presence are enabled to grow no older. The implication is that if one were able to dwell next to the Grail stone permanently then, as with any source of wisdom and spiritual attainment, life is endlessly prolonged. The sources for Wolfram's story, although largely derived through British and French Grail streams, seem to stem also from a Middle Eastern and Gnostic tradition.[79]

If we return to the British Grail tradition, we find that the Stone Hallow is most often represented by the chess-board. The *gwyddbwyll* board features as one of the Thirteen Treasures of Britain, and it is aligned to the Stone Hallow through its function of Otherworldly challenge. It is encountered by Peredur who finds the board's pieces playing against themselves. He settles down to support one side but it loses. In fury, he hurls the board and pieces out of the window. Immediately, a Black Maiden appears berating him for his action and telling him that he has cast away the Chess-board of the Empress and must immediately go in search of it.[30]

The appearance of the Black Maiden at this point is significant, for she usually appears to berate the Grail seeker for not asking the Grail question. The chess-board is, as we have already remarked, the symbolic analogue of the land. The pieces which move upon it are the major protagonists of the *Hallowquest*. The board really belongs to the Goddess of Sovereignty. And so we come full circle to the stone of inauguration upon which the king is proclaimed.

The Hallow of the Stone is the proper empowerment for the worthy seeker who has won through to the heart of the mystery, by means of experience and mastery of circumstance. It is the rightful place of the fully realized person, whose understanding of traditional wisdom enables him or her to overcome the challenge of the quest.

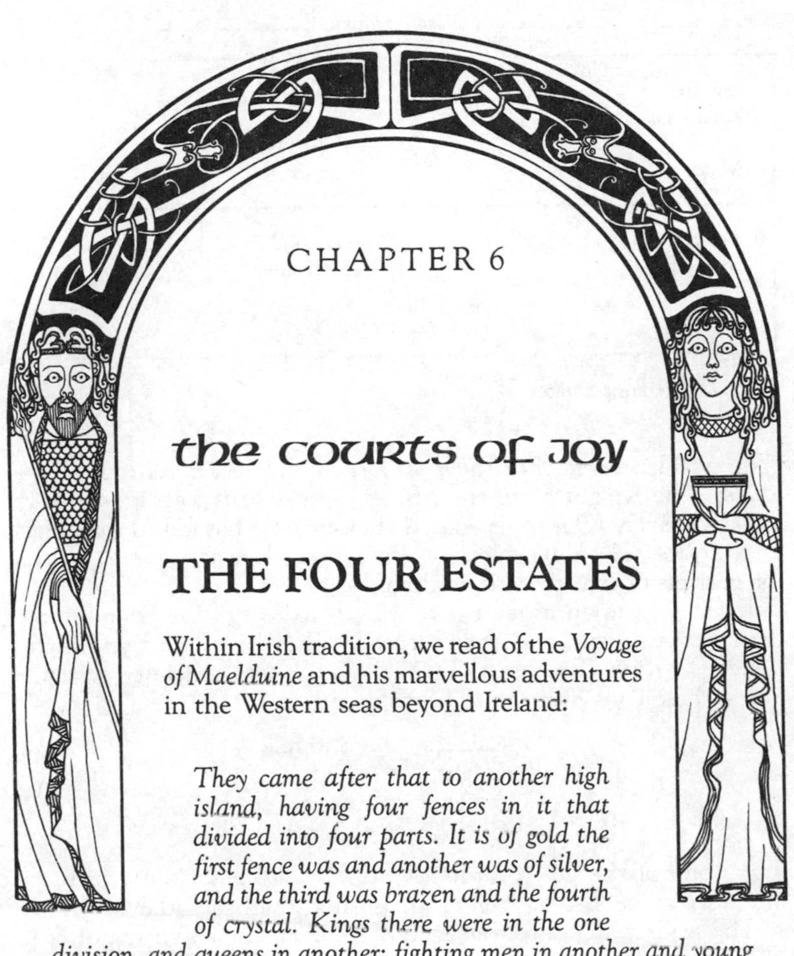

CHAPTER 6

the courts of joy

THE FOUR ESTATES

Within Irish tradition, we read of the *Voyage of Maelduine* and his marvellous adventures in the Western seas beyond Ireland:

> *They came after that to another high island, having four fences in it that divided into four parts. It is of gold the first fence was and another was of silver, and the third was brazen and the fourth of crystal. Kings there were in the one division, and queens in another; fighting men in another and young girls in the last.*[16]

These four enclosures represent an Otherworldly teaching which is most relevant to our study of the Court cards of the *Hallowquest*. (Since the following schemas are quite complex, read them over a few times until you grasp them thoroughly, especially if you intend to meditate upon them.)

Maelduine's vision of this fourfold island enclosure corresponds exactly to the four figures who represent each of the Hallow courts: the Maiden, the Knight, the Queen and the King. These personages represent each of the Four Estates. These are the conditions of humankind, on one level, while on another, the Four Estates can be seen as specific initiations related to the focused energy of the Hallows.

crystal enclosure Maidens	brass enclosure Knights
silver enclosure Queens	golden enclosure Kings

Fig. 6.1: The Four Estates

The Maiden represents the position of the seeker setting out on quest. The Knight represents the quester who is learning through adventure. The Queen represents the one who has found the object of the quest. The King represents the seeker who has become a master or mistress of that object's wisdom.

Each of us upon a quest corresponds to one of the Four Estates. Irrespective of gender, we each succeed to the roles of Maiden, Knight, Queen or King. (For those who like to work within defined gendural roles, these Four Estates can be polarized as:

Maiden → Squire
Knight → Lady
Queen → King
King → Queen

but none of the given forms of the *Hallowquest* Court cards are intended to be 'better', 'higher' or 'greater' than the others.)

The reader will notice that each of the Four Estates corresponds to a particular Hallow:

Maiden Sword
Knight Spear
Queen Grail
King Stone

But this is too simplistic a breakdown. The Four Courts of the *Hallowquest* represent the spiral journey of the seeker through the 16 portals of the Hallow Courts. (See Figure 6.3.) In this diagram we will see that the seeker journeys in a spiral through the Court of the Sword to begin with, passing through the portals of the Maiden, Knight, Queen and King in turn, until he or she reaches the Court of the Spear, and so on until all the portals are passed and each of the Courts traversed. See also the meditation on p.152.

THE 16 PORTALS OF THE HALLOW COURTS

As we have read in the previous chapter, each of the Hallows brings with it an initiatory experience which is on a different arc to that of the given correspondences of the elements, seasons, colours etc. Removed from its mundane correlatives, each Hallow can be seen as a variation of the interwoven Hallow powers.

The four Court card characters, while being figures of the Four Estates, are thus also exemplars of the interwoven Hallow powers. If we tabulate this realization, we will find that we have 16 separate initiatory experiences:

Court Card	*Initiatory Experience*
Sword Maiden	The Sword of the Sword
Sword Knight	The Sword of the Spear
Sword Queen	The Sword of the Grail
Sword King	The Sword of the Stone
Spear Maiden	The Spear of the Sword
Spear Knight	The Spear of the Spear
Spear Queen	The Spear of the Grail
Spear King	The Spear of the Stone
Grail Maiden	The Grail of the Sword
Grail Knight	The Grail of the Spear
Grail Queen	The Grail of the Grail
Grail King	The Grail of the Stone
Stone Maiden	The Stone of the Sword
Stone Knight	The Stone of the Spear
Stone Queen	The Stone of the Grail
Stone King	The Stone of the Stone

Fig. 6.2: The 16 Initiations of the Courts

These 16 initiatory experiences have been expressed elsewhere in elemental terms e.g Sword Maiden = Earth of Air, Grail King = Air of Water. (See p.255 where this schema is utilized magically.) In Figure 6.2 above, the correlations are very different, but in working with the *Hallowquest* pack in varying ways, we should learn to expect variety and further subtlety of correlation.

How may these 16 initiations be experienced? As each initiation represents a gradation of the Hallows' interactive power, the reader will find that direct meditation upon each of the Hallows to be of value, initially. In order to go beyond this, the reader will need to meditate upon where he or she fits within the Four Estates.

To pass through the 16 portals of the Hallow Courts, the reader needs to become a seeker in real earnest and meditate upon each of the Court cards in the order in which they appear above in Figure 6.2. Readers unfamiliar with meditation should read Chapter 8 before attempting the meditations in this chapter.

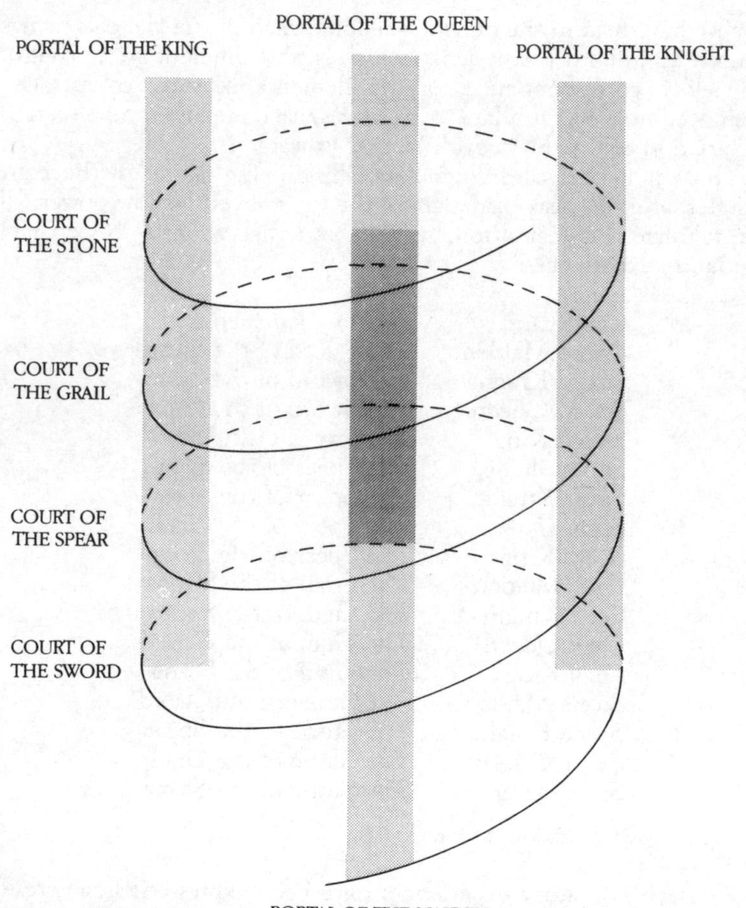

Fig. 6.3: The Spiral Journey of the Seeker

THE SPIRAL JOURNEY MEDITATION

Only the framework of this meditative progression can be given here, but once you begin it you will find it easy to pass on to the next part.

Although the journey depicted in Figure 6.3 is represented as an upward spiral, the reader should not be led astray into thinking that 'upwards' means 'heavenward' or 'superior progress'. The Spiral Journey is intended to be a *deepening* rather than an improving one.

Close your eyes and visualize the Court of the Sword as a circular hall with four rooms leading off a central courtyard. In the centre of the courtyard is a representation of the Sword Hallow. Over the door to the first room, the Sword Maiden's, is a shield with a sword on it. You first enter here and meet the Sword Maiden. Enter into interior dialogue with her and ask her about the significance of the Sword and the experience of the Maiden upon the quest. Listen to her answers. (If you cannot receive answers, try this meditation another day.)

When you feel you have understood the nature of this experience, the Sword Maiden tells you that the initiation of the Sword of the Sword will enable you to pass onwards on your Spiral Journey until you reach the next initiation.

You next enter the room of the Sword Knight in the same manner, succeeded by the Sword Queen and the Sword King. When you have completed one circuit in this way, you can pass onwards to the next Court — that of the Spear.

A good method of working is to take one Court card at a time: several sessions may be necessary before you are ready to go on to the next card. It will be pointless to complete the meditation one card a day for 16 days. It is far better to take your time and fully realize the significance of the 16 portal initiations over a period of several months rather than award yourself the grade of 'Stone of the Stone' unworthily.

The order of the sequence is as outlined in Figure 6.2. Make sure that you first visualize each Court clearly. The Courts of the Spear, Grail and Stone will each have a representation of the appropriate Hallow in the central courtyard. Write down the substance of your dialogues in your *Hallowquest* workbook and use your realizations for future research and work.

THE FOUR HOUSES

The four great houses which dominate the later Arthurian cycle, each in its own way represents the Courts of the *Hallowquest* and the four sacred objects which they guard. We may see each of them as later correlatives of the 16 Court cards of *Hallowquest*.

Thus the house of Pellinor, which numbers among its scions the Grail King Pelles, and one of the three achievers of the Grail, Perceval — as well as his sister, Dindraine, who also plays a major role in the quest — clearly represents the Court of the Grail. The house of Pendragon, of which Arthur is head, holds the Court of Swords,

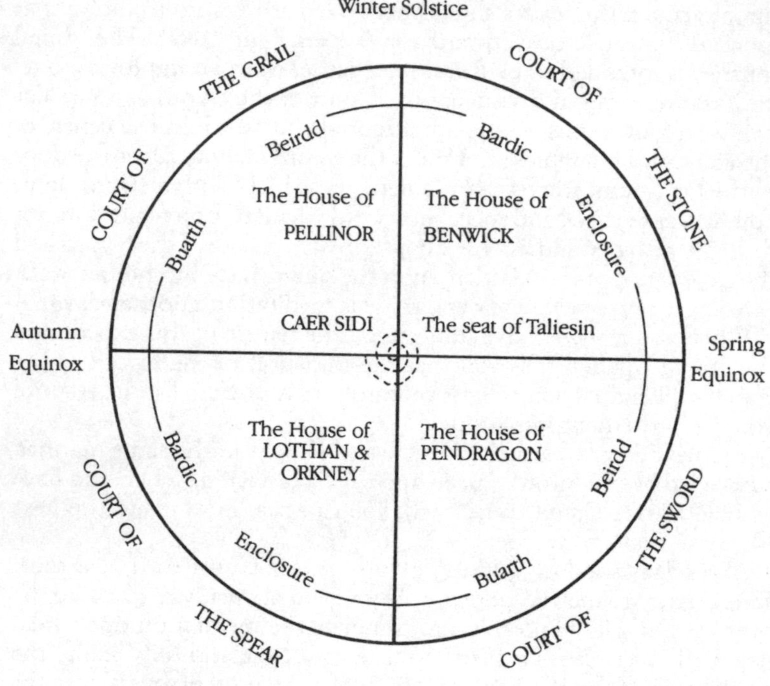

Fig. 6.4: The Four Houses

represented by Excalibur. The house of Lothian and Orkney represents the Court of Spears in the persons of the four strong, stern figures of Gawain, Gareth, Gaheris and Agravain — themselves like a sheaf of spears in the hands of a seasoned warrior. Finally, the house of Benwick, of Lancelot, and of Galahad and Bors, the other two successful Grail winners, stands for the four-square stone, the Chessboard of the land, of the Floating Stone from which Galahad, in emulation of Arthur, drew his own sword. (See Figures 6.5, 6.6, 6.7, and 6.8 below.)

The women of these four houses have frequently not come down to us from the cumulative Arthurian tradition, but have either been forgotten or appear merely as nameless ladies, mothers or sisters. But they can in no wise be discounted from the guardianship of the Hallows, for their part is crucial in the formation of the quest.

These four houses placed on the wheel of the year, (see Figure 6.4 above) circle and contain the mysteries of the Hallows, while at the centre, balancing and controlling, is Caer Sidi, House of the Otherworld and The Seat of Taliesin, the Hierophant. Around the circumference of the wheel of the year is the Bardic Enclosure: this is composed of the many story-tellers who have created and preserved the Arthurian mythos. This diagram is a cosmological glyph of the four houses. Within its structure lies the entire force and dynamism of the *Hallowquest*, set out in a manner that becomes accessible to all who wish to work with the later medieval archetypes of the Arthurian legend.

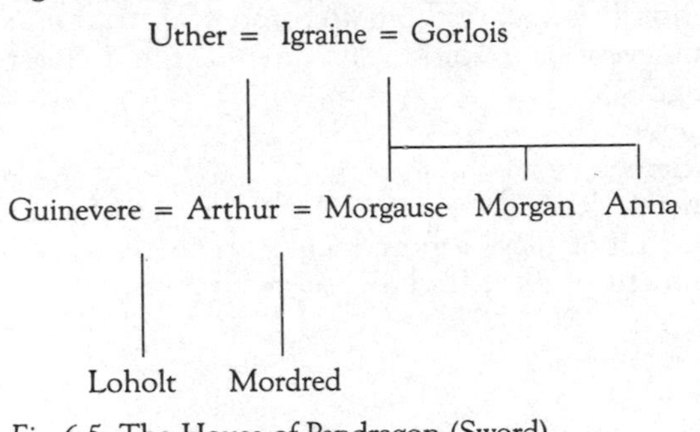

Fig. 6.5: The House of Pendragon (Sword)

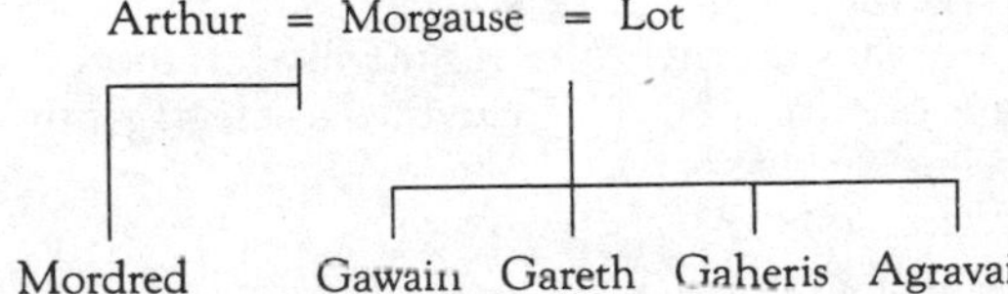

Fig. 6.6: The House of Lothian & Orkney (Spear)

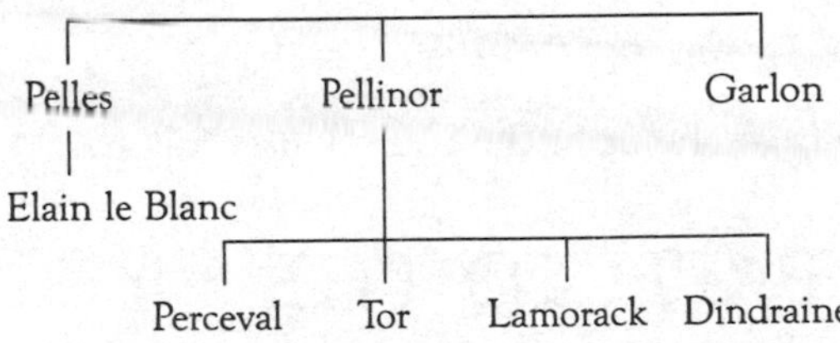

Fig. 6.7: The House of Pellinor (Grail)

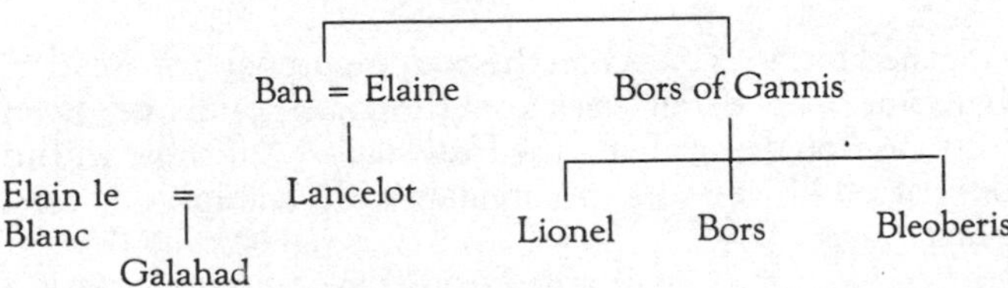

Fig. 6.8: The House of Benwick (Stone)

The *Arthurian Tarot* correlations are as various as the variants of these family trees, but the following suggested correspondences with the Court cards may be seen as the medieval octaves of the earlier archetypes depicted here. Readers will notice considerable departures between these correspondences and the suggested stories which underlie each of the Court cards on pp.76 through 116.

Court Cards:	*Medieval Arthurian Correlations:*
Sword Maiden	Dindraine
Sword Knight	Loholt (This almost forgotten son of Arthur and Guinevere is traditionally one of the boldest knights)
Sword Queen	Igraine
Sword King	Uther
Spear Maiden	Linet (Although not a member of the Orkney clan, Linet plays a prominent part in the establishment of Gareth's knightly reputation)
Spear Knight	Gareth
Spear Queen	Morgause
Spear King	Lot
Grail Maiden	Repanse de Schoy is one of her names
Grail Knight	Perceval
Grail Queen	Perceval's mother (She is unnamed in most texts, but one calls her Herzeloyhde — Heart's Sorrow)
Grail King	Pelles
Stone Maiden	Elaine le Blanc
Stone Knight	Lancelot
Stone Queen	Elain, Lancelot's mother
Stone King	Ban

Fig. 6.9: The Court Cards in the Medieval Arthurian Legends

A meditation related to this schema of the Four Houses follows.

THE PATH TO THE FOUR COURTS MEDITATION

The following meditation is based on the Four Houses above. Readers will note that some of the details vary from the correspondences given previously, but, as stated elsewhere, the *Hallowquest* is flexible within certain boundaries. If you are unfamiliar with meditation, read Chapter 8 first.

See before you a doorway of lintelled stone beyond which swirls a grey mist. As you step forward between the massive uprights, the mist clears and you see a rich land of wooded hills and green valleys through which run sparkling streams. Before you is a well-worn path of beaten earth, winding into the distance between the hills. The urge to follow it is strong and you set out eagerly for an unknown destination.

Soon you top the brow of a hill and see below you a sheltered valley in which is a long, low house of stone, roofed with rushes that glow golden in the light of the sun. Waiting to greet you as you descend is a powerfully built young man dressed in yellow. He smiles and bids you welcome:

'I am Tor. Welcome to the House of Pellinor.'

You follow him into the stone house and find yourself in a long narrow room with a low ceiling and whitewashed walls. On these walls are painted a number of scenes which you study as you follow Tor towards a dais upon which sits an aged, white-haired man. He is dressed in cloth of faded purple and there is a frailty about him which moves you deeply, even though you do not know him.

When you stand at last before his chair, Tor bows low and introduces you. 'This is my uncle, King Pelles, Guardian of the Cup of Life. If there is any question you wish to ask, do so now.'

You look upon the old, wise face of the king and see there deep suffering and yet great joy. You may, if you wish, ask him a personal question, but when you have done so and he has answered, you should ask again concerning the sacred object of which he is the guardian. In answer, the King points towards a painting upon the wall close by and you see there a picture which is somehow alive as you look at it.

It shows a young woman, her hair cropped close to her head, who carries in her hands a great shining Cup. As you watch she seems to hold out the Cup towards the aged King, and from its lip runs a stream of light which surrounds him.

You bow your head in awe and when you look up once more the chair before you is empty. Gently, Tor leads you back through the hall to the door, where stands a tall, dark-browed man, dressed in green, whom Tor announces as his brother, Lamorack. He is to be your guide to your next destination.

Lamorack holds out a hand to you and as you grasp it, the scene dissolves and then reforms. You find yourself standing before a high wooden gate in a fence of tall timbers. It is shut and barred against you, but Lamorack calls out to someone within and in a moment the door swings open. Waiting to greet you are four tall men, each of whom has a shock of red hair and a red beard. The elder of the four greets you with these words: 'I am Gawain, and these are my brothers, Gaheris, Gareth and Agravain. Welcome to the House of Orkney.' The four brothers lead the way through the gate and you find that you are inside a large stockade, in the centre of which stands a circular wooden hall with intricate carvings at door posts and lintel. You follow the brothers into this building and find yourselves in a round room, the walls of which are hung with brightly woven cloth. A fire blazes up in the centre of the room and you see by its light a single, ornately carved chair, in which sits the figure of a woman, clad in black, with her black hair drawn out around her shoulders like a cloak. Across her knees she holds a great Spear with a bronze head elaborately carved.

Gawain leads you to stand before her and introduces you: 'This is our mother, Queen Morgause of Orkney, Guardian of the Spear of Light. If there is any question you would ask her, do so now.'

You look up into the fierce dark face of the Queen and may, if you wish, ask her a personal question. But when you have done so and she has answered, you must ask her concerning that which she guards. In answer she lifts the Spear until it is pointing upright. At once a brilliant white light is emitted from the point, filling the hall with radiance. You seem to hear, though you cannot see whence it comes, a great voice declaiming: 'When the Spear is used to heal, then the Wasteland will be restored and all wrongful deaths undone.' You close your eyes to shield them from the brightness, and feel the strong hands of Gawain and his brothers guiding you back to the entrance of the hall. Outside, blinking in normal daylight, you see a man dressed in brown awaiting you. Gawain introduces him as: 'Bors, the Son of the King of Gannis. He will be your guide to your next destination.'

Bors is older than the four brothers and gravely courteous. He holds out a hand to you and as you take it once again the scene dissolves and you find yourself standing before a tall stone building built into the face of a tall cliff. The wind whines and tugs about you, but Bors is strong and sturdy at your side and at his touch a gate opens in the high wall of stone and you enter. Inside there is calm and stillness after the clamour of the wind. You find yourself in a high, vaulted room in the centre of which stands a four-square table marked out in squares of white and black. About this table sit four great figures and a place for a fifth at which Bors now sits, motioning you to stand at his side. Before you on the table are carved stone figures of great beauty and craftsmanship. The five men about the table watch eagerly as the pieces move of their own accord in an endless-seeming dance in which different patterns are formed and broken and again reformed . . . After a time you look at the faces of the four other men, and Bors murmurs their names aloud for you: Lancelot of the Lake; Galahad; Lionel; and last of all King Ban of Benwick, guardian of the Stone of Purpose.

You look upon the calm, wise face of the King, and may, if you so desire, ask him of some personal thing. But when you have done so you must ask him of that which he is guardian. He answers you thus: 'You see before you the Stone of Purpose, upon which the Game of the Quest is played out. Within this pattern is the meaning of the Quest and those who guard the Hallows move upon it as they must.'

As you look again at the board one figure amid the rest catches your attention. It is that of a woman, dressed in red, and as you look suddenly you are yourself transported onto the board and find yourself standing before her. The woman is of such beauty that you are at once in awe of her, but she greets you kindly: 'I am Guinevere, Queen to Arthur of Britain. Welcome to the House of Pendragon.'

Once again you are in the landscape of the Quest, and before you rise the massive ramparts of a great fortress and dwelling place. Led by Guinevere you follow a winding track up to a pair of great doors which are set wide and are unguarded. Within is a wide courtyard and beyond it a simple building of stone and timber, roofed with wattles. Striding to meet you comes a figure you know to be Arthur Pendragon, Lord of Britain and Guardian of the Hallow of the Sword. There is no need for introductions; you are expected and made welcome. Side by side Arthur and Guinevere lead you into the hall, which seems much larger within than without. In the centre is a circular table of stone, and on it, in front of the palce reserved for Arthur, lies a great Sword in a plain leather sheath. You know without being told that you are in the presence of Excalibur, the Great Sword of Truth, and you may ask if you wish what part you have to play in its work. When Arthur has answered, you ask further about the object of which he is guardian. Arthur answers you thus: 'In all the world there were not enough men and women of good faith to prevent the coming of the Wastelands. The Sword exists so that such men and women will begin their quest and come to me here in Avalon to learn what they may do to heal the torment of the world. Watch well and learn what *you* may do in this great cause . . .'

So saying Arthur draws the Sword part way forth from its sheath. At once it begins to glow, and you are filled with awareness of all that Arthur has told you, and with it the power and glory of all four Hallows. Listen as he bids you, that you may hear, the light of what part you have still to play in the work of the *Hallowquest* . . .

When you have heard all that you need to hear, the light of the Sword begins to fade, and as Arthur sheaths it again, all about you, and about the Round Table, stand those whom you have met on this journey, and others of the Four Houses and the Courts of the Four Hallows that you have not met. You stand for a short while in silence and contemplation, and then slowly the scene fades and you find yourself again before the lintelled doorway through which you entered. Step through it and find yourself once again back where you began this journey. You will find that much that you saw and learned will become increasingly clear to you in the days and weeks that follow. For you have walked in the Land of the Hallows and met with its greatest guardians, and you also become part of them through your journey . . .

THE VOICES OF THE WELLS

One of the great tasks which the *Hallowquest* is able to effect is the Restoration of the Courts of Joy. This term, used in many of the Arthurian legends, is analogous to the hermetic Great Work whereby the whole of creation is brought into alignment with the Otherworld, where potential ideals become reality. This is a state of perfection to which many people look in different ways.

Those following the path of the religions of revelation expect the coming of the Messiah or the Great Iman, or the Second Coming. But these visions are rather final in their implication: that the world will be brought to an end, cut off the loom, rolled up and sent back to God for sorting out. The *Hallowquest* vision — which stems from the lore of the native tradition or primal and originative mythology — is quite different. The Restoration of the Courts of Joy is a total overlapping of the created world by the Otherworld. In it, creation is perfected by means of blissful realization of our intrinsic wholeness and connection with the whole universe, manifest and unseen. Nothing is lost, sent to hell or cancelled, but brought to this blessed realization.

There are numerous stories which tell of a partial restoration within the Arthurian legends. Obviously, the Grail quest plays a paramount part in this scenario. So, also, do the many stories in which distressed ladies are rescued by Arthur's knights or restored to their rights. These stories have deeper esoteric meanings, however, which are not immediately apparent.

The major story which tells of the possibility of this restoration gives us an interesting light on the Celtic prefiguring of the Grail legends. *Elucidation de l'hystoire du Graal* is a French text of the early thirteenth century, clearly having its derivation from earlier British and Breton stories.

It tells how, in times past, an evil king called Amangons raped one of the damsels of the wells and stole her golden cup. She and others of her kind used to offer refreshment to travellers at the wells, but after this attack upon her and her companions, who were also violated by Amangon's followers, this service was discontinued. The immediate result of this was that the land became a desert and 'lost the voices of the wells'. The Courts of Joy, wherein the Rich Fisherman lived, were likewise lost and no one might find them.

In after years, King Arthur and his knights heard of this story and determined to recover the wells, but though they swore an oath to exterminate the kindred of Amangons, never did they see one of the damsels or hear the voices of the wells again.

One day, on quest, Arthur's knights discovered a strange company wandering in the forests — knights protecting their maidens. The Round Table knights fought them and Gawain captured one of their number who was a story-teller. He told how the wandering company were all descended from the line of Amangons and the damsels of the wells. They were fated to wander until the time when the Courts of Joy were found; then would all wrongs be righted.

In the ensuing quest by Arthur's knights, the Courts of Joy were found seven times. The finding of the Court and the Grail caused the land to be repeopled and the dry fountains to course with abundant waters so that the land was restored.

This fragment does not tell us more about the voices of the wells, but we may clearly see that the damsels of the wells are the representatives of Sovereignty herself. This story shows us a vision which is unlike any of the apocalyptic revelations of the world's cessation. We notice that the descendants of Amangons — the evil king — cannot be exterminated because they are likewise the descendants of the damsels of the wells — who we can see as the transcendent or Otherworldly women who minister to our own world. The voices of the wells which are lost in the times before Arthur's coming, signify the deep wisdom of Sovereignty, the voice of the land itself. Those who cannot discern this voice are not aligned to their own land and are powerless to restore the Wasteland.

A fuller synopsis of the story and commentary will be found in *Arthur and the Sovereignty of Britain.*[41]

The four Hallow Courts jointly comprise this state of wholeness and blessed realization. For those who wish to bring about the Courts of Joy among us, there is a ritual on p.254 which encompasses this restoration by means of the *Hallowquest*. It is a ritual for a large company for a good reason, since this work of restoration is best effected by many people of good will working together for the common benefit of the world. Lone readers may participate in this work also by means of creative meditation on the principles outlined in the ritual and scattered throughout this book.

OUTER WORLD ARCHETYPES

Lest it be thought that we give too great an emphasis to the inner quest, it is worth noting that the *Hallowquest* takes place as much in the outer world as it does on the inner.

The images of the Tarot are doorways indeed, but not only into inner worlds. It has been said that travellers on the inner planes often return like ordinary dreamers (which they most definitely are *not*!) with the answers to questions which have hemmed them in or given them cause for concern. In much the same way, however briefly, contact with the archetypes of the Tarot can, in themselves, offer a kind of immediately accessible wisdom. We may find ourselves aware of their presence in our lives, of the familiarity they produce within us when we see one of those living archetypes in the street. For we shall most assuredly do so, once we have learned to recognize them for what they are.

Charles Williams, in his novel of the Tarot, *The Greater Trumps*, saw them as akin to the Platonic archetypes — larger than life but still recognizably *of* the world. These Tarot figures are judges, policemen, road sweepers — the kind of people one might meet with at certain times and in certain situations and recognize them for what they are. These are *outer* world archetypes, the living shapes of the reality which surrounds us, just as the inner world archetypes are there in our explorations of the unconscious realm.[85]

We are all 'garments of the gods', according to esoteric tradition and there are many ways in which each of us enact or align with certain inner world archetypes at certain times. This can be by means of the roles we each play: our occupation, relationships, personal experiences all place us in different situations. It is important to realize that, whatever happens to us in life, we do not need to *become* the roles which we unconsciously enact. However, there are times when it is helpful to realize that the present pattern of our lives has placed us in alignment to certain natural archetypes.

The girl who leaves school to start work as a secretary is still the same as the woman who leaves work to have a baby, but she will have experienced different archetypal roles which enlarge her experience of life. In the course of a lifetime, many of us will have lived out most of the experiential archetypes of the Tarot. Very occasionally, we meet people who have become frozen into one or two chosen roles: they are noticeably dehumanized, static and rigid in their outlook. More rarely, we encounter someone who is a living embodiment of one of the Greater Powers or the Court cards: these people act as catalysts for purposeful action, becoming compassionate helpers and wise teachers. They are mature souls who have lived out their personal lives and have turned to a wider field of influence.

For we inhabit a realm of wonder just as potent, in its own right, as the inner planes, just as crowded with possibility, excitement, challenge, fear and love, as are those places we explore through meditation and magical operation.

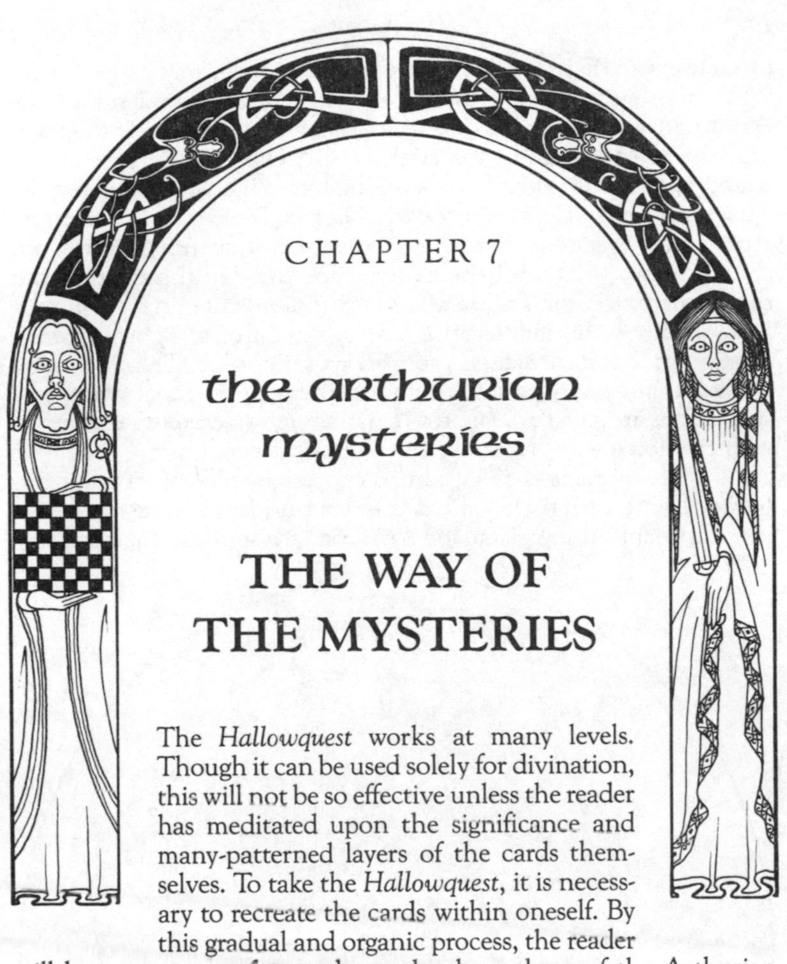

CHAPTER 7

the arthurian mysteries

THE WAY OF THE MYSTERIES

The *Hallowquest* works at many levels. Though it can be used solely for divination, this will not be so effective unless the reader has meditated upon the significance and many-patterned layers of the cards themselves. To take the *Hallowquest*, it is necessary to recreate the cards within oneself. By this gradual and organic process, the reader will become aware of even deeper levels — those of the Arthurian Mysteries.

The word 'mystery' has lost its traditional value in common parlance: now it merely means 'an enigma', but that is not how we use the word here. We have returned to its ancient value meaning 'an esoteric truth known only by divine revelation'. In this way, we can speak of the Eleusinian Mysteries of Demeter and Kore which were celebrated in Classical Greece.

To speak of the Arthurian legends in the same breath may seem strange, but we must consider that they arise out of the native mythology of the British Isles which long had its own set of mysteries. These mysteries, though they would have varied from place to place, nevertheless conformed to an intrinsic pattern of mythic archetypes and mystery initiations. Within this existing framework, the Arthurian legends have grown up and become fused with the native mysteries in such a way that they are indivisible from them.

In choosing to deal with the earlier, Celtic antecedents of the Arthurian legends, the authors seek to enable readers to find their way into this deeper level of material. In this chapter, the deeper correlations of the Greater Powers are manifested and shown in their archetypal light. Thus each of the Greater Powers is, in effect, an Arthurian power, of great authority and inner influence. Readers may choose not to work with the material presented in this chapter, but those who do so will find it rewarding and enlightening.

Here the Arthurian legends are taken beyond a mere literary creation and accorded their essential esoteric value. The Arthurian Triads on p.162 can be more fully experienced by ritual work, and suggestions are given in Chapter 11. There are two exercises connected with the Totemistic Triads on p.183 and on p.184.

Study the triplicities given in this chapter before you attempt any practical work with them. The deeper your understanding, the better you will be able to appreciate the Arthurian Mysteries in their entirety.

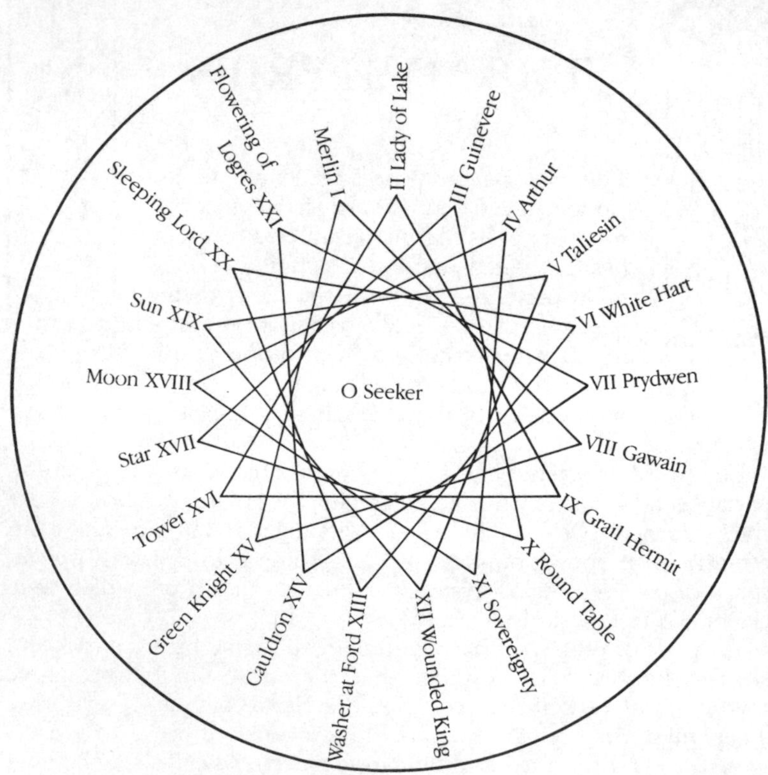

Fig. 7.1: The Eye of The Seeker

THE PATH OF THE ARTHURIAN POWERS

The foregoing diagram, The Eye of the Seeker, represents the mystical insight which you as the Seeker may have of the 21 major cards of the *Hallowquest* pack.

Each of the Greater Powers represents one of the Arthurian Powers or archetypes whose effect can be experienced in many combinations. The method for deeper reflection presented here shows how the 21 major cards, excluding the Seeker, interrelate in a sevenfold triplicity, or set of triads.

The Welsh Triads (*Trioedd Ynys Prydein*)[78] remain one of the major sources for early British myth and history. Within each triad, three events or persons are itemized under a single head e.g. The Three Unfortunate Disclosures, which tell of the uncovering of the head of Bran the Blessed by Arthur, the release of the dragons from under Vortigern's Tower, and the disinterment of Vortimer's bones. Each of these stories is separate yet their common theme is the guardianship of the land of Logres. The triads were compiled by the tradition-preserving poets of Celto-Arthurian culture; their purpose is to act as mnemonic of the various stories and as an aid to the transmission of tradition. Their deeper value is to enable the hearer attuned to their frequency to share by initiation the experience of each triad.

The triads concerning the 21 Greater Powers presented here do not of course derive from an authentic collection of British texts. They stem from the authors' own deep meditation upon the Arthurian Powers in their earliest, most archetypal forms. This is why the images depicted within the Greater Powers are not medieval but much earlier. The reader may, by similar meditation, experience the Greater Powers as a functional court of contacted energies.

You will note that each triad consists of three cards exactly seven cards distant from each other in the numerical round. While each card has its peculiar strength and function, a triadic set is even stronger.

If the reader wishes to comprehend the Arthurian Mysteries, then in-depth work on each of the triads will give you greater insights. The Arthurian Powers are not gods or ghosts, nor are they figments of our imagination. They represent the deepest levels of the *Hallowquest's* foundation. It is true that within each card lie traces of the earliest belief and that, if we had all the mythological correlatives, we might indeed be able to reconstruct the motivating mythos of the Bronze Age or the Stone Age. No matter what era or place or people, the saving story reappears in different forms. Within the Arthurian legends we encounter a rich amalgam of mythic levels: British, aboriginal, Celtic, Roman, medieval etc.

As a story which people have lived by, the Arthurian story is paramount in the English-speaking world. It is hero-story, chivalric poetry, racial myth, holy quest and recurrent narrative in our culture. Its archetypes, therefore, exercise considerable influence in our inner lives. For most people, this is at a puerile and even degraded level, where Merlin's magic no longer represents his guardianship of the land but as cheap conjurings, for example. The retelling of the Arthurian story by Marion Zimmer Bradley, *The Mists of Avalon*, has recently brought Morgan prominently into the consciousness of modern readers, many of whom are seeking feminist empowerment. This same book totally under-played the role of Guinevere, whom the author identified with the kind of fatuous and compliant woman that feminists scorn. Elsewhere, Arthur himself has been portrayed as a weak cuckold, and Taliesin has virtually become a stock 'bard' in fantasy literature. As for the other Arthurian Powers, they have suffered similar or even more obscure fates, becoming relegated to the subtext of our imaginative lives.[2]

In this book and the *Hallowquest* pack, we hope that the reader will find these forgotten levels again and activate them by making an inner world journey — not to the past, but to the ancestral level of consciousness where these prime protagonists reflect the wisdom of the land through all time.

There may be those who wonder about the viability of using what are, in effect, literary inventions, in this way. But this is not the case. The Arthurian Powers have, as we said, derived from many levels. At root they stem from the earliest and most commonly-delineated god-forms as perceived by our first ancestors. Their call sign or symbolic identification remains a constant within Otherworldly terms, and it is these values which have formed the core of Arthurian mythology. The succeeding traditions, both oral and literary, have built upon these archetypal forms, adding and sometimes changing the root impulse. This is why it has been so necessary to go to the earliest authentic levels of Arthurian tradition as our impulse for this pack.

The Arthurian Powers are presences having their basis in mythic and archetypal levels but able to transmit via the frequency of story, text and historical tradition.

The ways in which they can be worked with are outlined below and in succeeding chapters.

Sevenfold Triplicities in the Eye of the Seeker

Set One: I Merlin; VIII Gawain; XV The Green Knight.
Set Two: II The Lady of the Lake; IX The Grail Hermit; XVI The Spiral Tower.
Set Three: III Guinevere; X The Round Table; XVII The Star.

Set Four: IV Arthur; XI Sovereignty; XVIII The Moon.
Set Five: V Taliesin; XII The Wounded King; XIX The Sun.
Set Six: VI The White Hart; XIII The Washer at the Ford; XX The Sleeping Lord.
Set Seven: VII Prydwen; XIV The Cauldron; XXI The Flowering of Logres.

These sets of triplicities can be seen as triads of instruction, each revealing a mystery.

Set One: The Three Guardians of the Strong Door

The first was Merlin who enclosed the precincts of Logres.
The second was Gawain who by his strength kept the kingdom free of invasion.
The third was the Green Knight who challenged Arthur to defend his Sovereignty.

Set Two: The Three Otherworldly Retreats

The first was that of the Lady of the Lake who fostered the infant hero, arming and naming him in her islanded lake.
The second was that of the Grail Hermit who instructed the youth in virtue in the depths of the forest.
The third was the locus of Ynys Wytrin, the Spiral Tower which enclosed the body of the hero

Set Three: Three Shining Lights of the Island of Britain

The first was Gwenhwyfar, Queen of Arthur. She reflected the glory of Arthur's reign.
The second was the Round Table, made in likeness of the land and of the infinity of the heavens.
The third was the Star of Prophecy which flamed over the island the news of the Pendragon's coming.

Set Four: Three Renewing Sovereignties of the Island of Britain

The first was Arthur Pendragon, King of the Island, who will come again.
The second was Lady Sovereignty herself. Though she appear as hag, yet will she renew herself at the kiss of the rightful king.
The third was the sphere of the Moon which waxes, wanes and is reborn.

Set Five: Three Undying Streams of Radiance

The first was Taliesin who emerged from the waters of the cauldron with the radiant brow of knowledge.

The second was the Wounded King whose wounds watered the deep places of the island.
The third was the Sun whose beams reveal the path upon the waters, the track within the forest and which illumines the dark places of the heart.

Set Six: Three Dangerous Wonders of the Island of Britain
Brave the one who seeks to discover these:
The first is the White Hart who leads to love beyond death.
The second is the Washer at the Ford. Whosoever encounters her returns from battle upon his shield and is reborn in another manner.
The third is the Cave of the Sleeping Lord. Whosover wakes He Who Will Come must do so from the direst need of Logres alone.
Let him who must, blow the horn boldly and unsheath the sword.

Set Seven: Three Binding Oaths of the Island of Britain
Men swear by these three:
The first is the ship Prydwen which went burdened with men into the mouth of Annwn and only seven returned. Wherefore do men swear by the Underworld and the care of Arthur.
The second is the Cauldron of Rebirth which Arthur retrieved from Annwn. Wherefore do men swear by their hope of eternity.
The third is the Flowering of Logres, the healing of its waste places. Wherefore do men swear by the produce of the Island's bounty and the reign of Arthur which wrought its fertility.

COMMENTARY ON THE ARTHURIAN TRIADS:

Set One

1. Merlin

Within a late appendix to the Welsh Triads, Britain's many appellations through time are listed: it was the Island of Honey, and the Island of Prydein. But before either of these it was anciently called *Clas Myrddin* or Merlin's Enclosure. Merlin, at the end of the *Vita Merlini*,[9] enters within his glass observatory, having 70 doors and 70 windows, through which he observes the heavens. Tradition has then installed Merlin as Britain's ancient guardian. The watch around Clas Myrddin is still maintained today.

2. Gawain

The role of Gawain in the early texts is considerably more important than it becomes by Malory's time. A close study of the sources reveal Gawain as Arthur's *tanaiste* or elected successor. As Arthur's nephew, Gawain stands in the strongest place to succeed the King according to the laws and customs of king-making among the Celts, for Gawain is the king's sister's son, and the royal bloodline is understood to derive from the matriarchal side of the clan. In the earliest texts it is Gawain and not Lancelot who is the champion of the Lady Sovereignty. We see throughout the Arthurian legends that Arthur retreats more and more into his court, allowing his knights to represent him, rarely hazarding his person in combat or battle. Gawain is Arthur's primary representative on quests and adventures. *The Welsh Triads* speak of him as being one of the supremely courteous knights, and he frequently intervenes between the quarrelsome Cai (Kay) and his victims. Gawain represents the best of Arthur's fighting force, a man of skill and discernment who is deeply committed to the Goddess of the Land. His encounter with Dame Ragnell, the Loathly Lady, shows him performing the primary king-making act — he kisses the hag and transforms her by submitting to her will. His earliest name, Gwalchmai, the Hawk of May is investigated on p.175.

3. The Green Knight

The Green Knight represents one of the greatest challenges to Arthur's sovereignty and authority. He is the challenger, Sovereignty's Otherworldly champion, who emerges seasonally to challenge the might of the Lady's appointed king. It is only when Arthur himself offers to fight the Green Knight that Gawain steps forward in his place and takes up the Beheading Game. This story has its correlative in Cu Roi's appearance at the court of Ulster where Cuchulainn fulfils Gawain's role.[51] In another tale featuring Gawain, the Green Knight makes perhaps another appearance, in the shape of Gromer Somer Joure, The Man of Summer's Day, who threatens Arthur's life unless he can discover what it is that women most desire. Arthur is given a year to reply correctly, just like Gawain's contest with the Green Knight. The King meets the loathly Ragnell in a forest and it is she who tells him the answer, in return for marrying Gawain. Gawain accepts and later kisses Ragnell so that she changes into a beautiful maiden. It is discovered that both she and her brother, Gromer, were under command of Morgan who, in this story, acts as the challenging Goddess of Sovereignty.[41] The Green Knight is one of the most profoundly wild archetypes in the *Hallowquest*, but he is also the most important. Unless his challenges are met, the initiate cannot continue on the quest for the Hallows.

Set One tells then of the three guardians of Britain, which was also called the Island of the Strong Door. They are its gatekeepers and are at liberty to challenge all who seek entry into the inner Logres.

Set Two

1. The Lady of the Lake

The Lady of the Lake is primarily a figure deriving from Breton tradition, where Otherworldly women act as inspirers and as foster-mothers. She is of course a fusion of many archetypes which appear separately within Arthurian tradition, including Morgen (Morgan) in the *Vita Merlini*,[9] who has her Otherworldly island on which Arthur is healed; Nimuë or Niniane who appears in the French romances as the pupil and eventual seducer of Merlin; and the foster-mother of Lancelot.[80] The destined Grail winner usually follows a distinct life pattern which includes an unusual and obscure upbringing. The Lady of the Lake provides such an education for Lancelot and though this story is a late one, it shows a link with the Celtic custom of young men receiving their general and combat training with a woman. Cuchulainn is trained by the indefatigable Scathach, a woman warrior,[5] and is armed and given his invincible spear by her. The Lady of the Lake provides a safe environment for the destined Grail winner, who is often at risk from family enemies; she inculcates in him her wisdom and prepares him for the coming quest. She is the Otherworldly foster-mother.

2. The Grail Hermit

The Grail Hermit appears in many different forms within the Grail legends. His archetype stems from that of Joseph of Arimathea and the many Celtic saints and hermits who followed their particular ministry during the historical Arthurian period. Their function within the legends is to provide wise counsel and physical shelter for all seekers on the quest. In many instances, the Grail Hermit educates and fosters the Grail winner, and stands as patron for him at the Round Table, as King Pelles does for Galahad. He is the withdrawn foster-father.

3. The Spiral Tower

The Glass Caer or Spiral Castle is famed in Celtic mythology as the place of death and transformation. It is said to be under the rule of Arianrhod or Ceridwen, according to the testimony of Taliesin who suffered his poetic gestation within its confines.[30] The Tower is the place of changing where the Grail winner appears to come to grief, but yet is himself withdrawn to another plane of existence. Those who come under the influence of the Tower are indeed aligned to the Otherworld and become its denizens.

Set Two relates the upbringing and spiritual education of the Grail winner and his assimilation into the Otherworldly retreats from which he draws his strength.

Set Three

1. Guinevere

Gwenhwyfar or Guinevere is now seldom remembered in an honourable light and yet, within her person, she represents the Goddess of Sovereignty in her marriage to Arthur and is worthy of respect. She has fortunately been the object of reappraisal in many recent stories.[24,82] Throughout the Arthurian legends, from early times onwards, there are many stories telling of her abduction or near abduction. When these stories are analysed, we find that Arthur's queen is sought because she represents the intrinsic union of the king and the land: whoever possesses her has sovereignty over the land.[3] In the earliest texts, she is sought by Medrawt (Mordred). She is pulled from her throne and has wine dashed in her face by him, betokening an insult to the land itself via Sovereignty's representative. While Guinevere is at Arthur's side, no harm can befall the kingdom; when she is abducted or loves another, then the fertility of the land fails, as the later stories suggest.

2. The Round Table

The Round Table, says the *Didot Perceval*, was made by Merlin in the time of Uther. It is one of three tables, says Merlin, the first being the Table of the Upper Room at which the Last Supper was celebrated; the second was the Table of the Grail, made by Joseph for the Grail itself; and the third is the Round Table. There have been and will be many tables, but each aligns to the Grail which is both a withdrawn symbol of wholeness and an analogue of the cup of Sovereignty.[58]

3. The Star of Prophecy

The Star of Prophecy appeared in Uther's time to betoken the coming of the Pendragon's line. After a period of great instability and the usurpation of Vortigern, the Pendragons brought harmony and unity to Britain.[8]

Set Three signifies the restoration of the land and its harmonious alignment with primal principles of fertility and hope.

Set Four

1. Arthur

The legend of Arthur's return from the dead or out of the Otherworld is one of the most persistent claims of British mythology. The Stanzas of the Graves say that a grave for Arthur is an inconceivable thought,[59] but that has not stopped many places from claiming to have the Pendragon's burial place. The return of Arthur was so strong in medieval Brittany that a man might barely escape with his life for claiming the contrary.[27]

2. Sovereignty

The Celtic Goddess of Sovereignty is one of the great lost archetypes of Britain. Like many aspects of the Goddess which have been assimilated into lesser figures in both story and legend, she is clearly identifiable once one is alerted to her existence. There are few instances of her encounters with Arthur himself, but prime among these is Gawain and Ragnell (see p.165) where Gawain substitutes for his uncle. In Irish legend she frequently appears as a hag who guards a well or stream and will let no one drink until she kissed.[41] In British legend she is more often apparent as an enchanted queen in serpent form whom a kiss will disenchant.

3. The Moon

The Moon is considered to be the eye of the night sky. In both Welsh and Irish it is of feminine gender (*lleuad* and *gealach*) and its phases symbolically represent three faces of the Goddess: the Maiden, the Mother and the Cailleach. It governs growth and cyclicity and ever renews itself.

Set Four concerns the transformative nature of the kingly cycle and its relationship to the land. Nothing here is stable, but in continual rotation, for such is the nature of sovereignty.

Set Five

1. Taliesin

Taliesin's illuminating and obscure poems form the core of early Welsh verse. He boasts that he has been in many forms and knows the sum of knowledge. His name, Tal-iesin arises from the saying of his patron Elphin's men, when they pull the child in his skin bag from the waters with the cry, 'Behold the Radiant Brow!'. Taliesin is but one who drinks from a brew of wisdom intended for someone else. The same story is told also of Fionn mac Cumhail, whose thumb caught some of the juice of the salmon of knowledge which he was cooking for his master Finn Eces.[44] For ever afterwards, Fionn only had to chew his thumb to know the truth about anything.

2. The Wounded King

The sacrificial maiming of the Wounded King leaves him unable to die. The mystical insights of his willing sacrifice, which is no death, derive from earlier kingly immolations whereby a king would die for his people. The wounds of the Wounded King are the blood he sheds for his kingdom, which is laid waste. There is a sense in which Arthur himself fulfils this role for he too is unable to die but is borne to Avalon to find healing. He and the land are one.

3. The Sun

The Sun's illumination represents spiritual light and the manifestation of growth and inner purpose. Celtic mythology has no simplistic deities of sun and moon, for the greater and lesser lights are powers in their own right, though many gods reflect their radiance. The youthful Mabon rides upon the Moon-Mare to his appointed task.

Set Five represents the three Arthurian powers whose immortality is an enduring mystery: the poet, the king and the One Who Will Come.

Set Six

1. The White Hart

The hunting of the White Hart is the task specifically assigned to the Pendragon family only. In *Lanzelet*[80] and *Erec and Enid*[4] the task was established by Uther himself and a successful hunt meant that he could kiss the woman he designated. There are overtones here of a forgotten test of sovereignty: only the king can hunt the White Hart; only the king can kiss the Goddess of Sovereignty.

2. The Washer at the Ford

The Washer at the Ford in Arthurian legend is Modron, the Great Goddess herself, she whose son is to become the Grail winner. Those warriors who become her champions serve her as border-guardians and have another kind of existence, as we see in the *Didot Perceval* where Urbain (Urien) guards her ford. The Washer herself appears as a hag or sometimes in her totemistic shape of a raven, where she ravages the field of battle.[41]

3. The Sleeping Lord

The Sleeping Lord is the title which Arthur inherits from earlier mythologies — both native and Greek, for Cronos, the lord of time, was supposedly chained in these islands for the sin of attempting to eat his own son, Zeus. He ruled over a Golden Age, it is said.[44] Arthur's sojourn in Avalon, as recorded in Geoffrey of Monmouth and successive texts, seems to be a literary version of an older understanding of the King who will come again which was prevalent in Britain. There are numerous sites said to be the resting place of the great King and his warriors and if they are properly called they will return to aid the land.

Set Six concerns the kingly destiny of all seekers which is to establish communion with the Otherworld on all levels that the ways of access may be opened for the free exchange of energies between the kingdom of Logres and the ever-living realms.

Set Seven

1. Prydwen

Prydwen's journey to the Underworld represents Arthur's own deep establishment of his kingship among the realm of the ancestors. He goes there to gain the Otherworldly Hallows against great odds so that only few return. The poem which tells of this event, the *Preiddeu Annwn*, is one of the greatest poems of early Arthurian literature.[29]

2. The Cauldron

The Cauldron is one of the prime emblems of the Celtic peoples and makes many appearances in song and story. The cauldron of Ceridwen is one of wisdom; Bran's cauldron is one of rebirth; the cauldron of Diwrnach will not boil a coward's meat. (See p.136.) All cauldrons are in some part analogues of the Grail, for they each derive from Otherworldly regions and bestow their influence by means of some great mediator who is brave enough to bring through its power to the world. The cauldron of Annwn is tended, according to the poem the *Preiddeu Annwn*, by nine maidens; these are multiplications of the three faces of Sovereignty, the wise Maiden, the nurturing Mother and the gift-bestowing Cailleach.

3. The Flowering of Logres

The Flowering of Logres is the balancing point of all sovereigns and seekers. Here all is brought from potential into reality, the Wasteland is made fertile and the Grail is available to all.

Set Seven concerns the essential commitment of the seeker to the life of the land and its people.

PATH OF THE TOTEM BEASTS

You will have noticed that each of the Greater Powers have within them a bird, beast or fish. These do not appear by accident or as mere decoration. To those who are deeply tuned in to the magical and symbolic language of the inner world, these totem beasts are guides and indicators of different aspects of the inner wisdom. In fact these totems can be valuable companions on our quest for understanding in each card. See p.183 for a method for entering each card.

Within Celto-Arthurian tradition, we find the traces of earlier belief, especially concerning the movements of animals. Many bardic utterances which have come down to us seem to be framed in shamanic language, wherein the poet identifies with an animal or set of animals. Attempts have been made to correlate this evidence and explain it away as 'proof of reincarnation' in these shapes and guises, and, while certain Celtic characters — notably Fintan and Tuan mac Carill — do spend periods of their long existences in animal shape, we need to look to a more subtle explanation.

The poetic training lasted very many years, during which time the candidate would learn complex metres, long poems, genealogies and stories. This knowledge was not solely theoretical. In order to become a guardian of tradition, such as Taliesin, it was necessary to experience every level of life, both inner and outer. The poetic candidate was therefore taught the path of the totems, or the way of the animals. This mystical training method was probably inherited from a much earlier time and people, people to whom the totem beasts represented speaking symbols of the inner worlds.

In our own era when our relationship with the natural world is ruptured and in which we come to encounter animals only in their safe and tame forms as household pets or domesticated farm beasts, we have little sense of how powerful certain totems can be. Each of the totem beasts depicted within the Hallowquest cards represents the deepest level or inner world resonance of that card.

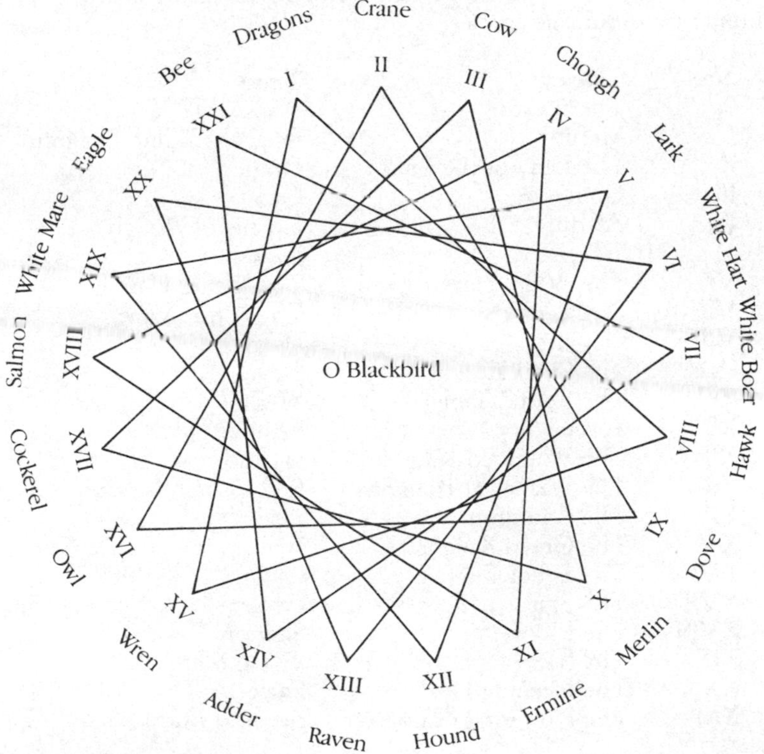

Fig. 7.2: The Totem Beasts

It will be asked, what are totem beasts for and how do they function? On one level they are analogues of inner world power or energy, represented in the form of a wild animal which can speak, guide or impart wisdom. At another they are a mode of transformation by which we share in their intrinsic nature, becoming, as it were, one of their species, on our inner journey.[17]

Throughout world literature and mythology, we encounter individuals who are natural hermits or wild people, or else 'civilized' people who run mad. In the Arthurian corpus we have the examples of Merlin, Lancelot and Owain who all run mad, inhabiting desert and forest places and purposely giving themselves to the 'therapy' of the wilderness. While they are in this state, they each encounter animals with whom they enter into relationships. When they emerge into sanity once more, the animals no longer approach them unafraid but flee as from other human beings. In the Sumerian myth of Gilgamesh, his friend, Enkidu, is one such natural wildman to whom the beasts congregate. When Enkidu is made human by the act of lying with a temple prostitute, the animals run away from him. This sad state of affairs is modern humanity's curse. But in the great chain of life, humanity is but one species.

No.	*Title*	*Totem*
0	The Seeker	Blackbird
I	Merlin	Red and White Dragons
II	The Lady of the Lake	Crane
III	Guinevere	Cow
IV	Arthur	Cornish Chough
V	Taliesin	Lark
VI	The White Hart	The White Hart
VII	Prydwen	The White Boar
VIII	Gawain	Hawk
IX	The Grail Hermit	Dove
X	The Round Table	Merlin
XI	Sovereignty	Ermine
XII	The Wounded King	Hound
XIII	The Washer at the Ford	Raven
XIV	The Cauldron	Adder
XV	The Green Knight	Wren
XVI	The Spiral Tower	Owl
XVII	The Star	Cockerel
XVIII	The Moon	Salmon
XIX	The Sun	White Mare
XX	The Sleeping Lord	Eagle
XXI	The Flowering of Logres	Bee and Butterfly

Fig. 7.3: The Totem Beasts in the Greater Powers.

Sevenfold Triplicities on the Path of the Totem Beasts

Set One: I Dragons; VIII Hawk; XV Wren.
Set Two: II Crane; IX Dove; XVI Owl.
Set Three: III Cow; X Merlin; XVII Cockerel.
Set Four: IV Chough; XI Ermine; XVIII Salmon.
Set Five: V Lark; XII Hound; XIX White Mare.
Set Six: VI White Hart; XIII Raven; XX Eagle.
Set Seven: VII White Boar; XIV Adder; XXI Bee.

The Totemistic Triads

Set One: The Three Winged Ones of Clas Myrddin

The first were the red and white dragons which Lludd enclosed at Dinas Emrys and which Myrddin Emrys released. They are the vitality of the land.
The second was the Hawk of May whose power was greatest at the sun's zenith.
The third was the wren, whose death released the Winter sun's fastness.

Set Two: The Three Winged Messengers of the Lady

The first was the crane, the guardian of the lake-island.
The second was the dove, the bringer of the Grail rejoicing.
The third was the owl, the announcer of the Glass Caer.

Set Three: The Three Portents of the Empress

The first was the cow, the wealth of Logres.
The second was the merlin, the watchful eye of the land.
The third was the cockerel, the hopeful voice of the kingdom.

Set Four: The Three Kingly Beasts of the Island of Britain

The first was the chough, the Emperor's own totem.
The second was the ermine, the totem of justice.
The third was the salmon, the totem of initiates.

Set Five: The Three Holy Hidden Ones of the Island of Britain

The first was the lark, whose voice announces freedom from the clouds.
The second was the hound who licked the wounds of the Fisher King.
The third was the white mare who bore the One Who Will Come.

Set Six: The Three Transforming Totems of the Island of Britain

The first was the White Hart, who changes hatred into love.

The second was the raven, who feeds off the flesh of the slain and they are reborn of her body.

The third was the eagle, which renews itself age upon age.

Set Seven: The Three Poisonous Healers of the Island of Britain

The first was the white boar who ravaged the lands until the Boar of Cornwall restored them.

The second was the adder by which befell the battle of Camlan and by whose virtue the king is healed.

The third was the bee by whose sting many die but whose honey brings life.

The Transcendent Set: The Three Singers Whose Song Binds These Three Sevens into One Harmony

The Blackbirds of Rhiannon who sang to the Noble Company of Bran and whose song enchanted Taliesin in the Glass Caer. Whoever shall follow them into the Otherworld, shall understand the meaning of these triads and come to blessedness.

COMMENTARY ON THE TOTEMISTIC TRIADS:

Set One

1. Dragons

The red and white dragons appear at critical periods of Britain's history. In the reign of Lludd, the King Lud of Geoffrey of Monmouth, they first make their appearance as energies which devastate the land by their shriek. Lludd is instructed to make them drunk and then secure them in a chest and bury them. This is done at the mystical centre of the land. They are then consigned and buried at Dinas Emrys in Wales where they lie forgotten until Vortigern arrives and intends building his fortress on this spot. The tower keeps falling down and his Druids say that only the sacrifice of 'a boy without a father' will be effective. The child Merlin Emrys is found, a boy whose mother conceived him in intercourse with a daemon or spirit. He challenges the Druids to tell him what lies beneath the tower but they cannot. He reveals the two dragons, who are released from their long captivity. He then utters many curious prophecies, in which he interprets the dragons as the embattled races of Britons — the red dragon — and the Saxons — the white dragon.[8]

However, the dragons do have a much deeper correlative, for they are the polarized energies of the land itself. Intrinsically they represent the male seed and the female blood, symbolically represented by the mystical union of the Goddess of Sovereignty, the Mistress of the Land, and the rightful King. In the reign of Lludd, these energies are out of control and he must find a means of safeguarding his realm until he himself has discovered the balanced use of government. In Vortigern's reign, we see a man unfit to rule placed in a position of supreme power which he then abuses. The coming of Merlin Emrys signals the end of his reign and prepares the coming of the Pendragons. The dragons, then, are the vitality of the land, ever circling the Island of the Mighty or Clas Myrddin — Merlin's Enclosure — as Britain was once called.[41]

2. Hawk

In early Arthurian texts and in the *Welsh Triads*, Gawain is known by his old name of Gwalchmai, or the Hawk of May. The quality of Gawain's mythos has shifted considerably over the centuries and from being the supremely courteous warrior who diplomatically intercedes between quarrelling knights, he appears in Malory as a truculent and overbearing knight. If we return to his original name, we will more speedily understand the totem power of this card. The hawk is able to fly above the land and see all that happens below with his piercing sight. He guards his domain, striking down invaders. Like Gawain, the hawk's powers of observation and protection are strongest towards midday, for then he can be champion of the land.[51]

3. Wren

The wren is known in Celtic folklore and mythology as 'the King of the Birds'. He acquired this title during the Battle of the Birds — a contest in which the various feathered totems battled for sovereignty. The wren was successful because he mounted upon the wings of the eagle and thus flew highest of all birds. The mystical reverence in which the wren was held was still observed in the rites of midwinter in both Ireland and Pembrokeshire, where a wren was carried about and properly mourned by being ritually shown in a wicker work house or attached to a pole and paraded about the village. In Welsh *dryw* means both wren and Druid and here we find the key to this power, for the Green Man is indeed the Green Man of Knowledge whose wisdom makes him king. In the Middle Ages, the wren was supposed also to be able to divine royal blood by his cry.[84] The Green Man is the inner guardian of knowledge but it is his chief desire to be overcome in the Beheading Game and bested by the opponent who was once his pupil and who will, eventually, outdo his master. The wren is thus the most powerful totem in this octave, since it humbles itself to what is truly royal and full of wisdom.

Set One is a triad about championship and the mystical connection between the land and its guardians.

Set Two

1. Crane

The crane has in Celtic mythology been associated both with transformation and with oracular power. It is no longer indigenous to the British Isles, but from early sources, as well as from the modern evidence in Europe where cranes still exist, they are clearly supposed to be bringers of luck. The crane's flesh was taboo among the Irish and probably also among the British. The crane is a transformative totem of the Lady, and many women in Celtic mythology assume this shape, including Miadhach who was in crane's shape for 295 years. Her story is substantially the same as that of Aoife who was bewitched into crane's shape and died so; the Otherworldly god Manannan made a treasure bag out of her skin, and this held the Hallows of Ireland, which passed into the keeping of Lugh and Fionn mac Cumhail. Thus the crane is associated with the guardianship of sovereign treasures.[44] The manner in which cranes fly gave rise to a particular form of divination, according to Hyginus, for Mercury was supposed to have invented some of the letters of the alphabet after seeing cranes fly. We can read this myth as part of the established divination by bird's flight practised among the Celtic peoples. The mysterious and aloof demeanour of the crane is particularly apposite to the Lady of the Lake, whose Otherworldly realm is a place of training and safety for the future Grail winner. It is a place where wisdom is imbibed and where the young hero may study the oracular knowledge which the Lady imparts.

2. Dove

The dove has ever been the bird of the Lady. In Wolfram von Eschenbach's *Parzival*, the dove becomes the supreme emblem of the Grail rejoicing. It is the device embroidered upon the clothing of Kundrie, the loathly yet wise Grail messenger, who accompanies the Grail knights and eventually announces the achieving of the Grail.[79]

3. Owl

The owl is the chthonic totem of the Lady and has ever been associated with ill-omen. The most famous instance of an owl in Celtic mythology is the story of Blodeuwedd, the Otherworldly wife of Llew who was conjured out of flowers by Math and Gwydion. It was her punishment to be turned into an owl for betraying Llew. The Welsh for owl, *blodeuwedd*, incorporates the joint qualities of Llew's wife — the owl and the flower. More usually the owl is *tyllfan* in Welsh or even *aderyn y coff*, 'corpse-bird'. In Scots Gaelic, the owl is called *Cailleach oidche* or 'Night-hag', signifying the Cailleach or dark aspect of the Lady.

The experience of the Spiral Tower, the Glass Caer, is likewise seen in two ways, depending on the observer's standpoint: it is a fearful thing, bringing death and oblivion, or a wonderful thing, signifying the complete transformation of the initiate. The owl is therefore the totem of this card, its shrill shriek announcing the coming of the Glass Caer.

Set Two is a triad about the Lady's totemistic appearances, each of which has different functions and appearances, but which represent the unfolding of her purpose.

Set Three

1. Cow

It is hard to appreciate just how central the cow was to Celtic society. It was the unit of currency and thus implied wealth. Many Otherworldly cows throng Celtic mythology; they usually are white in appearance with red ears, and each gives prodigious amounts of milk. Such a cow is captured on an Otherworldly raid by Cuchulainn but is stolen by Cu Roi mac Daire, his antagonist.[44] Such legends also surround Guinevere who, in the earliest texts, seems to be an Otherworldly woman, a sovereignty-bestowing maiden who is married to Arthur in order to endorse his marriage to the land. Guinevere is frequently captured or pursued by numerous lovers or would-be abductors, each of whom desires the wealth of Britain for himself.[82] The cow only ever appears when the king is in harmony with the land, for one of the first signs of the Wasteland — when the king's union with Sovereignty is ruptured — is the failure of the fields and the dearth of cow's milk.

2. Merlin

The merlin is one of the most humble of the hawk family, having no royal status, like the gerfalcon which might only be flown by monarchs. Arthur's Merlin came to be so called only as a result of the spread of the Arthurian legends into France where the British Myrddin was speedily translated into the more mellifluous and etymologically less embarrassing, Merlinus. So does tradition endlessly evolve. For though Myrddin's name had nothing whatever to do with a hawk once, now the merlin is indissoluble from this association. The assimilation of this totem was remarkably swift, for in the *Didot Perceval*, the text speaks of Merlin's *Esplumoir* or moulting cage, into which he retreats at the conclusion of the story.[58] The Round

Table was Merlin's conception, for the ordering of the land, but it derived from earlier and unseen prototypes. T.H. White made good use of Merlin's association with the least noble of the hawk family in his *The Once and Future King.*[84]

The earlier Merlin legends speak of Merlin raising Stonehenge as a monument to Ambrosius.[8] It is well known that many previous henge monuments were erected on the site and that the latest ediface was erected much earlier than the fifth century AD. But the idea of the circle as a gathering place is one long established. The Round Table was said to be Guinevere's dowry and this is significant in itself since she represents the land. The eye of the merlin keeps in sight the good of the land on all levels concurrently, for he has seen what once was and what is yet to be in the stars, and he ever serves the empress.

3. Cockerel

The cock, along with the goose and hare, was one of the sacred totems of the British, according to Julius Caesar. It also appears in Romano-British reliefs in connection with two deities — the Celtic Mercury and an unnamed goddess of Sovereignty.[57] Both cock and goose have been regarded as admonitory birds, warning both of day and of unwelcome visitors. In the Star, the cock warns of the Pendragons' coming just as the starry comet announces this news to the skies.

Set Three is a triad concerning the sovereignty both of Guinevere and of the land itself. These three humble beasts keep watch over the kingdom of Logres.

Set Four

1. Chough

The Cornish Chough, a member of the crow family, has traditionally been associated with Arthur, as the totem by which he appears before his final reappearance and recall from Avalon. This bird is fitting, with its red bill and red feet — a true inhabitant of the Otherworld. Bran the Blessed's totem was the raven, but Bran's head was disinterred from under the White Tower because Arthur felt that only he should guard the shores of Britain from invasion.[78]

2. Ermine

The coat of the stoat turns white in winter in northern latitudes when it is called the ermine. The white, black-tipped pelts of the ermine traditionally adorned the robes of judges and of royalty. Lady Sovereignty also changes her appearance, appearing as the loathly hag and as the queenly bestower, as the Flower Bride and also as the admonitory Black Maiden. This last, warrior maiden is fittingly represented by the totem of the ermine.[41]

3. Salmon

The salmon is traditionally one of the oldest animals in Celtic myth. It is the totem of many initiates, including Taliesin, Fintan, Tuan mac Carill and others. Its great struggle to re-enter the waters where it was spawned make it the supreme totem of initiatic effort.[44]

Set Four is a triad concerning the royal totems of the Island of the Mighty, and they confer unique freedom and responsibility at once.

Set Five

1. Lark

Taliesin's totems are as many as the shapes he entered into during his poetic initiation, but the lark is the premier bird of Summer's gladness and release from restriction. Its endless song, like that of Taliesin, sounds perpetually, though the bird is itself unseen, but hovering above high in the clouds. It is Taliesin who knows supremely the language of the birds, the ancient knowledge of the totems.

2. Hound

The faithful hound is almost a cliché in folklore, and yet there is another level on which the dog represents a possibility of the relationship between humanity and all animals. The hound was the symbol frequently found in the temple of Nodens (Irish Nuadu) at Lydney in Gloucestershire. Nodens was a wounded god and king who lost his hand in battle. Since a maimed king was automatically dethroned, because a healthy man was necessary to maintain the mystical links between the kingship and the land, Nodens/Nuadu ceded place to the god Lugh.[44] At Nodens' temple, there were *abatons* — sleeping cubicles in which the sick would spend a night in holy sleep, while in the morning their dreams and their illness were interpreted by his priests. The hound frequently appears in connection with therapeutic rites in Celtic mythology and the appearance of the hound in connection with the Wounded King is profound. In the folk carol which stems from this mythos, *The Corpus Christi Carol*, is the verse:

And at the bed's foot there lieth a hound;
Licking the blood as it daily runs down.

The hound is thus the totem of the Wounded King, bringing healing and restoration, while he lies in a state of suspended animation.

3. White Mare

The White Mare is primarily the totem and ritual appearance of Rhiannon who, with the Celtic goddess Epona, shares the emblem of the mare and her foal. Rhiannon's first appearance to Pwyll was riding a white mare which, though it went very slowly, could never be caught. Later, when accused of having killed and eaten her son, Pryderi, she was sentenced to stand at the mounting block and offer to bear guests into the hall on her back, after having told them her story. Rhiannon is a prototype of Modron, the mother of Mabon, who seeks for her son through all adversity and brings him at last to his appointed place.[44]

In this card, the white mare literally is the bearer and mother of the youth. The White Horse of Uffington in Berkshire stems from pre-Celtic times, but represents the same abiding strength and purpose.

Set Five is a triad concerning the liberating and helping totems who are crucial to the initiate's development.

Set Six

1. White Hart

The White Hart, like the mythical unicorn, is one of the guiding totems of the seeker. The hunting of animals for food represents one of the greatest exchanges between humanity and the natural world. In the hunting of the stag, venery became a royal and ceremonial art, one which figured largely in early and medieval literature. The famous Unicorn Tapestries of the Metropolitan Museum, New York, and La Dame de Licorne tapestries of Cluny in Paris, represent pictorially this very event. Whenever white beasts appear in Celtic mythology it is as Otherworldly messengers and guides. The White Hart is the supreme mystical totem that stands at the heart of the transformative exchange: it makes that which is mundane, Otherworldly, and gives experience of the greatest of virtues, love itself.

2. Raven

The raven is alter-ego and totem of the Goddesses Badbh, Macha and Nemhainn who form the triple-aspected goddess of battle, the Morrighan. This carrion bird figures largely in Celto-Arthurian literature as the taker of the slain, for whom the battlefield is the larder. This katabolic function of the Goddess is little understood, but she assimilates death and transforms it into new life. The raven is also the totemistic messenger of the Goddess to her champion, if the mythos of Lugh is anything to go by. The parallels between this association of ravens with Lugh and that of ravens with Odin is remarkably similar. In *The Dream of Rhonabwy*, Owain ap Urien is aided by ravens in his gaming-board combat with Arthur.[41]

3. Eagle

The eagle is one of the oldest animals and is associated with the finding of Mabon in *Culhwch and Olwen*.[30] In Romano-British cults it seemed to be the attribute of Taranis, the thunderer, who was seen as the

Celtic Jupiter. Fintan, the oldest man, spent some of his long existence in eagle shape. Llew was transformed into an eagle after his betrayal at the hands of Blodeuwedd and her love, Gronw. His sufferings and virtual physical dissolution are but a prelude to his healing. This seems to have been a Celtic tradition, possibly native, partly influenced by the biblical saying 'They shall renew themselves as eagles', since Maelduine and his companions discover much the same on their great wonder voyage to the Isles of the Blessed where they discover an aged and moulting eagle which plunges itself into a lake of immortality and is renewed.[16] Arthur himself had a long dialogue with an eagle, in which shape his nephew, Eliwlod ap Madog was transformed.[28] Geoffrey of Monmouth reports that Arthur's grave (perhaps he means resting place, because 'a grave for Arthur is an inconceivable thing', according to the Stanzas of the Graves) was guarded by a pair of chained eagles.[8] The eagle thus renews itself and is the totem of the Sleeping Lord.

Set Six is a triad in which we seek the deeply transformative power of the Otherworldly messenger, the Lady of the Wheel and the Sleeping Lord: the three inner guardians.

Set Seven

1. White Boar

The White Boar, like the White Hart, usually betokens an eruption of the Otherworld into the earthly realms. Pryderi and Manawyddan follow a white boar in their hunting and Pryderi is enticed into an Otherworldly castle in which he becomes stuck to a golden basin. His mother, Rhiannon, suffers the same fate, until Manawyddan is able to release them and rescind the enchantments which are upon Dyfed. These are caused by an Otherworldly adversary, of which the White Boar is but an appearance.[30] Arthur's own encounter with a white boar, Twrch Trwyth, is one of the most impressive adventures of the early texts. He follows the devastating boar to Ireland and there grapples with it in single combat for nine days and nights, before the creature escapes to Britain and there begins its devastation again in Arthur's realm. Pursued by a great number of warriors, Twrch Trwyth eventually plunges into the sea at Cornwall and is seen no more. This pursuit, like Arthur's passage to Annwn, causes the king great anguish since he loses many men. But the White Boar is the guardian of a set of magical treasures which the giant Yspadadden requires before allowing Arthur's nephew, Culhwch, to marry his daughter. Arthur and his men obtain these and Culhwch marries Olwen. Yspadadden is beheaded and the joint devastation of boar and giant is no more.[44] Arthur's earliest title is the Boar of Cornwall, which became his emblem, possibly as a result of his association with this totem. The boar represents the chthonic powers of the Underworld which are overcome and controlled by Arthur.

2. Adder

The adder plays a very significant part in the dissolution of the Arthurian world. It is primarily the totem of Morgan who acts as a catalyst for Arthur's manifestation as king and his downfall. When Medrawt (Mordred) and Arthur are drawn up in parley at the Battle of Camlan, it is proclaimed that no man draw his sword. However an adder darts from the undergrowth, frightening a rider who draws his sword to slash at the serpent. This is taken as the signal for the onset of hostilities. The adder is Britain's only venomous snake and it is the prime totem for the Goddess of Sovereignty in her dark phase. She is Queen Dragon, the serpent that traditionally appears from her mound on Candlemas Day in order to battle with the Spring Maiden, Brighid for the governing of the land.[41] The venom which causes Arthur's downfall is also his healing, since it is to Morgan's island that he is borne to be healed of his wounds. The dichotomy represented by the Goddess's totem of the adder is reflected in a character frequently appearing in Celtic folk-story: the old hag who plunges the hero into a cauldron to cure, to heal his wounds, and then into a cauldron of poison to 'harden him up'.[6]

3. Bee

The bee is properly the totem of the land's fertility. It can only produce honey when there is blossom on the trees and flowers, and so its presence in this card betokens the healing of the Wasteland. Like the adder, it is beneficial but also harmful. The true cost of kingship is acknowledged by every sovereign; the land is fruitful only to those who industriously tend it. The bee's hive is a microcosm of what a kingdom should be: every citizen working harmoniously for the good of the hive.

Set Seven is a triad where the totems reflect the delicate balance of the land and its people. After Summer, the snows of Winter; after the rigours of Spring, the fruits of Autumn.

The Transcendent Set

This reveals the three blackbirds of Rhiannon who announce to all seekers the way into the Otherworld. These same birds sang in the hall of Bran, after his head had been stricken off; while their song continued, the Company of the Noble Head enjoyed the company of their lord as though he had been alive, but one opened the forbidden door and the birds sang no more. All were aware of their mortality and from that time Bran's head began to decay. They are the totem of all who seek to understand the mysteries at the heart of the *Hallowquest*.

MEDITATION ON THE TOTEMS

There are many methods of 'entering' the *Hallowquest* cards. Some of these are explored elsewhere in this book. But it is also possible to explore another level of each of the Greater Powers, by means of the totem beast depicted on each of them. Each of these totems is the 'voice' of the card. This is especially helpful in the case of the Greater Powers which do not depict a character e.g. XVI The Spiral Tower or X The Round Table.

To start your meditation, choose one of the Greater Powers. You will also need one of the Lesser Powers: the Stone Nine. This card forms the setting of the visualization. Set the card before you, establish your meditation space and prepare yourself by breathing and relaxation. Having studied the card before you, close your eyes and visualize the evergreen clearing. There is nothing within it, save the central stone.

Walk forward to the stone and place your hands upon it, calling upon the totem of the card you wish to learn about. From along one of the many paths leading to this clearing, your totem will appear. Greet it courteously, and ask it to lead you into deeper understanding of the Greater Power in question. It will answer your questions and also set some questions of its own. It may also lead you along one of the paths to another place and show you different things. Eventually, it will lead you to the scene depicted on the card of its origin and introduce you to the character in that card. (If you chose a Greater Power which has no character depicted on it, this will not apply, but you will be given a deeper understanding of the card.)

When you have gained your realizations from this meditation, re-establish consciousness in your own time and place and write down your experiences.

This meditation is only given in outline here. You may personally experience events in a slightly different order than stated here, and you may be led to different scenes and understandings. The setting of the evergreen clearing is the place of sanctuary for all created things, wherein you are given the space and time to learn from the totems.

You may initially experience some reluctance to enter into a dialogue with the totems, but you can remind yourself that the totems are not 'just animals', they are supra-bestial, representing the cognizances of a deeper realm than we inhabit. Their memories and knowledge are older than ours, for they have been existent through all the ages of humankind. We may have lost access to our racial memory, becoming creatures of order and reason rather than instinct, but we can share through an interspecific communion with the totems.

FINDING THE PERSONAL TOTEM

The path of the totem beast leads us back into communion with the source of our spiritual strength, our creative belonging to the earth. Each of us has a natural affinity with at least one totem animal which acts as our bridge to the primal and originative worlds of our creation. Some people are clearly aligned with and aware of their totem, others are not. The following exercise enables the reader to find their personal totem, a factor which will assist further work with the totemistic triads.

In order to find our totem, we need to switch off the 'rational watch-dog', and alert the 'instinctive tracker dog'. We use another part of our brains in order to find our personal totem: the brain stem, which lodges the genetic code and instinctive memories. This is activated by simple exercises which bypass the rational faculty and connect us with our deep memories.

The teaching of the totems is a pre-Celtic one, but in the *Hallowquest* pack we can approach it under the aegis of two of the Greater Powers — V Taliesin who, as chief poet of Arthur, comprises the fullest range of totemistic experiences; or Mabon, (XVIII The Moon and XIX The Sun) whose captivity has been from before the ages of recorded time and whose existence is remembered only by the true totems. You can ask the help of either of these totemistic guardians in this exercise.

A. Taliesin as guardian

Visualize yourself in the hall of story-telling as in Greater Power V. You are sitting before Taliesin, about to listen to his skilful telling. Ask him to help you discover your personal totem. He bids you look into the smoke and fire while he tells you a story. Listen to his words carefully and watch the smoke and flames for the images which will form themselves there.

B. Mabon as guardian

Visualize yourself in the landscape of Greater Power XIX. You await the coming of Mabon upon his white mare. As he rides up, you ask him to help find your totem. He bids you mount behind him and together you travel the land until you come to the scene of Greater Power XVIII. He takes out his harp and begins to play, bidding you look in the waters of the weir and the stones of the riverbed. As his music weaves its spell, watch for the images which will form themselves there.

With each of these meditations, be aware that it may take a few sessions before you are sufficiently 'tuned in' to the task in hand. It may take several months of steady and persistent meditation to realize your totem. Do not be dismayed; there is a right time for everything, and it may be that you have to assimilate other realizations before this one will emerge.

As a rough set of guidelines for this exercise: when you start to see images of the totems always accept the *first* image which you see — this is usually the right one; watch your dreams for recurrent images; be mentally adaptable; keep a compassionate heart for yourself, as well as for others; listen for the voice of wisdom, your mother-wit or instinct throughout the day.

Your totem may be any created beast, bird or fish. It will rarely or never be a mythical animal such as a winged horse, or griffon. Your totem will not necessarily be drawn from the list which comprise the Greater Powers. More usually, it will be derived from your native land. If your ancestry is from another land, even though your family may have lived in Britain or America for several generations, then expect animals from that place.

When you have discovered your totem you will instinctively know whether you have realized it correctly. The interchange of energy between you will already be established and you will 'recognize' it immediately as your own.

It is possible to work with the Totemistic Triads in a ritual format. Guidelines can be found for working the Arthurian Powers on p.252. These can be adapted by the reader for use with the totems also. In this case, your own totem will act as a central mediating agency between you and your ritual experience, in much the same role as Taliesin and Mabon act in the exercise above.

THE MYSTERIES OF THE TAROT OCTAVES

Fig. 7.4: The Greater Powers Expressed as Musical Octaves

The cohesion of each triad may be demonstrated if we express the Greater Powers as music. In the example above, we see the 21 Greater Powers equated to a note of music. The Seeker (0) is not shown here for that card represents the sacred silence of the student. In the school of Pythagoras, new pupils were not permitted to speak for at least two years but expected to keep a listening and learning silence. It was only after this time that they were allowed to participate in dialogues. During this time they would have learned what questions were worth asking.

The range of notes shown above in Figure 7.4 represent the normal range of the human voice, from bass, baritone, tenor and contralto to soprano. Likewise, the Greater Powers represent the normal range of archetypes which will be found underlying any major mythology.

By expressing the cards as music rather than as specific characters from any mythology, we can appreciate their universal quality, since the language of music transcends the babel of tongues which keep nations separated. The mystical power of music to overcome divisions is indeed great, whether we look to the power of Orpheus over the wild beasts or to the international cohesion created by the massive fund-raising of Band Aid in 1986. Similarly, the Greater Powers are resonating notes which go on sounding whether or not we are attuned to their qualities.

Even non-musicians will be aware that if, say, the note of D is sounded on a harp, all the corresponding D strings of other octaves will likewise resonate. D strings of different octaves, although they express 'the quality of D-ness', nevertheless cannot be confused with each other, since each expresses a different level of tonality. In the same way, the Greater Powers of one octave cannot be confused either.

There is no reason for the reader to accept the exact musical correlations of this example, for the musical expression of the Greater Powers may be transposed according to personal needs and wishes. But if we equate the note G to the first card of the sequence, we arrive at the following octaves:

Octaves of G. I Merlin; VIII Gawain; XV The Green Knight.
Octaves of A. II The Lady of the Lake; IX The Grail Hermit; XVI The Spiral Tower.
Octaves of B. III Guinevere; X The Round Table; XVII The Star
Octaves of C. IV Arthur; XI Sovereignty; XVIII The Moon.
Octaves of D. V Taliesin; XII The Wounded King; XIX The Sun.
Octaves of E. VI The White Hart; XIII The Washer at the Ford; XX The Sleeping Lord.
Octaves of F. VII Prydwen; XIV The Cauldron; XXI The Flowering of Logres.

If the reader wishes to accept these correlations, then the following mnenomic may help anchor the key word of each octave:

Octave Note	*Key word*
G	Galvanizing
A	Attuning
B	Beginning
C	Creating
D	Defining
E	Enhancing
F	Finalizing

The G octaves are concerned with instigating action.
The A octaves promote interior assessment.
The B octaves establish foundations.
The C octaves manifest creatively.
The D octaves define and limit.
The E octaves suggest new patterns.
The F octaves conclude the action.

Musical readers will doubtless find many other ways of working with these octaves in creative and ritual ways.

CHAPTER 8

the secret door

EVERYDAY MEDITATION

The Tarot has been primarily associated with divination. However, there is another, neglected level to the cards which can be very rewarding: meditation is the secret door to an undiscovered realm. This secret door is not hidden in a temple inaccessible to non-initiates; it lies within each of us.

There is much mystification about meditation and so many misconceptions surrounding it that many people automatically consider it to be an activity best left to others. Many meditational techniques do, of course, stem from specific religious traditions and these often require a special posture, mantra or complex format. But most Westerners do not have experience of such techniques, since they are not adherents of those religions; they are more likely however to have some contact with yoga or martial arts than they are with the mystical traditions of Judaism and Christianity, both of which possess their own meditational skills.

There are also many esoteric meditational techniques, usually requiring some knowledge of specific symbolism and experience of inner worlds. But again, few people are aware of such complex systems and even fewer have any sense of inner geography — the archetypal realms of which our outer life is a manifestion.

It is not hard to see why meditation should therefore be considered so obscure. However, all of us have experience of certain forms of meditation, although perhaps we have never thought of these activities as using 'meditational skills':

1. day-dreaming
2. visualizing
3. dreaming

Let us consider these in order:

1. When we day-dream, we are visualizing our desires imaginatively, allowing our thoughts to create our dream house, an ideal partner, a new job, whatever. Our day-dreaming is a powerful magical tool which, if used creatively and positively, can dictate our circumstances. Day-dreaming is not a childish or time-wasting occupation, though certainly it can be used in a counter-productive manner, whether it be the creation of 'Walter Mitty'-like impossibilities or a depressive brooding on 'what might happen' scenarios. Everyone is aware that such fantasizing can be harmful, but few seem aware that day-dreaming can also aid us.

2. All of us are used to visualizing scenes: this happens when we hear an anecdote or story, or when we listen to a radio play or read a novel: our brain supplies visual images to accompany what we are hearing or reading. We are thus able to reproduce images. But another person's visualization will often be totally different from our own.

3. Now many people swear that they are unaware of dreaming, but it is something which we all do. Everyone dreams, but those who have no recall of doing so, probably pass from deep sleep into immediate consciousness. Those of us who do recall our dreams will know that there are many kinds of dream, just as there are many different forms of narrative. Sometimes we passively watch scenes unfolding, as though we are watching a film; sometimes we actively participate in the scenario. Sometimes we appear as ourselves, sometimes we know we are someone else — someone known or unknown.

The variety of dream types seems to be a psychological need. For instance, people suffering deprivation — in prison, during war etc — dream vivid, comforting and fulfilling dreams in which their homes, families, and good food figure largely. The desire to stay in bed in the morning is very often a submerged need to recall the tail-end of a dream which we were enjoying. In this state we approach a semi-conscious state.

If we analyse these three activities we find that:

1. In daydreams we voluntarily create our own images and live them out imaginatively.
2. In visualization, we reproduce visual images from a set narrative, but these images will be coloured by our cultural and social education.
3. In dreams we participate in involuntary scenarios, often expressed in universal or archetypal symbolism.

These three abilities are the basis for the kind of meditation you can achieve using the *Hallowquest* pack.

ESOTERIC PRINCIPLES OF MEDITATION

This is all very well, but what is the purpose of meditation? The benefits of meditation have been vastly overstressed in the wrong way for, though they do undoubtedly include increased perception of oneself, one's goals and relationships, meditation by itself will not necessarily bring luck in love and money, health or magical powers. All esoteric skills have what might be called their 'productive' side, in the sense that they incidentally provide a sound basis for a better life, but that is not primarily their function.

Meditation is about clear perception and about the alignment of one's physical, psychic and spiritual natures with the deep archetypal inner world. This inner world is not a psychological state or complex which we each personally inhabit, but a timeless, ever-present inner reality. It has been called many different things: paradise, heaven, the kingdom, the collective unconscious, the place of peace, the Other-world — these are all valid names. You will have your own word for this place which lies beyond the secret door which is within you. In this book, it will be called the Otherworld.

We may think of this reality as the ultimate source of our life, both physical and spiritual. All knowledge, all wisdom, derives from this place. If such a reality is not immediate to you, take time to day-dream about the inner world: let the images rise from your own needs and desires — your picture need not derive from any existent cultural analogy or spiritual archetype. It is primarily a place of ultimate resources where every thing, idea, concept etc. is available and approachable. Belief in a spiritual never never land is not required here; merely take time to act 'as if' the inner world existed for you. Here all symbologies have their source and are often represented by archetypal inhabitants — both human and animal.

When we meditate, we enter this reality, and this is often a source of great anxiety to those who have never meditated before. What exactly happens when we meditate? What part of me is actually meditating? Few books on meditation give any notion of what we might expect, but it is important to retain our common sense and apply exactly the same principles to esoteric practices as we do in our everyday lives.

Before you read on, try the following exercise exactly where you are sitting now. No one will notice anything strange about you. All they will see will be someone reading a book with eyes lowered. Turn to the picture of one of the Greater Powers which appeals to you and study it carefully, noting the archetype depicted, the surrounding landscape or interior. Now close your eyes and 'see' in your mind's eye the picture you have been studying. Make a conscious effort to see the picture in colour, now see it framed by a doorway and let the image grow until it is life-size. That doorway is standing right in front of you and you can 'walk' straight through and meet the person within. You have 'stepped' through the door. Now 'look' down and see your own body, hold your hands out in front of you to establish that you are really doing this and not just visualizing yourself, projecting your own image as though you were on a TV screen.

What is the weather like? Is it day or night? Feel the ground beneath your feet. Now approach the figure before you and greet it. 'Hear' its reply. If you can't think of anything to say then ask questions, e.g. what does this card signify? 'Listen' to the answer. If nothing happens, don't worry. When you feel you've got the idea, then say goodbye and come back through the door to where you are sitting.

What happened while you were doing this? Your physical body never moved, but some other part of you 'travelled'. At no point were you confused about which reality was which, as sometimes happens when you dream. You were totally in charge of the experience you had. Though if you 'heard' answers, then you may be wondering where they came from.

The kind of visualization you have just attempted started out as a voluntary meditation in which you were reproducing an established image: just as you do when you read a novel. But you actively entered into the picture and interacted with it: this is nearer to the process of dreaming, when you are actively participating yet the scenario is not scripted. At the conclusion of this visualization, you came back to yourself without difficulty, just as you do when you wake.

The mystery about 'where you go to' and where 'what you experience' during meditation comes from is not such a difficulty. What you have done here is cross the boundaries between one reality and another and come back again. What you experienced while you were there is as a direct result of interacting with the deep symbology of the card you chose. By concentrating on the symbolism of the card you have 'made contact' with its archetypal message. There is no mystery in this for we perform much the same perceptual act when we interact with another human being: the way they dress, their body language, what they say etc. all determine how we view them. When we get to know them, we may be said to touch a deeper level of communication with their individual soul — so it is with this exercise.

All mystical teaching systems, such as the *Hallowquest* pack, act as archetypal messengers conveying information only to those who are sufficiently *aligned* with its deeper levels. By meditating or visualizing we so align ourselves. In this way, the cards can come to mean much more to you than the mere casual acquaintance of occasionally handling them and doing a weekly reading. Like people whom you pass in the street every morning, each card has more to tell you about itself.

PREPARATION FOR MEDITATION

There are a few essential basic requirements which will prepare you for meditating. These basics have no magical cachet, but are all grounded in practical common sense. If you prepare yourself properly you will meditate more productively, clearing the way between yourself and the object of your visualization.

Regular breathing and relaxation of body and mind are the first things: these are so basic that most of us skip over them to get on to the meat of the exercise. Believe that these are the very plates on which your meditation is served — and yes, you can eat with your fingers — but it isn't so convenient or orderly. Centring and stillness are the result of good breathing and relaxation. They create the space in which to meditate and sustain the experience you will have. If your brain is busy compiling a shopping list of things to do, or your body tense from another activity, your breathing is going to be irregular and you will achieve no depth of meditation.

Meditate where and when you will not be disturbed. The place is not important otherwise. If you have a special quiet place, then use that, but it is not essential.

Sit in a comfortable chair which supports your back, so that your body is in its most natural alignment of easy relaxation. If you lie down you will probably fall asleep. Being upright usually ensures that, however deep you go, you will remain in semi-wakefulness at the very least.

Several of the exercises following use a simple entry and exit technique: this device merely asserts your intention of entering the meditation and your return from it, and is a useful orienting method for those who feel anxious about aligning with the Otherworld. You can make your own visual or verbal passport, if you wish.

Your use of the entry and exit technique will establish good practices from the very start. Before meditating and after relaxing and breathing in a regular way, close your eyes and visualize before you an ancient door. Say:

As a seeker I stand before the secret door.
May the way be open to me,
May no hindrance stay my steps,
For I take the way within.

Then visualize the door opening and begin your meditation. When you have finished meditating, see the door before you again, only this time it leads from the inner world to your own time and place. Say:

A traveller I return through the secret door.
The way is plain to me,
And my steps were led.
From the world within I return.

Pass through the door and gradually re-establish consciousness slowly. Become aware of the chair you are sitting on, of the ground beneath your feet. Open your eyes and take a few deep breaths. Stretch, lean forward and touch your feet, if you are able. Then write down your experiences.

Use your own form of words to open and close your meditation, when you are a more experienced traveller in the Otherworld.

Rarely, some people find it difficult to return from meditation. Normally, sleep overcomes the meditator who awakes in the normal way after a very refreshing slumber, but sometimes, the meditator remains briefly in a state of consciousness between full awareness and sleep in which the limbs seem heavy, the blood runs slowly and there is a reluctance 'to come out of it'. If this should happen, do not panic. You are not being gripped by malign forces but merely suffering from the psychic equivalent of cramp. As with pins and needles which pass after a while, this condition will also alleviate. Make a conscious effort to speed up your breathing and to stretch the limbs, since this condition is usually purely physiological in origin. You can also forcefully bring to mind any physical image which will help you 'earth' yourself again, e.g. peeling potatoes or digging the garden. Immediately on recovering, take a hot drink and have something to eat to fully earth yourself.

PATHS TO VISION

There are many ways in which you can acquaint yourself with the deeper meanings of the *Arthurian Tarot*. The path of meditation and visualization demands time and commitment, of which not everyone has excess. If you decide to start meditating on the *Hallowquest* pack, then set time aside — preferably about 20 minutes daily — and organize your study material into manageable blocks. If you decide to work on the Lesser Powers, then establishing a meditation programme to take in, say, just one Hallow suit or the Court cards, is going to be more encouraging and more likely to be fulfilled than a decision to work systematically through all 56 cards.

There follow various meditations for you to attempt. Some are complete in themselves, being short journeys into the world of the

Hallowquest, others are quite long and complex, requiring deep meditation upon each card. You will find it useful to record some of all of these on to a tape recorder, reading each one slowly and leaving sufficient pauses at the points indicated by an asterix to allow for independent visualization and assimilation. Using a tape recorder frees you from the necessity of having to remember the sequence of the meditations given here. If this is too much trouble, most of the meditations in this book have been recorded by the authors and are available from the address on p.294.

When you begin meditating, go slowly and carefully rather than jumping in at the deep end. Meditational skills are acquired over many years' practice, and even the most experienced meditator still has to observe the basic rules of breathing and relaxation, of patient visualization and the chasing away of distracting thoughts.

THE KING'S PROGRESS

The following visualization is intended to give experience of each of the Hallow suits. Only the framework is outlined here, but each reader can adapt this to each of the Hallow suits in turn. It will be useful to refer to the diagram on p.118, Figure 4.1 for this meditation, which shows the Court of Arthur (Llys Arthur) at the centre of the land and the four Hallow courts at the four quarters. For this meditation, the Court of Arthur is placed at Caerleon on Usk (the ancient stronghold of Arthur, according to early tradition) or Camelot (if you prefer the medieval tradition); either of these castles is at the centre of your own land.

Visualize the Court of Arthur before you as a mighty stronghold. You have come as a guest to this castle. At the door you are greeted by the steward and led to your place in the Hall of the Round Table. He presents you to the King and Queen.

The King greets you, saying: 'I am about to go on progress about my kingdom. Do you wish to accompany me?'

You are eager to go. You are seated between the King and Queen as their honoured guest. The Queen speaks: 'On this journey we will see many wondrous sights. If you wish to remember them clearly, you have only to gaze upon the ring which is on the King's hand and you will recall them all.'

(Throughout this meditation, which can take in one or many of the Lesser Powers, you have only to look at Arthur's ring — a massive ruby — in order to return to your own time and place.)

After a magnificent feast, members of the court prepare to set out on the King's progress. The castle is left in the charge of Gawain. You find yourself riding in the company of many of the knights and ladies of Arthur's court. If you wish to understand anything better upon your way, you have only to ask the King or the Queen.

The first part of the progress is towards the eastern part of the kingdom, towards the Court of the Sword, and the landscape you encounter is that of the Sword cards. (The sequence is, on each part of the progress, from Hallow Two to Hallow King.) As you set out it is Spring. (In successive journeyings, you will pass through the whole year, as well as through the four directions.)

The court travels on, with Arthur and Guinevere concerned and watchful over the state of the land and its inhabitants. At each card, the court halts to rest. You are free to explore, to ride or walk, as you choose, in the unfolding landscape. You will not get lost, for you will hear the sound of the horn which is blown to signal that the court is moving onwards.

At each stopping place you may meet people or animals with whom you speak or interact. Each inhabitant of this land has a message to give concerning the place which you are in. Listen carefully to them and, if you do not understand them, ask the King or the Queen.

In this way you journey onwards until you reach the Hallow Ten, the castle of your destination, where you encounter the four royal persons of that court: the Maiden, Knight, Queen and King of that Hallow, from whom you may learn further of the land you are in.

At the conclusion of each visit, you enter the chapel or sacred place of the Hallow court where, with Arthur, Guinevere and the rest of Llys Arthur, you are given a vision of the Hallow in question. After this, it is time to leave and travel on to the next court: that of the Spear, which lies to the south of the kingdom.

Take time to complete your entire progress. At the commencement of each new session, rejoin the court of Arthur wherever you left them on your journey. You will end up at the Court of the Stone in the north; it will be Winter. (If however, you live in the southern hemisphere, you may wish to change the directions. See note on p.246.)

At the conclusion of the whole progress, you return to Caerleon/Camelot and there celebrate Midwinter/Christmas with the court. You have circled the year and learned much about the nature of the land in which you live.

This meditation is obviously very adaptable and can be as long as it needs to take. It is not something to do all in one session, but over a long period. Ideally, it would be good to start it at the Spring Equinox and take a whole year to work through it, but there is at least three months' intensive meditation work here, for those who need a programme to work to. You may find that you occasionally encounter characters from the Greater Powers, apart from Arthur and Guinevere. The Grail Hermit, Merlin, Sovereignty and the Green Knight seem to turn up most often, but you may see others.

The ring of memory on Arthur's hand is taken from an authentic tradition found in *The Dream of Rhonabwy.*[30]

THE QUEST FOR THE SPEAR

The intention in this meditation, apart from its intrinsic object, is to show how a single episode from one of the Arthurian texts (in this case *Perlesvaus*) can be built up to create a scenario to enable you to participate directly in the actions of the Hallows — in this case the Spear. Other incidents can be used in the same way, and you will find that with a little practice you will be able to extract a great deal from even the most minor-seeming incident. Malory's great book *Le Morte d'Arthur*[31] is one of the best for this, since it contains so many strange and wonderful moments which repay deeper study. On the Celtic front probably no better example can be found than the story of Culhwch and Olwen from the *Mabinogion*.[30] Either of these texts, or indeed any other, can be utilized for powerful meditational work, which will both broaden and deepen your understanding of the Arthurian mythos and the *Hallowquest*.

See before you a room, high and square with carpet underfoot and tapestries on the walls. All of one side is windowed, giving access onto a balcony. You step out onto this and find you are looking out over the sea. It is night and a strong, fresh wind blows inland. The sky is dark and moonless, but as you look you see a single bright star far off in the darkness, and as you watch it, it seems to grow larger, nearer, until you see that it is not a star but a ship, floating serenely on the wavetops, with a dazzling light at its mast-head. It is drawn by a great white swan with a collar of gold.

Below you, you see a flight of stone steps cut into the face of the cliff, leading downwards to the beach. You hasten down this way until you stand on the shore. The ship has come to rest, high and dry on the fine sand. The swan stands close by, its great wings folded, watching. The boat is really a flat-bottomed barge, draped in rich, dark material which flows down from a high canopy and falls over the sides of the vessel. At either end, prow and stern, burns a great candle. They cast a strong, unwavering light upon the scene. You climb aboard and raise the edge of the dark pall to look within. In the midst of the ship is a wide bed, draped in rich cloths. On it lies the body of a kingly man, dressed in gold and brocade. He is partly covered to the breast with a heavy scarlet cloth, but from his breast, high up, protrudes the haft of a spear, stuck fast there and broken off short. The face of the dead man is serene and noble: you have perhaps never seen so fair a face except in dreams. Pity wells in you as you look upon him. Then you see a parchment, rolled and tied with scarlet cord, lying at his side, and you take it up and unroll it. It is a letter. This is what you read:

To the one who finds this letter, greeting. Know the story of this knight whom you see lying before you. For I was once known in life as Balin le Sauvage, and one day I came to a forest, and within the forest was a castle of emerald with strange beasts carved on the walls, and within the castle was a tower of silver, and within the tower of silver a fair table of gold set for a feast. And there I sat down and was served right royally by invisible hands. And at the end of the meal a fair and kingly man came before me and asked how I fared. I answered him well and he led me outside again into the courtyard of the emerald castle. And there I saw a fair well-head and by its side stood a most beauteous damsel who spoke not but smiled upon me until my heart warmed towards her and was full of desire. My host led me to a warm and comfortable room where I was to lodge that night and so left me.

But that night I could not sleep for thinking of the damsel of the well and at last I rose and went forth into the courtyard of the castle to find her. And she was still standing beside the well-head and still she smiled upon me, so that I was driven near to madness with desire for her and so had my way with the damsel who cried out most piteously at my shameful treatment of her.

At that there was a great outcry and the noble man who was my host ran forth from the castle crying that I was an evil man to so betray his hospitality. Then he drew forth his sword and being all unarmed I fled before him through the castle seeking refuge. At last I came to a room and saw before me a great spear that hung upon the wall, point downwards above a little basin of silver, and I believe some drops of blood fell from the point. But I was in great fear for my life and so snatched the spear from the wall and turned at bay there. When my host came through the door with his sword raised I struck him with the spear, a terrible wound through the thighs so that he fell down and cried aloud. And in that moment the spear turned in my hands and struck me in the breast as you see here. And then I felt my death come upon me and tried to pull the spear free. That I could not do, and the spear broke off leaving the rest imbedded in me. I know not how I went from that place, but remember only that I found myself by the shore of the sea and this barge pulled by a swan floating there. And I went aboard into the ship and wrote this letter with my last strength. If you who discover it would set right the evil that I have done and give me rest, go you and seek the spear that is broken and bring it here, for only then shall the two parts be reunited and my spirit freed from a terrible doom.

All this you read, standing on the deck of the black-draped barge by the side of the dead knight, then replacing the letter as you found it you go back to the prow of the boat. At this point you may return by the way you came and take no further part in what follows, or you may remain on the barge and participate in the next stage of the journey. There is no blame to those who decide to depart . . .

Those who decide to continue, feel the barge move beneath your feet. The swan claps its wings and gives forth a ringing cry. It begins to tow the barge swiftly across the water and in no time at all you have reached the farther shore. A gentle shelving beach stretches before you and you leave the barge and walk up inland until you meet a wall of dark trees. They look dark and forbidding, impenetrable and wild with long thorns growing from them, but you press forwards without fear and they part before you allowing you to go deeper into the wood. Soon you come to a clearing and see before you the towers of a castle whose walls are made of green emerald and its gates of ivory. The gates open before you and you pass within, walking softly on lush green grass.

Before you now you see a tower, high and round that gleams softly and seems made all of silver. In the wall is a door through which you pass and find yourself in a high, lofty room with doors leading off at several places. All are tightly shut save one and through this a steady light comes. You advance towards it cautiously, not knowing what lies beyond, until you are able to see within. There you see a great bed hung with purple cloth and on it lies the body of a noble man, kingly in stature with a high, noble brow. His face is waxen and pale and he moves restlessly upon the pillows against which he is propped. At his side sits a woman clad in a gown the colour of apples, her hands are clasped before her and she seems unaware of your presence.

You enter the room and stand by the bed of the sick man. You see that he bears a strong resemblance to the man whose body you saw earlier in the barge. They might almost be brothers indeed, and the woman their sister. At the side of the bed is propped the shaft of a great spear, broken off near the head. You realize clearly what you must do, and without hesitation, despite any natural reluctance you may feel, you pull back the cover from the sick king and putting your hand to the head of the spear which you see sticking from the depths of the wound you pull it forth. Immediately the kingly man's restless movements cease and he seems to sleep deeply and peacefully. The spear-head is not bloody and you take it to where the haft rests against the wall and place the two parts side by side. Immediately they are drawn together and become one, so that you can see no break. At which the kingly man opens his eyes and sits up, and the maiden at his bedside cries aloud with joy. Then through the door comes the knight whom you last saw lying dead in the barge. He is clad in silver armour and the badge at his breast is a swan with open wings. He takes up the spear and joins his brother before a small altar which you now see is in the corner of the room.

The two kingly men place their hands one above each other on the haft of the spear, which suddenly seems to have grown very heavy. You become aware that it is now a part of a great current of power and energy which links earth and sky together. For several moments the two figures stand thus, supporting the great weight of the spear, then the woman who seems to be their sister comes forward bearing in her hands a silver dish or bowl which she places on the altar before them. Now you see drops of blood welling forth from the point of the spear. They fall into the silver bowl which begins to glow brightly — so brightly that you cannot look at it for long and are forced to turn away. You concentrate instead on the device of the silver swan on the back of the knight of the barge and as you do so you begin to relinquish the scene from your inner mind and become slowly aware again of your surroundings. Feel the ground beneath your feet and the chair on which you are sitting and allow yourself to return in your own time to this place and this time.

THE BEACON OF THE LAND

The Tarot is a landscape. We have made much of this idea throughout this book, especially in the Minor Powers, because the dimension of wandering in a place which is not this world is important for the way it enables us to get a fresh view on the place we normally spend our time. If the landscape happens to overlap with the primal places of the Otherworld so much the better. The experience will be that much more powerful, the insights gained that much deeper, the journey that much more exciting. The meditation presented next is designed to give one view of that wondrous inscape to which the *Hallowquest* pack offers so many opportunities of access. If your home is outside Britain you should adapt the setting to suit your own place: the meditation will work just as strongly wherever it is set.

Slowly let the walls of the place where you are dissolve. As they do so you find you are standing outside in deepening twilight. Before you is a path which leads upwards towards some trees. You follow it and find yourself climbing up a steep wooded hillside. As you go you pick up one of the many fallen branches which litter the floor of the wood. Soon you emerge near the top of the hill, where you see the beginnings of a great fire has been laid. You place your own branch on the pile and climb on to the summit.

On all sides save one stand huge sentinel trees. The way to the south is open however, and you look out across the valley below you, seeing the lights of hamlet and town laid out like jewels in the darkening land. The sun has already set, leaving the sky afire with orange and green light, but as you look out across the land you find that your own sight has been enhanced, and that you are able to see great distances. Below is spread the heartland of Britain, league upon league of rolling country in the gathering dusk. Here and there a few pin-points of light shine forth, marking the dwelling places of the people. But this is an ancient land and you are no longer certain what period of time you are in, whether some impossibly distant past or future, where all is different.

The darkness hides such details from you, but as you stand in wondering silence, you hear, distantly at first, but growing stronger, the call of a horn. Again it sounds, and again, and far off in the distance you see a spark of light that grows steadily brighter, until you are able to see with your enhanced sight, a group of riders travelling with the speed of the wind across the distant miles of the land. At their head rides a tall, proud figure who wears a sparkling diadem alight with gems and carries a flaming torch high in one upraised hand. He is a figure of such power and beauty that you are scarcely able to watch him for long, but turn your eyes instead to those who follow him. You see a strange band of people, men and women who ride, hair and clothes streaming in the wind of their going. People of all ages and conditions are there — children and youths and maidens and old grey bearded men and aged women. All have one thing in common — the look of wonder and joy that is written upon their faces and which shines out from their eyes. Each one, like their leader, carries a flaming torch.

As you watch they reach a place where a tall hill rises from the misty land, and they begin to circle around it. So fast do they go that it seems as though a spiral of fire encloses the hill. At length they reach the summit and with a great cry, audible even across the distance which separates you from them, each flings his flaming brand into the centre of a circle marked out on the hilltop, where they form a blazing fire. Higher and higher the flames leap, while around them the riders hurtle and turn. Then the great figure who is their leader reaches down into the heart of the fire and plucks a blazing brand — except that it is no longer the branch from a lopped tree but a sword which flashes in his hand. Thrice he brandishes it above his head, then leads the way off the hill, leaping outright into the air and leading the great throng of riders, who stream out behind him like the tail of a fiery comet. In scarcely a moment they are overhead, and as you look up in wonder, one of the riders lets fall a globe of fire which bursts a little below you on the hillside where you had laid your branch ready for the lighting of the fire. It bursts into flame with a great roar and as you stand in its light and warmth you feel deep contentment, and the knowledge comes to you that all across the land at this moment similar fires are burning, with a flame that will keep alive the energies of the earth and channel them to balance the sundered parts of the Island of the Mighty.

The riders have gone now, passing from sight with a great blast of air and a shout of joy. Slowly, as the fire you saw lit continues to burn steadily, you turn away and begin to descend the hill. A light burns quietly in the distance, beckoning you home. It burns in the room from which you began this journey . . . in which you now find yourself again, safely returned. Open your eyes and look around, re-establishing contact with your room. Remember what you have seen this night, and understanding will follow as time passes.

THE SEEKER'S JOURNEY

The following meditation is written in the form of a pathworking — a form of visualization derived from following the paths on the Qabalistic Tree of Life whereby one goes on a journey, following the symbolism as it appears within a landscape. The most valuable way of doing this meditation, which is quite long, is to record it on tape, leaving a good 10–15 second pause at the points which are asterisked. During these pauses you should be visualizing independently of the script.

Read it like a story, fairly slowly and descriptively. When you listen to it, close your eyes and allow the images to arise. Try to 'be there' as strongly as possible, because you are supposed to be an active participant in this scenario. Alternatively you can read the text and perform the meditation in sections. Breaks are indicated by this sign >.

To end each section, merely visualize the secret door before you and return. To begin again, visualize the secret door and then walk through into the last scene of your former session. Some parts of the visualization have more than one outcome and require that, if you are unable to pass the Greater Power confronting you, you return to an earlier scene. In visualization, such alternative outcomes are both usual and normal, so expect them. Merely return to the scene indicated and proceed forward as before: but do this in a fresh session. This is indicated by this sign <. You have not failed totally but just need to recapitulate the scenes you were unable to assimilate or respond to the first time. It is not recommended that you perform the whole meditation unless you have recorded it on tape, since this interferes with concentration and becomes a mere cerebral exercise.

As the secret door opens before you, step within. You stand in a dry, infertile land. Withered trees, cracked riverbeds, and parched fields are all about you. A well-trodden trackway lies before your feet and you step on to it. Ahead a rainbow path joins the way and standing at the end of it is a young man in ragged clothing. Though he is poor and the prospect about him is bleak, he looks cheerful, even hopeful. He greets you and asks you your name and destination. You tell him that you are on the seeker's journey to discover all that you can about the great powers which animate the world. When you ask him his name he says: 'Call me the Seeker in the Wasteland, for I cannot have a name until I have achieved my quest. But we are on the road together: will you join me on this journey?' You gladly accept and fall into step beside him.

As you walk through a silent valley you ask your companion: 'Why is the land like this?' Before the Seeker can answer, a voice nearby says 'That is a good question!' The speaker is a rugged man with piercing eyes. He stands in the entrance to a cave and before him is a stone table on which is a map. As you approach you see that it is a map of your own country. * Imprinted in the vellum or superimposed upon it, you cannot tell which, you see four objects shimmering. They seem to be far away and diminished.

The Seeker greets the man respectfully: 'Reverend Master, will you tell us the meaning of this mystery and how you are called?'

'Welcome, Seeker in the Wasteland! I know both you and your companion. I am Merlin, the guardian of the Stone Hallow. In the land which you see depicted on this map there is great disorder, and we Hallow guardians await the coming of one who will liberate the spirit of the land and restore it to fertility. The objects which you see here are but likenesses of the Four Hallows by which all countries are held in balance.'

The Seeker says: 'Give us understanding of the Hallow which you guard, for we know nothing of its power.'

Merlin holds both hands before him, the right over the left, and between them you see a mighty stone, emanating powerful wisdom. He says: 'This Stone Hallow is the abode of wisdom; it represents the element of Earth. Without this treasure, the land and its people lack stability. It is my task to mediate its power to all who ask in good faith, and theirs in turn to mediate it to the world about them. Do you truly desire the initiation of the Stone Hallow?'

You answer in your own words. Merlin then holds up the Stone and you allow its power to pass into you. * He then says: 'I have three fellow guardians who keep the other Hallows. Do you wish to see them?' You are both eager to do so.

'If you wish to understand the mystery of the Hallows, you must enter into the life of the land at a deeper level. Are you ready for such adventures?'

The Seeker says: 'It is for this that I came.' You must decide whether you wish to continue your journey or return to your own time and place at this point. If you wish to leave now, then make your answer to Merlin and return via the secret door. > If you wish to continue, make an answer and go where he sends you.

Merlin points at the map. 'I send you first to the Lady of the Lake.' Instantly you are transported into the map itself which grows, extending all round you to form the landscape. You find yourselves on a marshy island. It is night and the wind rustles the stiff reeds. Before you, upon a throne of reeds, is the Lady of this place. She is clothed in blue and she has the air of a wise woman. You instinctively feel that, like Merlin, she is not of mortal race, but of older stock.

The Seeker kneels to her, ‘Blessed Lady, we come for your guidance.’

‘Welcome seekers! I see that you have been sent by Merlin. I am the guardian of the Sword Hallow, which represents the element of Air. It brings strength and truth to its bearer, and those who uphold its power. Without this treasure the land and its people lack justice. Do you truly desire the initiation of the Sword Hallow?’

You answer in your own words. The Lady holds in her right hand a blade whose light is reflected in the waters of the lake and which seems to outshine the moon above. You allow the power of the Sword to pass within you. * >

‘There are two other guardians who keep the Hallows, but their mediation is of a different nature from that of mine or my brother’s. If you would experience the treasures which they guard, look within the waters of the lake.’

As you gaze into the lake you see not your own reflections, but a rich water-meadow with grazing cattle. And you are standing within it. Before you is a woman who sits spinning beside a blossoming tree.

The Seeker greets her: ‘Sovereign Lady, we come for your guidance. Please give us understanding of the Hallow which you guard and tell us how you are called.’

‘Welcome, seekers. I am Guinevere. Did the Lady send you to me? I am the guardian of the Grail Hallow which gives the blessing of fertility; it represents the element of Water. Without this treasure the land is laid waste and its people are without compassion. Do you truly desire the initiation of the Grail Hallow?’

You answer in your own words. Out of her lap, Guinevere draws a cup of great brilliance, brimming with light and power. You allow its power to pass within you. * >

‘There remains but one Hallow guardian for you to meet: my lord Arthur. Watch the thread as it winds on to the spindle.’ And taking up her spindle and distaff once more, she spins a fine thread faster and faster until your vision blurs and you find yourself standing on a mountainous prominence.

Before you is Arthur himself, dressed for battle and with his dragon standard flying behind him.

The Seeker bows, saying, ‘Greetings, Sovereign Lord. We come to seek your guidance and to have understanding of the Hallow which you guard.’

‘Welcome, seekers! I guard the Spear Hallow which both heals and wounds. Without this treasure the land and its people lack vitality. Do you truly desire the initiation of the Spear Hallow?’

You answer in your own words. In Arthur’s hand a great Spear of scintillating brightness shines. You allow its power to pass within you. * >

Arthur speaks, ‘You have experienced the power of each of the Hallows, but the guardians cannot give you understanding. I give you leave to pass through this realm until you fully comprehend the mystery of the Hallows and the Powers who mediate them.'

The Seeker asks, 'Sovereign Lord, where should we begin?'

'My poet, Taliesin, is the wisest man alive. Go to him and he will set you on the road.'

So saying, he holds up his hand on which is a brilliant red stone. As you look within it, you see a firelit hall in which a man in a feathered cloak sits with two children at his feet. They are listening to the story which he is telling. Seeing you, he breaks off and invites you both to be seated.

'All seekers who go on quest should first discover who they really are. You have seen the four Hallows and their guardians, but these will mean nothing to you unless you become aware of the action of the Hallows in your life. Sit, hear and become even as these children: receptive and eager to discover.'

You sit down together and become drawn into the vivid weaving of his narrative. As he tells the story of his transformations, you see before you your own life and the ways you have changed since you were a small child. Take time to consider the constants of your life's direction to date: what has been the source of your strength? * >

Taliesin's story seems to be coming to an end and another story is beginning. In the wreathing smoke of the fire other images come clear. You see a forest clearing before you. The White Hart stands unafraid of the hunter's bow because the hunter is gazing transfixed at a beautiful woman. But although the woman is aware of the kneeling man, her gaze is upon the White Hart.

'Welcome, seekers in the forest!' It is the White Hart who speaks. 'Do not be afraid. Come closer. You will not disturb these lovers for they are under a mighty spell. He loves the woman, but she loves the idea of love itself. He sees only her, she sees what lies beyond physical attraction. They have much to teach each other.

'If you would learn discernment and justice in your relationships hold fast to the chain about my neck and close your eyes.'

As you do so, you become aware of your friends and lovers, and those who are dear to you. Take time to consider how you abuse their trust and how many levels of your relationship are still to be explored. * >

'How deep is your trust in the power of love?' asks the White Hart. 'Are you willing to test it? Hold fast to the chain, and I will take you upon a journey.'

The White Hart leaps into the air and, still holding fast, you find yourself plunging down and down until you land on a cliff top overlooking a twisting and rock-strewn inlet.

'You see the ship Prydwen making its entry into the portals of the Underworld. My lord Arthur is upon it, as is Taliesin, his poet. They seek the cauldron of Annwn for the good of the land.

Theirs is a perilous journey, and though you have another quest to achieve, your search is likewise perilous.'

Gazing down on the plunging ship below, you sincerely wish your own journey to be less hazardous. The White Hart says: 'This is the first gateway which you must face. You must decide quickly which of your abilities will be of most use on this journey. Which of your qualities is your strength?' You take time to consider this. * >

As Prydwen passes out of sight into the Underworld, so you too find yourself fading from the scene. When you open your eyes again you stand in a mountain pass. The sun is beating down and before you, guarding a ford, is a warrior.

'Greetings, mighty warrior!' says the Seeker. 'We are seekers in this place. Will you be our guide and tell us how you are called?'

'It is well for you that you greet me so, for I am Gawain, the king's champion. While he journeys to the Underworld, I hold the land in his place and let no one pass who cannot give account of himself. You must tell me: what is your purpose and by what right do you go upon quest?'

You take time to consider your commitment to the Hallowquest and what you wish to gain. Then answer Gawain in your own words. *

If your answer is satisfactory he will let you pass. If he refuses to let you continue on your journey, then return to the hall where Taliesin sits and begin again from there. <

Gawain lowers his sword and says: 'Pass on into the forest beyond and there you will find the guide you seek.'

Together the Seeker and yourself journey on by foot until you come to a forest clearing where a hermit sits writing in his book. At the sight of you, he holds up a hand and says: 'Here begin the terrors! Here begin the mysteries! Welcome, seekers upon the road!'

Despite his fearsome words, he looks kindly upon you and invites you to sit with him. He asks to hear of your travels and says: 'Is there anything which you have experienced which you did not fully understand? Ask and I shall answer you.'

Take time to review your journey and ask the Hermit to enlighten you: anything upon your life's journey which seems puzzling or incomprehensible you may ask him about. Ask and listen to his answer. * >

The Hermit says, 'I wish you a rewarding quest! I shall send my dove on before you to show you the way. Follow her.' And the dove which has been perched upon the stone in the clearing wings away and you are enabled to follow her in the shape of doves likewise.

You soar through the air, passing from twilight to evening. Below you is a great plain with a stone circle of trilithons in its midst. The dove speaks to you: 'Bravely flown! If you wish to understand this mystery you must hear the merlin.'

A small hawk flies near and, hovering over the plain, says to you both: 'Greetings, shape-shifting seekers! Below you see the first meeting place of your kind. But look before you, and see the second.' You see the Round Table, seemingly floating over the stone circle. 'There are many meeting places for humankind, but these two are round in likeness of the world itself and the cyclicity of the eternal laws. Yet there is a third of which you should be aware.' And you see the heavens above you clear and a ring of stars with a crystal cup at its centre appears.

'There are greater things even than this, but neither birds nor mortals may know them yet. When the three worlds are in alignment, then all shall know the purpose and motion of creation. But before you can continue on your journey, you must judge whether you are fit for the mysteries yet to be unfolded. Think now: in what ways are you unyielding? How do you need to change? Are you able to adapt yourself to the quest?'

You consider these questions and make your own answers. * If they are unacceptable to the merlin, return to your own shape and retrace your steps until you come again to the mountain pass where Gawain guards the ford, and proceed from there. < If your answer is acceptable, you follow the dove, still in birdshape and fly down to where a stream flows swiftly out of a mountain side. You resume your own shape again. >

Beside the stream sits a noble woman in a red dress. The Seeker bows to her and says: 'Mighty Lady, we give you greeting! We are seekers on the quest. Will you guide us and tell us who you are?'

The woman speaks: 'I have been with you already upon your journey in the form of a dove. But now you behold me as I really am. I am Sovereignty: royal rule herself. I am she who guides and inspires. My cup gives empowerment but whoever would drink of it must offer something in exchange. What would you offer?' And she holds up her four-sided cup.

You consider what is the greatest thing you possess. Could you offer this up freely in exchange for a draught from Sovereignty's cup? Take time and make your offer to her. *

If it is unacceptable, the cup breaks into pieces. If this happens, return to the Hermit's forest clearing and proceed until you are successful in reuniting the cup by your true and willing offer. < If the cup remains whole, drink from it.

As you drink, you hear Sovereignty's voice: 'Look upon the Wounded King. He too was once a seeker like you.'

And you find yourself in a sombre clearing which is hung with banners. Upon a bed of golden cloth lies the Wounded King. He lives but his wounds are terrible, the blood falling to the ground where it is lapped by his hound. Sovereignty accompanies you but is silent. The sufferings of the Wounded King are so terrible that you are struck dumb and want to turn away, but the Seeker asks on your behalf: 'What is the meaning of this, Lady Sovereignty? Can his wounds never find healing?'

She answers: 'They can, but only you can find the way.' In your inmost heart, you consider the ways of healing. There seem to be only two possibilities: that the Wounded King should be healed of his sufferings or that he should cease to suffer by dying. But how can you effect his healing? You find two solutions. Either you realize that only by continuing your quest can you help him, because his task is not yet complete. You must finish what he began. Or you can take the Sovereignty's cup and give him a drink from it. Take time to choose which you shall do. *

If you decide to offer the cup to the Wounded King, then do so. He will sit up and you can ask him about the nature of the quest and the real cost of following the path to the end. Listen to what he has to say and then return to the vision of the Round Table and proceed on from there. <

If you decide to continue your quest, make your vow of commitment to the Wounded King, that you will take up the task which he is unable to accomplish and strive to achieve it. He will raise his hand in blessing and point the way through the woods. >

You follow and find that outside the forest night has fallen and that a swiftly-flowing river stands between you and the way ahead. Moreover, kneeling at the river bank is a fearful woman washing bloody linen which stains the waters red. There is no way across the river, for it is deep and treacherous.

The Seeker steps forward and calls across the waters: 'Mother, we seek a way across the river, do you know a way? For we are seekers on quest and the path lies ahead. Can you help us and tell us who you are?'

Distantly the call of dogs howling comes to your ears and fear grips your heart. The woman raises her ghastly face to you and replies: 'All ways are known to me, yet not all travellers seek them. Do you truly wish to cross the river, for this is the second gateway which you must face? You may not know who I am until you cross the river, though I am known as the Washer at the Ford. See, I will make a bridge for you.' And she throws a linen sheet upon the waters which floats towards where you stand. She asks: 'What can you give up to lighten your passage? For only the one who comes freely and without freight can come to the other shore.'

You consider the ideas and notions which you bear about with you on your journey. Is there anything which is unnecessary, which is slowing you down? Decide what you could lose and make your decision to cross the river. *

If the linen bridge does not bear your weight, return to the near bank and then start again from Sovereignty's mountain stream. <

If the linen bridge bears you across the river, the Washer comes forward with open hands to help you to the far bank. As you take her hands you see that she has changed. No longer a frightful hag, she has become Sovereignty in her red dress. >

'You have accepted the task of the Wounded King and passed the river of death, which is the second gateway. You are ready to descend into the Underworld.' And she sets her hand upon you both in blessing and sets you upon the way which leads down into the rock face nearby.

Together you descend, deeper and deeper, until you emerge in an underground cavern. It is hard to see what is happening because the air is heavy with steam which billows up from an enormous cauldron. It is tended by three women: one very young, one mature, and the other very old.

'Here are two who have come to be made new,' says the old one.

'Do you seek the mysteries of the Cauldron?' says the young one.

'These are the seekers who have crossed the river,' says the middle one.

'Sisters, we have come beyond death to seek life,' says the Seeker. 'Who are you and what do you do here?'

'We are the Keepers of the Cauldron, the sisters who are three times three.' They chant. And you suddenly see that each woman has three aspects and appearances. Before you can blink this ninefold sisterhood are dancing about the cauldron, singing faster and faster until the reverberent echoes confuse you. With the Seeker you are seized and thrown into the Cauldron.

You slowly sink down and down. You are totally permeated by the liquid within the Cauldron, but the vessel seems bottomless and you can still breathe. You land suddenly and safely on a great pile of autumn leaves from which eager hands pull you and brush you down.

Servants bring you in out of the Winter wood where you have landed into a warm chamber where you are tended and given fresh clothes. Then they lead you into a feasting hall. At the high table sit Arthur and the men who sailed on Prydwen to fetch the cauldron. You are welcomed and bidden to sit and eat with them, for you, like they, have survived the dreaded journey to Annwn.

You have been feasting but a short time when the hall door bursts open and in strides a great figure, attired in leaves. He is massive, like a living tree. He speaks: 'Lord Arthur, I give you and your men greeting! But who are these and by what right do they feast with you?'

Arthur replies, 'They are seekers who are on the Hallowquest. They are empowered and initiated by myself and my fellow Hallow guardians. Who are you to challenge them?'

'I am the Green Knight, the Lord of the Wood, the Challenger at the Crossroads. You know me as the Lord of the Underworld, Lord Arthur, for was it not my cauldron that you came to seek?'

'It was indeed, Green Knight,' says Arthur. 'And out of courtesy I will allow you to question these seekers.'

The Green Knight fixes you with a piercing stare. 'I have a game, if you are brave enough to play it. Tell me are you willing to risk everything you have gained upon this journey?'

You look to Arthur for an answer: 'You must make the answer for yourself. If you truly trust your own experience, then we also place our trust in you . . . Tell us the rules of your game, Green Knight!'

'That they first behead me and in return I will behead them,' says the Green Knight. 'Here is the axe!'

'That seems fair,' says Arthur. 'Are you willing to play?'

If you are unwilling to play this game, you must return to your own time and place now and start your quest from the very beginning. <

If you wish to play, then pick up the axe. The Green Knight will kneel for your stroke. Behead him. He rises up, picks up his head and says: 'Well struck! Now you must kneel for me.'

If you are unwilling to suffer the axe, you must return to your own time and place, and start your quest from the very beginning. < As you kneel for the stroke, you seem to see the Green Knight in another guise altogether, but you are unable to see what, as at that moment the axe falls. >

You are quite whole but you are standing on a hillside alone. The Seeker is no longer by your side. It is night and before you is a spiral hill with a tower upon it. As you look, lightning strikes the tower and masonry begins to fall. But even as the physical tower crashes down, you see stretching upwards, in its place, a Spiral Tower of crystal light. Around you the heavens turn, beneath you the earth turns. You hear the voice of the Green Knight: 'A good game, my friend! Enter this tower and be my guest.'

You pass within the Spiral Tower and ascend its winding stairway until you reach the top. There you find the Green Knight, changed beyond all recognition. He is dressed in clothes of green and he appears to be a man from the realm of faery. He says: 'Here I am called the Lord of the Wheel, to complement my Lady of the Wheel.' And he gestures to where a woman, also in green, sits before a great mirror. If she is familiar to you, it is no surprise, for it is the Lady of the Lake whom you see before you in another aspect.

'You are welcome to the Spiral Tower which some call the Glass Caer. Here you stand at the beginning and end of the ages of the world. Here time is not. You have had the initiation of the Hallows and pursued the path of the quest. Have you any questions now?' >

You ask about the Seeker and what has become of him. For answer, the Lady of the Wheel bids you look into the mirror. The mirror is a vast crystal dish framed by representations of the Zodiacal signs. As you look into the glass, the signs revolve and you are drawn into the mirror.

You see a fortress and two men on watch — or rather one is on watch and the other is asleep. The Lady says: 'In every age there is the expectation of a seeker who will accomplish the quest for the Hallows.' You see the great comet which announces the coming of the one — a man or a woman — who will empower the land by wielding the Hallows, and so align all three worlds for a short space. You see the dragon star falling through the night sky and hear the excited shouts of the watchman. Two streams of brightness shoot from the dragon's mouth: 'The son and daughter of the prophecy,' she explains. 'But the times are dangerous for such a one, and the expected one is born in obscurity and brought up secretly.'

The image changes and you see the full-bellied moon shining over a dark landscape. In the moon is the promise of the child to come, while in the waters below a salmon fights to return to the source of its birth. The Lady continues: 'When the time is right the expected child grows up and goes forth as a seeker, taking no name, until he or she has earned one.'

The scene changes. Night becomes day and you see a naked youth mounted upon a white mare, innocent and unafraid. In the features of the youth you recognize the same innocence of your erstwhile friend. 'But the deeds of the seeker are his or her name, and the challenges of the quest cause the seeker to take a perilous journey, into the inner realms and beyond death. And for that time, the seeker is the Sovereign of the land and its people. And at the end of the quest, the sleepers awake, the land is healed and the deep wisdom of the Hallows is once more wielded in the land.'

You see the youth, standing upon the outstretched flank of the Sleeping Lord who is the land itself. And in that giant hillshape you recognize both the Wounded King and Arthur himself. The sound of a horn shatters the stillness of the mirror image. And you see at last the identity of the seeker in the mirror before you. The king, the land, the seeker — all images dissolve and only your reflection alone remains.

You are no longer in the Spiral Tower, but in the mouth of the cave where Merlin's stone table shows the map of your country. He stands before you, his glance wise and thoughtful.

'And have you found what you sought, Seeker in the Wasteland?' he asks.

Answer him in your own words. He says: 'Your quest is over for this time. But remember, there are other quests and other journeys yet to be taken. Go with the blessing of the Hallows!'

And before you are Merlin, the Lady of the Lake, Guinevere and Arthur, each holding the Hallow of their guardianship.

You turn to go on your way back to the secret door, but as you do you see on the plains below you the figure of the Seeker dancing with the two children whom you met in the hall with Taliesin. The land about them is no longer barren, but blooming with the freshness of Spring.

This is your land. Make your blessing now upon it and then return to your own time and place.

There is a blessing on all who serve.

GOING BEYOND THE BEGINNING

Meditation is a progressively organic process. Most people do not meditate daily or even weekly: they do so when they have need, and then usually in intensive blocks of work. Perhaps this will be so with your *Hallowquest* work. But it is preferable to keep up a regular and steady daily practice if you can. What you obtain from meditation will be unique to you. If you compare notes with a friend or partner who has meditated from the book independently, you will both find divergences and similarities. There is nothing odd in this, since there is no 'right way' to meditate, no standard set of results. Not having any form of yardstick to refer to makes meditation and ritual work very difficult for some people, who may feel that they are deluding themselves. But if you always preface your meditation or ritual with a firm statement of ethical intent or an invocation for divine guidance, then you will be proceeding along the right lines, excepting rare cases of paranoia or severe mental illness.

It may be that you will never refer back to this meditative work at all, but if you ever want to do so, you will need a record of your realizations. There is no virtue in keeping a record for the sake of it, but in your initial meditations you will probably touch deep levels, moments of balanced alignment with the inner worlds, which will be precious to you or which you may wish to explore further in years to come. What we experience at the archetypal levels is not always understandable at the time, and it often takes more maturity and experience for these realizations to come to fruition and manifestation in our lives. Like seeds, they may lie dormant for years.

After each meditation session, therefore, keep a legible and full account of your experiences. You may also wish to write down features of the cards as these occur to you. Do not hesitate to write in this book, adding your own realizations to the descriptions given in Chapter 3 and elsewhere.

People who work alone can often get very hung up on their realizations, believing them to be the greatest thing since the Bible, since they have been personally dictated by their inner teacher, by Merlin or the Lady of the Lake. Working with others does give one a sense of proportion in this work. Other people also have valid realizations and it often helps to share your findings with other students of a meditation system, since these bring to light aspects and methods of working you have not thought of yourself.

Meditation can be a lonely business and you may wish to work with other people, using the *Hallowquest* Tarot as a group training system. Chapter 11 gives ways on how you can work with the Tarot in a more ritual way. If ritual does not appeal to you, then try using the cards as a method of story-telling (Chapter 12). In the Afterword, you will find an address to write to if you want to know more about courses or tapes relating to the *Hallowquest* Tarot.

Above all, devise your own journeys, find other ways of exploring your ever-unfolding inner world. Meditation is by far the best way of familiarizing yourself with the deeper levels of the cards, but once you have acquired the rudiments of meditation skills, you will be ready to take other journeys. With practice and application you will be laying the basis for deep divinatory work which will take you beyond the trite levels of fortune-telling, into the true quest.

CHAPTER 9

the diviner's art

ESOTERIC PRINCIPLES OF DIVINATION BY TAROT

The Tarot user will be most familiar with the use of Tarot solely for divinatory purposes. While the Arthurian Tarot *can* be used in this way, this is not its prime function. Divination can, in the hands of a skilful operator, become a useful tool, if used sparingly. Unfortunately, divination or fortune-telling, as most non-Tarot users call it, is a very much debased art surrounded by superstition and misunderstanding of esoteric principles.

The Arthurian Tarot, like most other packs, is a symbolic means of contacting the archetypal worlds where deep understanding of the inner and outer worlds can be gained. Anyone working with a traditional symbology soon begins to perceive certain correspondences and meaningful patterns which intermesh with their personal, group or inner life. It is within the potential of anyone to discover these patterns with the help of a craft such as Tarot divination, so that one becomes a life-spinner, a pathfinder, a pattern-maker.

No mystical system or divinatory tool can ever replace personally observed patterns, since these alone are the inner messengers which convey to us the guidance and sustenance which we each need. However, sometimes a divinatory tool can help us *trigger recognition* of these patterns. It is only the innately lazy who rely upon the Tarot as a daily crutch or decision-making process. Hence the warning in many Tarot books about over-use of the Tarot for divination.

The primary use of Tarot in divination is that of a symbolic messenger which helps us read the underlying patterns of our life, conveying potent images from the deep inner world of archetypal reality to the everyday world in which we function. The Tarot user's task is to become skilful in this art of interpretation, both personally and for the benefit of others who are unskilled in perceiving their personal life patterns.

FATE, DESTINY AND THE WILL OF GOD

Quite how the Tarot works as a divinatory system is a matter of extreme interest to sceptics who are quick to quote statistics and numerical permutations about the fall of cards in certain positions. It is not the purpose of this book to offer authentication, whether scientific or otherwise, for the Tarot as a primary divinatory method.

The Tarot seems to offer a number of possibilities and permutations which, when configured in a certain way, give insights into an overall pattern which had not been previously clear to us. The act of consulting the cards at all does, of course, distance us from our problem or question and enable us to see it from another angle. This usually comes about as the result of consulting a Tarot counsellor, but how does this vary from consulting, say, a psychotherapist?

It is by asking a question that we start to assemble the components of our problem. 'What is wrong?' 'Why is this happening?' 'What should I do next?' are questions which will enable us to move on to the next step in our life, if we answer them seriously. Other questions may arise as a result of their answers and deeper areas which we never saw may emerge. This process seems very little different from psychotherapy, but the fact that we consult an oracle — in this instance the Tarot cards — puts the whole process on a different level. When we consult a psychotherapist, however well trained, he or she remains a human being. When we consult the Tarot we are asking questions of a symbolic system which uses the esoteric language of the Otherworld. In common parlance, we have consigned our question 'into the lap of the gods'. The Tarot consultant merely acts as a priestly interpreter of the symbolism, one who is skilled in the imagery and mythos and whose duty is to give us the message.

But what exactly happens when we consult the cards? If the Tarot counsellor is a good one, does he or she give us the message of the gods? Is the message unavoidable, or fated? Do we have any effect on the predicted outcome? These questions lie at the back of our minds because, at root, we are uncertain of our ground. Our cultural conditioning and education vie with the remnants of various spiritual traditions concerning fate. One of the major esoteric differences between the mystical traditions of East and West is the concept of fate. In the East there is a distinct cosmic order in which humanity has its place, especially within Hinduism. The so-called passivity or fatalism of the East seems to derive from this sense of humanity's place in the cosmic order of things. In the Classical world, we still perceive a concept in which individuals are convinced of their destiny — a god-given vocation to fulfil — while at the same time being aware of the cosmic order whose boundaries they transgress. In Buddhism we see an evolving interest in the karmic duty of an individual who, while he or she has been born in certain conditions, may yet achieve a totally different destiny by mystical alignment.

The sense of fatalism — being bound by the gods to a predestined life-pattern — and a sense of destiny — being able to change one's fate through alignment of opportunities — have been at loggerheads within our own historical era. On the one hand we find the propitiation of luck — once a Roman goddess — on the other a serene acceptance of the will of God. Certainly, we are in a great muddle about our life direction. The lack of sound esoteric principles underlies this confusion: the West has a record of ignoring its mystical traditions — whether these have been Christian, pagan or magical — and so has failed to assimilate a sense of fate in its truest sense. As a result the West seems to generally consist of two kinds of people: those who lie down under the weight of circumstance and are beaten by life, and those who struggle against circumstances to achieve their desires. Neither has any esoteric sense. A third kind of person is also emerging, although is by no means common, as a result of emerging esoteric influence: the one who is able to bend when the wind blows but who is able to make opportunities work for them too. Nearly every New Age and esoteric book proclaims ways in which to live more effectively: this sells books more than anything else, for people desperately need to know how to live their lives. If there is a way in which they can consciously change their life circumstances, they will do it, if they are determined enough. Hence we find supposedly esoteric books advising us about prosperity consciousness, or how to magically influence people — such writings are dishonest since they blatantly draw upon the manipulation of personality and psychology. They do not attempt to address the archetypal levels of the spirit, but are about the use of power over individuals and events from a totally non-esoteric standpoint.

It is only when we can perceive the person we really are that we can effect change. This means first of all a basis for self-knowledge. See p.229 for a spread which will enable you to know yourself better. You may also want to do the 'Clearing the Way' ritual on p.218 before undertaking a series of consultancy sessions.

PRINCIPLES OF ESOTERIC COUNSELLING

At some point someone is going to ask you to do a reading for them: it is then that you will be in the position of an esoteric counsellor. This is a responsible role and one you should seriously consider before you set up in business as a Tarot reader of this or any other pack. Such a statement may seem baffling to anyone who has been reading the Tarot for years, or merely over-cautious to someone thinking of using divination as a counselling method, but we live in times when traditional mystical systems have no 'official' guardians.

If we look at the history of divination, it will become clear that while ordinary people have occasionally used divination for themselves, it has always been a skill administered by the priests or priestesses of a particular deity. The Roman state officially employed augurs to divine auspicious occasions from such things as the flight of birds or the entrails of a ram. Navaho elders still interpret and diagnose problems by consulting the sand paintings in southern America. But Western society has no sustained mystical tradition in which properly trained counsellors still practise.

In the revival of the Western esoteric tradition, each person has to find what training he or she can, augmented by personal experience and interaction with disparate traditions. This has brought about a great many so-called and self-proclaimed counsellors who claim to give healing therapy, possess magical powers or interpret the messages of the gods through various divinatory systems. It is in the best interests of all concerned that you seriously consider your own ability and resources as a potential counsellor, as well as establishing that you really do work from a sound ethical basis.

The average person who comes to you for a reading will want to know some crucial information concerning their future life or their next step along that road. They will not be interested in your ethics so much as in how much you charge. They will probably imagine that you possess secret powers, that you are psychic and can predict the future in intimate detail. These and many other common misconceptions will confront you as you start divining from the *Hallowquest* pack. You, as reader and counsellor, will be in a position of trust. You will also be a representative of the divinatory system and the mystical tradition which lies behind it.

Implicit here is a double respect: one to the tradition in which you are working, and one to the querent who will be put in touch with that tradition, for however short a time. Obviously, the longer you have spent in preparing yourself for this task, the better you will be as a counsellor. If you have meditated on each pack of the cards, steeped yourself in the mythos surrounding the *Hallowquest* pack and thoroughly assimilated the diverse meanings of each card, then you already stand in the place of guardian of the British mysteries, for you have worked first hand with the mythic archetypes underlying that mystery system. The querent who comes to you for help will feel correspondingly more confident in consulting you, for you will 'know your stuff', and be able to relate the archetypal messages of the *Hallowquest* pack to the everyday problems upon which you will be called to give advice.

Being a counsellor does not make you God. If someone has come to ask the cards a question through your interpretive skills, then you can only respond to the best of your abilities. You do not have to be highly psychic to read for someone, although the reading process generally draws upon most people's latent psychism. At no point should you imply or let it be understood that you are possessed of magical, occult or special powers; this is untrue. The only thing you can perhaps claim is a true affinity with inner world energies, or that you have the ability to align yourself with them — and that is probably overstepping the boundaries of humility by a long chalk, for such moments happen rarely in the lives of human beings!

Perhaps most basic of all principles of esoteric counselling is the need for the counsellor to seek counselling! You will probably consult the *Hallowquest* in your own needs and crises, but you may find that you yourself need another person to help you. Recognize this need and seek an experienced Tarot consultant, if that is the kind of help you want. Being at a point of crisis in your life will make you better appreciate why people come to consult you and how muddled they feel about their lives and how unable they are to initiate the next step without focused guidance.

You, as Tarot counsellor, must act as a transparent window through which the querent may gaze at the configuration of events and their possible outcome. You are an objective interpreter of the cards, able to elicit the needs and desires of each querent sympathetically and confront them with the blocks which they themselves have set up in the way of those needs and desires. You remain professionally uninvolved in the sense that you personally do not give advice nor take responsibility for someone else's decisions. However, it is important that you give a psychic space for the querent to come to grips with the situation at issue by first creating an atmosphere of trust and relaxed objectivity.

As a Tarot counsellor you will be asked multiplicitous questions about different aspects of 'the occult'. Fear, credulity and ignorance seem to be distributed in equal proportions, as you will find. The fact that you read the cards immediately aligns you with other mystical or nefarious practices in people's minds. It will be your responsibility to give esoteric counselling a good name by your professional scrupulosity and adherence to esoteric ethics. If, by the way, you are able to dispel some of the misconceptions relating to aspects of mystical or esoteric living, then so much the better, but never pretend that you know more about something than you actually do. Be clear, concise and practical in your remarks. If someone wants advice on whether to join an esoteric group about which they feel uncertain for example, ask two simple questions: 'Would you leave your child overnight with these people?' or 'Would you invest money in a joint account with this person?' These common-sense questions generally evoke common-sense responses at a gut level.

On the question of taking money for your Tarot consultations, we would ask, 'Are you offering a professional service, based on sound esoteric ethics?' If your answer is a whole-hearted yes, then by all means charge a reasonable consultation fee. If you are still learning your craft, it may be better to offer free readings to friends and acquaintances, in order to gain experience. You will have no shortage of clients if the readings are free. You may hold deep esoteric precepts about not charging for mystical services, whether these be divination, therapy or ritual, treating the whole act on the level of prayer freely offered and spiritually effected. Such people generally do not offer divination casually, quite rightly if they hold these views, but as a special act of alignment between the querent and the gods. There are currently few people who make a living from esoteric practices, but the day will soon dawn when esoteric counselling will be considered a professional calling. When that happens and ethical standards are established by an officially authorized body, it will be interesting to see exactly where Tarot consultants will stand.

CLEARING THE WAY RITUAL

This mini ritual is something which you can perform at any time before you undertake a reading for a client, preferably before they arrive. One of the glaring problems of the New Age and its many alternative therapies and disciplines is the way in which the interpreters and healers seem always to be in such turmoil themselves. Who heals the healers? is a question which has been reasonably asked.

Of course, we cannot expect to live smooth, trouble-free lives. but, on the other hand, we must be sensitive to the troubles of other people if we are going to do Tarot counselling. This ritual clears the way between you and your concerns, putting you in readiness for your client and theirs.

Take a smooth stone — a pebble from a beach would do — and hold it in both hands. Close your eyes. Allow your mind to focus only on the stone and its smoothness. Do not permit any other thoughts to arise. Allow your breathing to reach a steady, even rhythm. When you feel sufficiently centred and calm, visualize the Greater Power card of the Wounded King.

Enter the card and go to his side. He opens his eyes and speaks to you; listen to his words, acknowledging his insights, wrought of suffering and experience. His wisdom is for your ears only. Thank him for his advice. He then lays his hand upon the nape of your neck in blessing, commissioning you to return to the world with healing wisdom.

Lay down your stone and open your eyes. Take up the *Hallowquest* pack and dedicate both yourself and your Tarot to the service of others. Do this in words of your own choosing, making this ritual your own personal affirmation of intent.

HALLOWQUEST QUALITIES

Each card in the *Hallowquest* pack has its own quality which can be borne in mind as you interpret a spread. These qualities may enhance the face meaning which, taken cumulatively, may give a clear overall message to the spread. They can be summarized as follows:

The Greater Powers

These cards represent archetypal or universal energies. When a number of these appear in a spread it indicates that the querent's life is currently governed by inner world direction. It may be that the querent is perfectly aligned with his or her destiny or that the energies ruling this alignment are so strong that they are being brought into play through the querent's life circumstances.

The Lesser Powers

Hallows signify initiating energies. The querent will experience the elemental quality of the Hallowcards which appear in a reading at a deep level; this will manifest perhaps in an unformulated way as a desire to create or bring about an idea in a concrete manner i.e. a painting, a book, a garden or a crêche. A Hallow will often focus a reading quicker than any other card since it frequently gives a key to the querent whose creativity is blocked. The Hallows signify deeply desired change.

The numerical values of the other Minor Arcana cards may also be significant in a spread, especially where two or more cards of the same numerical value appear, i.e. two or more Nines may signify that the querent is currently on the final stages of integrating plans or preparing for the final manifestation of an idea. The reading may indicate how he or she may most effectively bring this about. Individual numbers have the following qualities; as well as indicating the particular path which the querent is travelling.

Twos signify finding direction. The impulse for change which was experienced in the Hallows now makes its first move, sometimes tentatively, sometimes finding reciprocal response as it moves. The impulse to find wisdom.

Threes signify formalization. The idea has received its first impetus at Two but now requires a form or concept to give it shape. The understanding of personal experience derived from the outset of a project.

Fours signify the first attempts to manifest one's idea. Like all try-outs, something positive is always gained in terms of experience, whether the attempt is wholly successful or not. One is administering one's concept and taking responsibility for it for the first time.

Fives signify modification and adjustment. After the first trials of Four, the idea meets problems which have to be solved if the concept is to work effectively. This may seem like a setback, but the necessary adjustment will only come about as a result of facing the obstacles against it.

Sixes signify harmony. After the modification of Five, the idea has found its feet and is a true creation, capable of functioning in all respects. A sense of satisfaction is present.

Sevens signify specialization and extension. It is time to take the idea a step further and experiment with a variety of applications. This sometimes results in an over-extension of energy, but imagination and potential are stretched and the idea will be fully explored for the first time.

Eights signify organization. After the expansive expression of the Sevens, it is time to pull in one's horns and re-assess the situation. This necessary retrenchment is valuable to re-establish one's priorities.

Nines signify integration. With the experience of Seven and Eight behind the idea, it can now be fully integrated. It is at this point that it becomes obvious whether this is the path for you — having seen the idea through all its stages, it must now become part of your life or pass on.

Tens signify culmination. The idea now becomes part of the larger world affecting friends, family and neighbours. The creative impulse of the Hallows is now firmly established on earth as manifest idea-in-action. The world inherits your brainchild which is no longer your responsibility.

Court Cards

Can signify people relating to the querent, aspects of the querent him- or herself, or archetypal messengers of the Hallow court they represent. Their qualities are as follows:

Maidens signify sensation, the way in which you physically perceive things. They are messengers whose advice offers ways out of blocked situations, though this sometimes means taking risks. They open new paths on the Hallowquest.

Knights signify the way in which you intuitively perceive things. They are prime movers who actively demonstrate the strengths and weaknesses of their Hallow. They are companions upon the Hallowquest whose help you may call upon.

Queens signify the way in which you feel about things. They are the bearers who channel the energies of their Hallow. They represent stability and dedication to the quest.

Kings signify the way in which you think about things. They are the guardians of their Hallow, giving experience of its wisdom to all who seek it. They represent insight and authority on the Hallowquest.

The Court cards depict the Maidens and Queens as female and the Knights and Kings as male, but these face values do not necessarily denote gender, rather the quality which they bear, i.e. a mystical and idealistic woman who is teaching esoteric wisdom to others might be represented by the Grail Knight, while a practical young man who has just opened a garden centre might be represented by the Stone Queen.

SIGNIFICATORS

It has been traditional to draw a card from the pack to indicate the querent at the commencement of a reading. This is normally one of the Court cards; however, there is nothing against drawing one of the Greater Powers instead. If your querent is very self-contained or unwilling to choose a card for him- or herself, then choose one according to your most effective criteria: appearance, emotional feedback from the querent, the nature of problem to be focused upon. If, however, the querent is enthusiastic about the reading process, let him or her shift through the pack until a card is found which seems right.

The *Hallowquest* pack depicts only British racial types because its mythological impetus is from the Arthurian legends. If you or your querent are of another race, do not hesitate to draw whatever card seems most appropriate to you, using the *Hallowquest* qualities or the meanings of any card as a guideline for your decision.

TIMING AND INTERPRETATION

Many querents require exact timing from their readings, e.g. 'When will I get married?' 'How long will it be till I get another job?' The Tarot does not seem to be a very accurate device for telling time, but following the example of Gail Fairfield's method[7] it is possible to use the *Hallowquest* pack for this kind of detail.

Swords	Spring
Spears	Summer
Grails	Autumn
Stones	Winter

For more precise interpretation, the Greater Powers from Hallow to Queen may be signified in the following way:

Sword

Hallow	21–27 Mar
Two	28 Mar–3 Apr
Three	4–10 Apr
Four	11–17 Apr
Five	18–24 Apr
Six	25 Apr–1 May
Seven	2–8 May
Eight	9–15 May
Nine	16–22 May
Ten	23–29 May
Maiden	30 May–5 Jun
Knight	6–12 Jun
Queen	13–19 Jun

Spear

Hallow	20–26 Jun
Two	27 Jun–3 Jul
Three	4–10 Jul
Four	11–17 Jul
Five	18–24 Jul
Six	25–31 Jul
Seven	1–7 Aug
Eight	8–14 Aug
Nine	15–21 Aug
Ten	22–28 Aug
Maiden	29 Aug–4 Sep
Knight	5–11 Sep
Queen	12–18 Sep

Grail

Hallow	19–25 Sep
Two	26 Sep–2 Oct
Three	3–9 Oct
Four	10–16 Oct
Five	17–23 Oct
Six	24–30 Oct
Seven	31 Oct–6 Nov
Eight	7–13 Nov
Nine	14–20 Nov
Ten	21–27 Nov
Maiden	28 Nov–4 Dec
Knight	5–11 Dec
Queen	12–18 Dec

Stone

Hallow	19–25 Dec
Two	26 Dec–2 Jan
Three	3–9 Jan
Four	10–16 Jan
Five	17–23 Jan
Six	24–30 Jan
Seven	31 Jan–6 Feb
Eight	7–13 Feb
Nine	14–20 Feb
Ten	21–27 Feb
Maiden	28 Feb–6 Mar
Knight	7–13 Mar
Queen	14–20 Mar

Using this method it will be seen that each of the Hallow cards fall within the weeks of the Spring and Autumn Equinoxes and the Summer and Winter Solstices. Leap Year Day, 29 February, always falls within the card of the Stone Maiden. The Kings, if they are drawn using this method, signify the season rather than an exact week. If one of the Greater Powers is drawn, then this signifies that a crucial factor has yet to be determined: either the querent has not resolved the matter to allow the free flow of the problem in hand or else an outside factor is at work. Study the cards drawn carefully for their surface value and meaning.

THE READING PROCESS

You have decided to set up in business as a Tarot consultant or counsellor. How do you proceed? Word of mouth is your best advertisement, but you can always advertise locally in order to get your consultancy on the road. Where are your clients going to consult you? If you cannot spare a special consultancy room, then ensure that you have a clearly designated corner of another room especially set aside, uncluttered by your family's belongings. Make it welcoming and comfortable, whether you have cushions on the floor or a good sized table with two chairs. Decide whether your querent is going to sit beside you, so as to be able to see the cards, or facing you.

Your first client arrives, perhaps uncertain or anxious, sceptical or expecting to hear only the worst, distressed or waiting for confirmation of what he or she already knows. Break the ice with tea or coffee and get to know your client a little better. Find out what his expectations are exactly, so that you will know how to pitch your reading. Outline the service you can offer, stressing truthfully that it will be up to the querent to implement what the reading tells him. For the worried or stressed client, ensure that he is aware that the reading is confidential. Allow all querents to feel that they are safe in your consultancy room and that they can consider it a free space in which they are temporarily free from the anxieties which beset them. This is very important, for it frees the querent's mind, enabling it to be receptive to the message of the reading.

Now many clients approach a Tarot reading with the attitude of seeing 'how good you are', meaning that they have come in the spirit of an audience attending a spiritualist meeting or a mind-reading performance. If you are psychic, they will get the message anyway, but if you are not, say so. The most important thing for the Tarot counsellor is to know the nature of the problem or issue in question, how the querent feels about it and what they need to know about it. Feedback is essential for the non-psychic, for it helps relate the message to the querent's immediately perceived needs.

It may be that the querent does not really know what question should be asked and here a short general reading 'How things stand at present' may suffice to elicit the querent's response, so that you can both focus on a particular problem. Most people are not constructively introspective or aware of the fears which beset them at a deep level. One short reading will uncover the topsoil sufficiently for the counsellor to delve deeper.

Don't be afraid to write down the querent's question/s; get the querent to do this if he seems to have difficulty focusing his needs. There may be specific questions arising from a central issue, concerning time, involvement, commitment or obstacles. Devise your own spreads to accommodate these questions. In Chapter 10 there are a number of suggested spreads and guidelines for devising your own with the querent's help.

When the question is established, get the querent to shuffle the cards while mentally repeating the question. The cards are the oracle, you are only their interpreter. The shuffling should last as long as seems right for the querent who should then place the cards face down on the table and cut them, if this is your practice. Now lay them out in your chosen spread. During the shuffling and spreading try to discourage the querent from talking, which many will do nervously, thus distracting themselves from the divinatory process.

Now scan the cards, noting how many kinds of Greater or Lesser Powers and their numerical values. Take into account the surface meanings as well as the hidden qualities possessed by each card. Next notice relationships between cards which seem to reinforce the overall message of the reading. Next relate the individual cards to their positions.

Analysis and interpretation is a very personal thing, and you may find that your style of presentation varies considerably between different querents. You will probably want to examine the cards silently before making any comments. If you find it hard to break into the reading then tell the message like a story, making a string or chain of events which grow out of each other. At other times the words will just rise in you, and the overall message will be an obvious one. When the message is unclear to you as the interpreter, it may mean that the querent has not sufficiently focused on the issue at hand. At other times, a reading will seem inconclusive and raise other issues which you may wish to explore using a different sort of spread.

The most important thing is to be flexible. If a card which you have previously filed in your brain as being broadly beneficial in effect appears in a negative position then read it as such, e.g. the Empress appearing in the 'What is hindering you' position would indicate that the querent is spending too much time looking after other people to the detriment of his or her own well-being, or that the querent has allowed him- or herself to get domestically cosy at a time when he or she needs to be more adventurous.

Don't be afraid to state what the cards relate to you, but be sensitive about the way you phrase this to the querent. If you read an accident as a result of careless driving as a possible outcome, then reinforce the message of the cards by advising the querent to improve concentration when driving, or to refrain from driving if tired. Similarly, if an operation or illness seems lurking on the horizon of possibilities, look deeper into the reading to discover the causes of this and whether the querent can improve his or her own health by the avoidance of stress.

Divination is not about doom and gloom, although most of the historical examples we possess, e.g. Julius Caesar's Ides of March warning, the witches' prophecy that Macbeth would never be killed by 'one of woman born' etc. seem to be of this variety. It is true that humanity usually remembers the bad rather than the good news. 'Sufficient unto the day is the evil thereof.' It is not the Tarot consultant's task to add to the burden of life's cares, but to help the querent steer between the reefs and find the most effective way of living by means of the Tarot.

Tarot counselling can be a very rewarding process. You as the reader will be putting clients in touch with the influences of the Otherworld perhaps for the first time. You will be responsible for helping other people to help themselves by pointing out the message of the cards. The querent will draw clues and important keys from your interpretative skills which will empower him or her to focus major life directions. This reciprocal reading process thereby passes beyond the superstitions of fortune-telling into the deeper realms of real divination, where the cards speak directly to the querent bringing their message of guidance and hope.

CHAPTER 10

paths through the forest

THE GRAIL QUESTION

There are as many ways to spread the *Hallowquest* pack as there are readers of this book. Each of us can devise our own methods and ways of divining with the Tarot, and there is no necessity to stick to the same spreads over and over, unless you are learning your craft.

Making your own spreads is like finding your own paths through the forest: an adventure in discovery. The time-honoured spreads, like the Celtic Cross and the Zodiac spreads have not been given in this chapter, since there are many books which repeat these time and again. The spreads which follow are suggested uses only: your own spreads are as good as these, if not better, since they will be tailored to suit your needs and those of your querent. Gail Fairfield's book *Choice Centred Tarot* gives many suggestions on how to formulate your own spreads.[7]

The only traditional spread given here is the Tree of Life spread, p.233. Before deciding to read for a querent, the most important thing is to gauge the kind of spread you will need: this will depend very much on the nature of the question to be asked. (See Chapter 9.)

You may wish to start the reading with a three-card spread to give the general drift of the consultancy session or to help clarify an unfocused question. You may start with one reading and go on to use another to further define the querent's problem. Tarot consultants are not made of cast iron, however, and two readings a client per session is probably quite enough. Occasionally clients can be very pressing. If they wish to know more, get them to book another appointment.

To help you decide which of the following spreads would be most useful for your purposes, here is a breakdown of their uses:

General clarifying spreads:	*Prydwen's Anchor*
	Tree of Life
Identifying who you are, the real self:	*Merlin's Mirror*
Escape from self-limitations:	*Mabon's Gate*
Finding your elemental balance:	*Sovereignty's Spread*
Uncovering past karmic responsibility:	*The Excalibur Spread*
Revealing unconscious potential:	*The Three Worlds*

You will undoubtedly discover that these readings will not always fit your needs and you can adapt and reshape them as necessary. Perhaps the most important thing in divination is 'the right question'. Like the Grail question which, when asked, can resolve all problems, the querent's question must be correctly phrased for the diviner's art to have any effect.

Questions like 'Will I marry Jim or Bert?' will just not do, because they are not sufficiently defined. Questions like 'Will I get a new job?' may be inadequate because other questions have not been posed first, such as, 'What has caused me to be without work?' Much of divination is concerned with self-knowledge and this can only be elicited by questioning. This is hard enough for oneself; eliciting such answers from querents can be uphill work, especially if they have resigned responsibility for themselves into the hands of providence, the state or your Tarot cards!

Your divinatory skills should foster self-responsibility in your querents as well as a healthy degree of incredulity and hard questioning. Our mother-wit or common sense is sadly neglected, no more so than in esoteric areas of life where credulity and resignation of personal responsibility are frequently paramount. The Tarot consultant needs to bear in mind the fact that many people are spiritually impoverished to the point of starvation and that they will seize on any prop to support their life-style, including the Tarot. Therefore, it should be with compassionate insight that the consultant should choose the most appropriate method of questioning the querent.

It is so that the most appropriate spread should be sought, for the ground of divination by Tarot is the questioning spread. The spread demarks part of the querent's spiritual journey, his or her personal quest for meaning and truth. So do not be afraid to abandon your favourite spread if your querent's needs are specific, even if it means you must invent one for that one session.

It is by means of the Grail question that the Wasteland is healed, but until it is asked, nothing can be restored to its full potential.

PRYDWEN'S ANCHOR SPREAD

Many Tarot consultants find that they need a good, general spread to answer general questions like 'What is happening now?' Such a spread should present the prevailing circumstances and surrounding factors in such a way that the querent can clearly see how their present life is configured. Prydwen's Anchor is such a spread and like the anchor on that enduring ship of Arthur's, it shows the factors which give the querent a hold on everyday life.

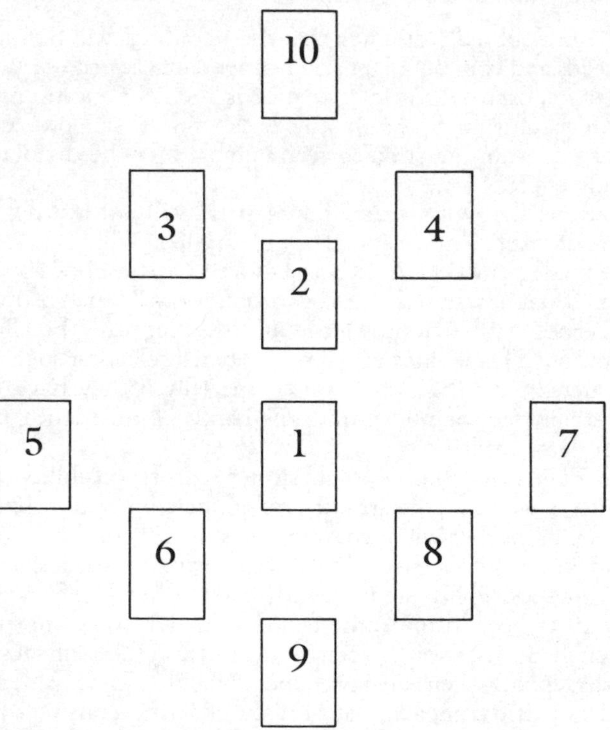

Fig. 10.1: Prydwen's Anchor

Meanings of Positions

1. General circumstances prevailing. What is happening now?
2. What is my current direction?
3. How am I preventing the free flow of my life?

4. What opportunities are currently available to me?
5. Home/family factors.
6. Job/vocational factors.
7. Relationship factors.
8. What should I become self-aware of?
9. The past.
10. The future/possible outcome.

MERLIN'S MIRROR SPREAD

We each of us need to know ourselves better: this is the prime directive of esoteric living and without it we are directionless and unhappy because we can never solve the reason why things do not go right with our lives. Some people spend their whole lives blaming circumstances or other people for their misfortunes, but fail to register their own inadequacies as being at the root of the matter. The Merlin's Mirror

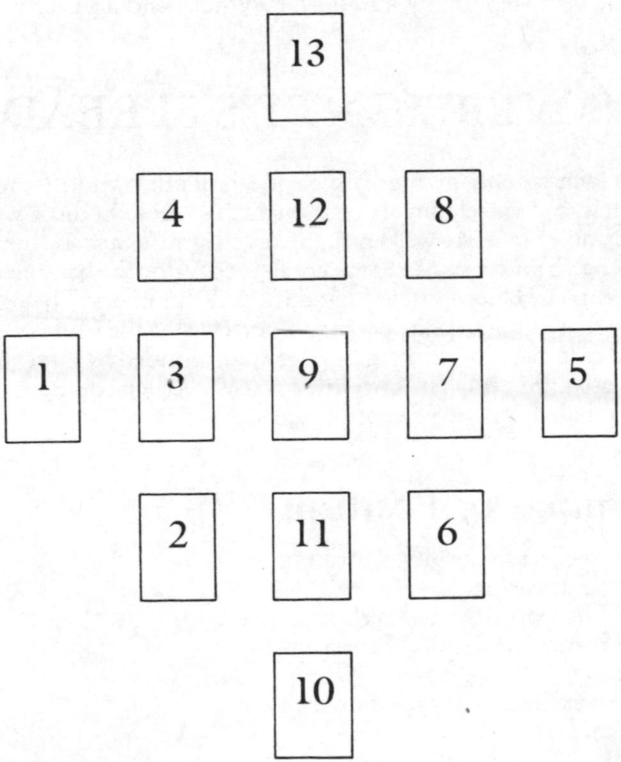

Fig. 10.2: Merlin's Mirror

Spread reflects our three faces: the one we show to others, the one we would like to be, and the real self which often lies hidden at the centre.

Meanings of Positions

1. The face I show to the world.
2. The reasons why I assume this mask, my hidden fears.
3. What I expect to gain by presenting this persona.
4. What am I doing with my life?
5. Who I would like to be.
6. What is preventing me from becoming this person?
7. What opportunities am I avoiding?
8. How do I envisage my life becoming?
9. The real me.
10. What is my life purpose?
11. What still needs to be assimilated into the real me?
12. What inessential part of my persona am I shoring up?
13. The next step on my life journey. What I should bear in mind.

SOVEREIGNTY'S SPREAD

We are each potentially the king or queen of our own inner realm of awareness, but we seldom act as though this was so because we really do not know ourselves well enough. Sovereignty's Spread shows how our strengths and weaknesses are configured, using the basic elemental ascriptions of Hallow positions and the four humours. The resultant reading shows us 'the body politic' — ourselves as the realm of Logres, centred at its heart as the king or queen, surrounded by our empowering or disempowering Hallows, and subject to crucial decisions which must be based on our perceptive faculties.

Meanings of Positions

1. The Intellectual faculty. Thinking.
2. The Intuitive faculty.
3. The Emotional faculty. Feeling.
4. The Instinctive faculty. Sensation.
5. Fears.
6. Unconsidered, hasty decisions.
7. Hopes.
8. Considered, introspective decisions.
9. Oneself as sovereign.

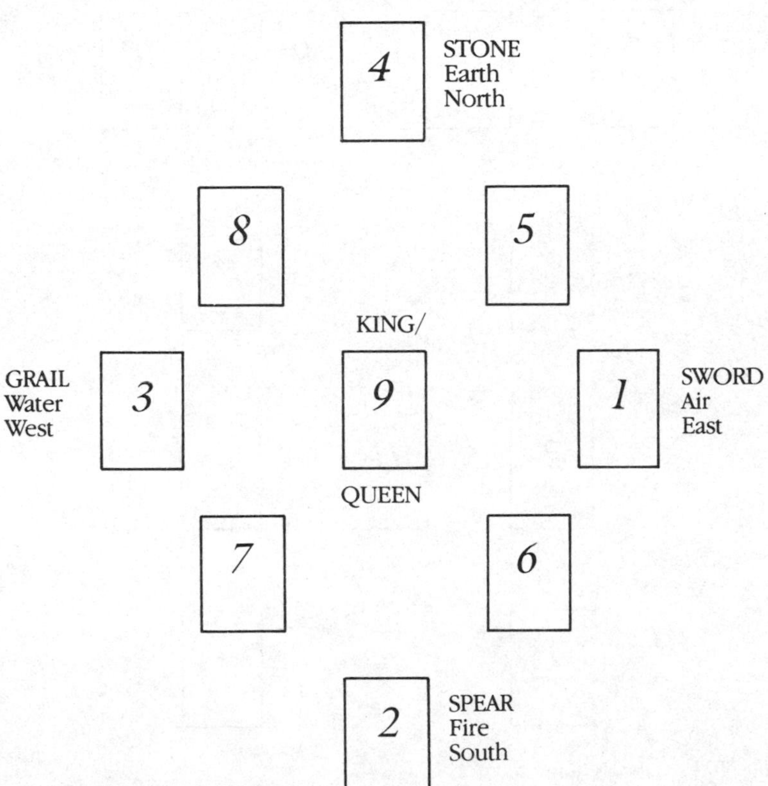

Fig. 10.3: Sovereignty's Spread

MABON'S GATE SPREAD

Most of us have ideal situations which exist in our heads but which never come to fruition because we cannot pass through the door which leads beyond our everyday lives. This reading helps clarify the means by which we can both block and help ourselves to achieve our aims, giving a key to unlock that door. The release of Mabon from his long imprisonment was the basis for this spread.

Meanings of Positions

1. What I would like to achieve.
2. What is blocking me from achieving it?
3. How I unconsciously block myself.
4. What I have already achieved.
5. What helped me achieve it?

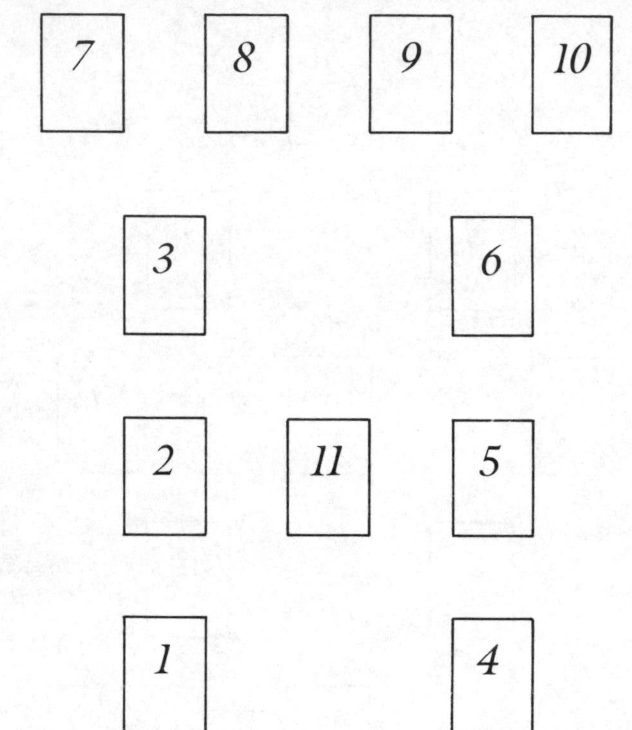

Fig. 10.4: Mabon's Gate

6. How have I helped myself?
7. The way my idea is received by others.
8. Who will benefit from my idea?
9. How I can revisualize my idea.
10. The next step.
11. The key which will unlock the door to achievement.

THE EXCALIBUR SPREAD

Sometimes a conventional spread is not sufficient to pin-point the querent's difficulties. They may be too deep-seated, possibly stemming from karmic factors from past lives. The querent may be finding recurrent difficulties, all variations on a theme. If such information crops up either as a result of a reading or in conversation with a client, be very sensitive and listen hard. If the querent states, for example, that people are *always* letting him down, or that he *never* seems to be able to hold down a job, then be suspicious. The 'nevers' and 'always'

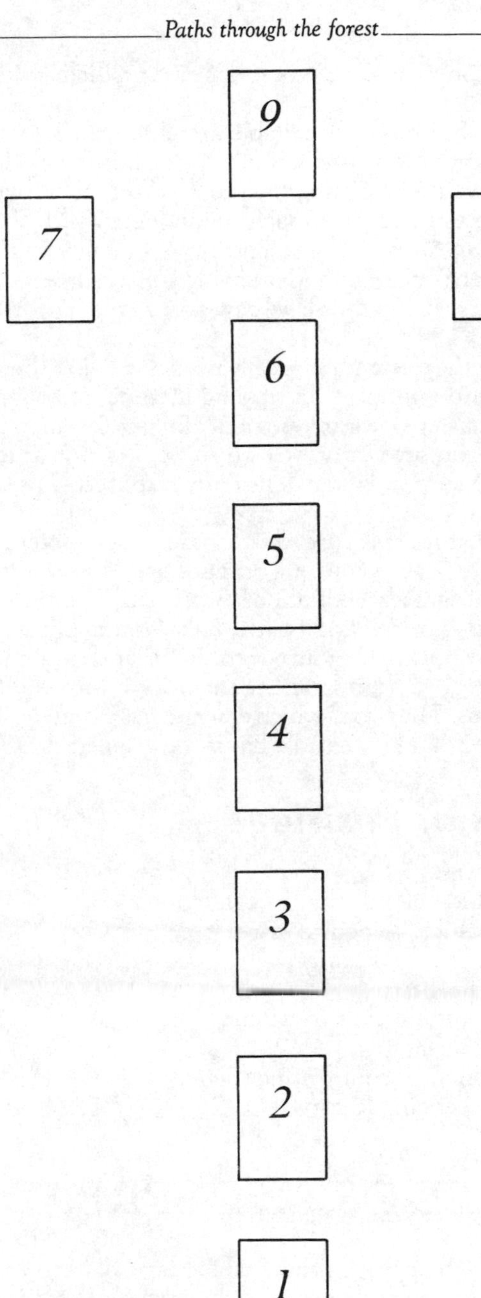

Fig. 10.5: The Excalibur Spread

which occur in conversation denote ingrained problems which are not being faced.

The Excalibur Spread is not suitable for all querents. Not everyone believes in reincarnation, and some who do are so credulous and gullible that it would be a disservice to confront them with such a reading. This spread does not touch in any detail with the previous incarnation/s, but gives a general and overall quality to the kind of person the querent once was and probably still is, since incarnational lessons recur in our present life if we have passed them up in a previous one.

If you feel that the querent may really need regression therapy which can be a powerful and often distressing method of shifting karmic problems into current awareness, then do not attempt to do this yourself unless you are really well qualified. Do not send them to anyone who you suspect is not sufficiently responsible or well-versed in esoteric ethics.

You will probably only use this spread with esoterically-aware clients, in which case, you might conduct the reading in the framework of a simple meditation. Since the sword of Arthur's kingship is guarded by the Lady of the Lake, you might well conduct the querent to a short inner journey to that island, using the card to trigger the imagery if necessary. Let them look into the lake while shuffling the cards. The sword which emerges has a double-sided blade of great sharpness, and its handle has to be gripped decisively.

Meanings of Positions

1. Who I once was.
2. The lessons I learned in that incarnation.
3. The lessons which I failed to learn.
4. Who I am in this incarnation.
5. The things I find easy.
6. The things I find difficult to accept.
7. Recurrent problems.
8. The best method of confronting them.
9. This life's challenging lessons.

TREE OF LIFE SPREAD

The readings which appear in this chapter have all been aimed at the querent him- or herself and how he or she reacts to the circumstances. This spread has been included to demonstrate how one may appraise a situation, a project or a plan. The Tree of Life is the prime symbolic system of Qabalah, which is a study in itself. For that reason, the

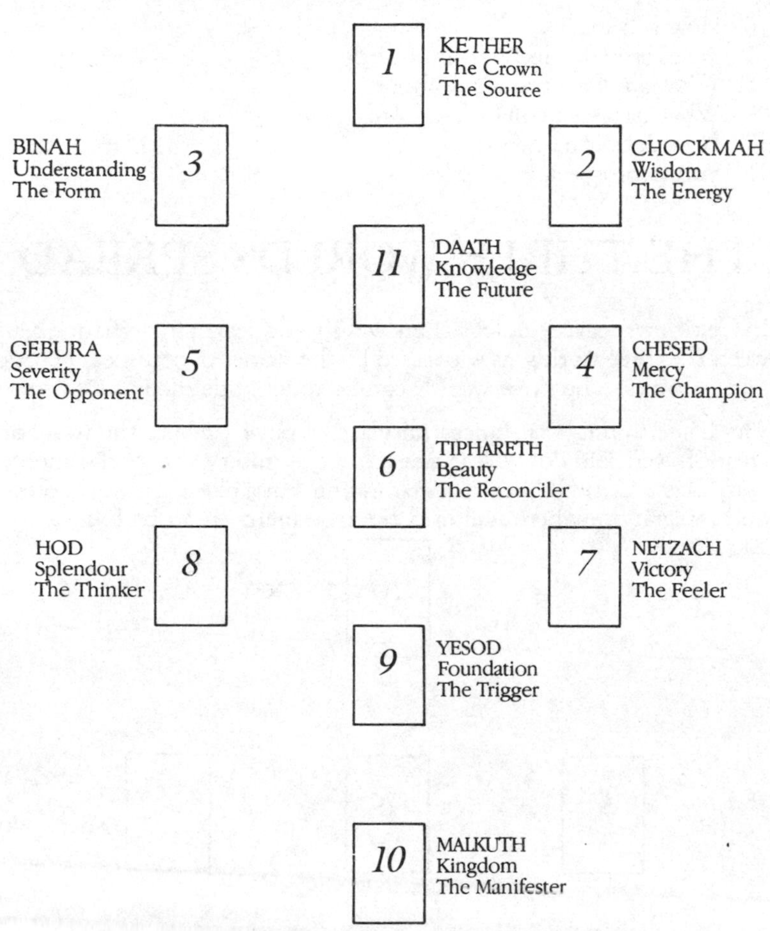

Fig. 10.6: Tree Of Life

spread positions outlined show the Jewish title of each sephira with its English counterpart. Beneath these are the adapted titles which derive from the qualities and functions of each position.

Meanings of Positions

1. What is the source of the matter?
2. What energy impels it?
3. What form does it take?
4. How is it promoted/assisted?
5. How is it opposed?

6. How is it expressed?
7. What are your feelings about it?
8. What are your thoughts about it?
9. What triggers its manifestation?
10. How does it manifest?
11. Future prospects?

THE THREE WORLDS SPREAD

In Celtic mystical cosmology there was a great deal of interchange between the three worlds, as witnessed by the stories of countless heroes and heroines. The three worlds can be roughly defined as follows:

The Underworld — the ancestral place of power, where the roots of creation were laid down. It is not a place of misery and punishment, as in Classical and Biblical understanding, but a place of primal power and integration, where skill and empowerment are to be found.

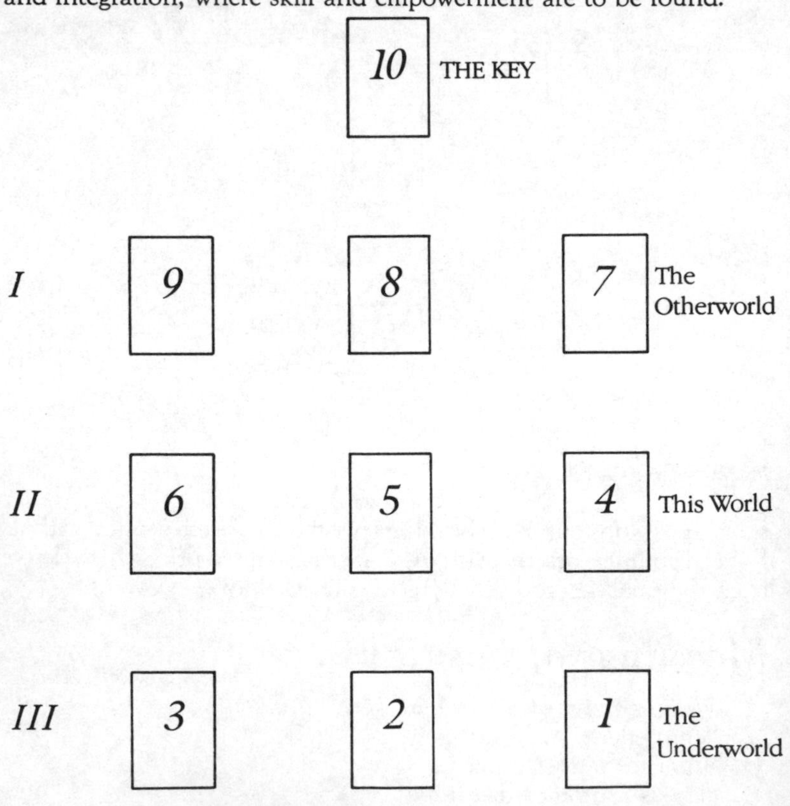

Fig. 10.7: The Three Worlds Spread

This World — the created, terrestrial world in which ordinary people are born, live and die. It is closely associated with the other two worlds.

The Otherworld — the blessed world of the gods and archetypes, of which mortals had visions, and into which they frequently ventured for enlightenment. It is the burning glass through which eternal light filters into this world.

This spread is particularly valuable for putting people in touch with the hidden alignments of the three worlds, which are still operative for those who perceive them. The Otherworldly level often provides the guiding 'story' which animates the reading.

This spread is quite flexible and does not have a fixed or designated meaning for each card. The three levels are read in order and also in alignment, so that cards 1, 4 and 7 may reveal an interesting or significant factor which the querent is ignorant of or somehow suppressing. The 10th position, the key, gives the keynote of the reading, either expressed as a cumulative factor or else as a way of proceeding.

CHAPTER 11

RITUALS TO LIVE BY

This chapter outlines a few of the ways in which you can utilize the *Hallowquest* pack as the foundation for ritual work. If you have fully entered into the world of the Arthurian Powers, into the landscape and related to its associated inhabitants, you will be part of another country — an inner one. This shared understanding can be further deepened by the use of ritual.

Throughout this book, you will have had the opportunity to become acquainted with forms of meditation, visualization and divination. Each of these disciplines enables us to mesh more closely with the world of the *Hallowquest*. The practice of meditation and visualization can help us to be more skilful and more sensitive on our spiritual journey. The practice of divination can sharpen our insight and deepen our compassion, as we come into contact with clients who need counsel and encouragement.

Very slowly, if you choose to work closely with the *Hallowquest*, you will find that you are creating rituals to live by: ethical ways of behaviour, insightful realizations, and the manifesting power of the Hallows in your life will be sure signs that this is happening.

The work of ritual takes us beyond our personal lives, for it is centred in the inner world, from which its influence is manifested and broadcast to the rest of the world. Some of the rituals appearing in this chapter are clearly of this nature, others are not. But even in the 'Eye of the Seeker' ritual, which is mainly a training ritual, there is a dimension beyond that of personal progress or enlightenment.

The action of ritual focuses and channels a pool of collective potential energies and makes them available to a wider frame of reference. The impossibility of describing the action of ritual brings us beyond the boundaries of language. In terms of esoteric science, we can say that ritual is a means by which the microcosm (our own physical world) can penetrate the macrocosm (the Greater, imaginal or Platonic world).

We may imagine our own world and the inner world as being divided by a thin, elastic web. If we push our hand against it, a corresponding handshape is discerned on the inner worlds. Likewise, if some being on the inner world side were to lean against the wall of the web, we might discern its shape and formation. This is, of course, the language of analogy, but it may help to think of ritual in these images.

The reciprocation of the worlds — both outer and inner — is something that few of us have any notion of, since it is not taught outside orthodox spiritualities or esoteric traditions. Anyone who has received a marginally religious education may have visions of angels running up and down celestial ladders, assisting the work of creation. This is not a bad image, since it derives from the classic mystical Christian study *The Celestial Hierarchies* by Dionysius the Areopagite.

It is unfortunate that the humanistic centred universe is the one currently holding sway in our cosmological orientation, for this fosters no sense of interdependency between the worlds. Ritual acts as a corrective, for our participation in ritual work enhances our understanding of this two-way flow. Standing in our demarked sacred space, we are aligned with the inner world, which is, logically, also aligned with our outer world. We speak words of intent, move in formal patterns, all the time receiving visualizations and subtle impressions of our ritual action. During this timeless action, we may also be aware of the inhabitants of the inner world — not always in the persons of the Arthurian Powers and Court cards.

Such an experience may be traumatic to a person raised in the belief that he or she is the highest species of creation inhabiting the earth. Perhaps this kind of shock is necessary for, if we look to the primal civilizations and primitive cultures still flourishing in far-flung pockets of the planet, the interrelation of the worlds is a basic understanding by which people live. The fact that Western civilization has abandoned this fundamental premise perhaps shows how seriously it has departed from wholistic living.

The corrective function of ritual is to enable us to live more harmoniously, to bring into alignment that which is out of balance.

Its effects will be personally felt as well as made universally available to those in need. At the end of each ritual action, provision should be made for this active mediation. This prevents the ritual operator from becoming ego bound and reminds him or her that the all-inclusive nature of ritual must be mediated to everyone in need, whether friend, family or foe.

There follow basic guidelines for the performance of rituals and an introduction for those who are unfamiliar with this manner of carrying on.

WHY PERFORM RITUALS?

The whole of our life is a set of personal, social and cosmic rituals, though we seldom perceive it as that. When these rituals are disrupted due to holiday or a stay in hospital, then we realize that we are at the mercy of other people's rituals, often at variance to our own. But it is not on this level that we wish to remain here.

A ritual is an outer endorsement, a sealing or manifestation of an inner concept. The sacrament of the Mass is the ritual remembrance and re-enactment of the redemptive sacrifice of Christ in which participants — in this case, baptized Christians — share in a mystical way. This is not a foreign concept to religiously-minded people, although it is an unfamiliar one to people who are not initiates of a spiritual tradition.

We live in a society which finds spiritual matters embarrassing. It is considered abnormal to see a person pray in public, for instance, unless it be at some religious gathering. Within the circle of friends and acquaintances, it is rare to hear a serious religious discussion which is not automatically earthed by one person's scepticism or nervous laughter. We are, as a people, unused to ritual in its spiritual forms. The shallowness and alienation so often exhibited in the presence of deep belief is a sure sign that our society is sick to its soul. And yet, strangely enough, in place of firmly-held religious belief, many people turn to the fringes of occultism for a quick panacea to this sickness. The Tarot is one of the first touchstones for such people, who approach it as a fortune-telling cure-all. What they fail to see is that even the most specious form of fortune-telling stems from a major branch of the mighty Tree of esoteric tradition. We are forgetful that yoga is a discipline of Hinduism, that the runes were the powerful symbols of the Norse gods, and that the Tarot is a wisdom-bearing sprig of the Tree of Knowledge.

Ritual is more often referred to as 'magical ritual' — the adjective is really superfluous since all ritual actions are 'magical'. No one suddenly announces one morning, 'I'm going to do a ritual today' with the air of someone set on taking a bath. Rituals always have a reason, a motivating purpose. People unfamiliar with esoteric ethics should note this, since it is frequently assumed that by even owning a Tarot deck one is 'dabbling in the occult'. Magicians do not dabble, they work — hard. And all of us are magicians according to our capabilities and insight, potentially speaking.

In this chapter there are outlines for working ritually with the *Hallowquest* pack. If you have already attempted some of the meditation work in Chapter 8 you will be ready to try one of these rituals yourself. If you haven't tried any meditation yet, then leave the exercises in this chapter alone until you have. Read through this chapter to familiarize yourself with its contents and especially do not attempt any ritual work until you have read the next section.

The reason for performing these *Hallowquest* rituals is a very simple one in most cases — you require a deeper understanding of the cards and a ritual will supply you with insights which you will not receive from merely reading this book or even looking contemplatively at the cards. You already know for yourself that it is one thing to explain a task to others and another to show them by performing that task practically. Ritual and meditation are the practice: reading and thinking about the Tarot are the theory. It is a good and proper thing that they should precede practice, and that practice should be replaced by perfection. To that end we invite you to read on.

Please read the next section very carefully and check that you understand its contents before performing any of the ritual exercises.

RITUAL ETHICS

If you found the previous admonition annoying or bewildering, stop and think. You always read the warnings on the side of medicine bottles before drinking because you want to know what kind of side-effects might result. The medicine has been prescribed to help cure you, but it might result in drowsiness, indicating that you should refrain from driving; it might be dangerous to exceed the stated dose. The same common-sense measures apply to ritual. Ritual action is remediable in its effect, but it does sometimes result in certain side-effects about which you should be warned.

As stated above, a ritual is performed for a reason, never for a whim. When you decide to perform a ritual, you prepare for it properly. Your first considerations should be as follows:

1. Have I understood the principles of the ritual action so that I am clear about procedures?
2. Am I in good health and in an unstressed state?
3. Have I prepared myself in accordance with the procedures below on p.244?

4. Can I ensure that I will be undisturbed by callers, family or the telephone before I start?
5. Do I have time to perform the ritual in a relaxed manner?

The questions above are straightforward enough. They imply that you are seriously intent, that you are in a fit state to do a ritual e.g. you have not taken drugs or just had an argument with your partner.

Within the ritual action you will be contacting the Otherworldly levels from which the archetypes of the *Hallowquest* derive. This will bring you into contact with these Arthurian Powers at first hand, and this may make you feel disorientated or strange. Switching levels of consciousness suddenly can cause all manner of temporary aberrance and delusion. If you follow the ritual procedures outlined below on p.244, you will be all right.

It is true to say, however, that the levels of power you contact are usually in proportion to your experience and knowledge. In other words, the levels of stress encountered by a beginner will rarely exceed those encountered by an experienced hand.

No one can explain to you what anything is like, let alone what participating in ritual feels like. Only *you* can experience this and come to terms with it on your own level. If you go slowly and follow the copious directives of this chapter, you will gradually enhance your insight and understanding of how these things work. An experienced communicant will, for example, relate that rarely will they personally experience dynamic changes or level-shifts during Mass, but that their daily experience is more mundane and indeed, sometimes boring to the sensual perception. We are not always able to perceive the flow of energy; indeed, it may not even be there, but in time we will experience something and get a sense of how ritual works.

If at any time you feel ill or severely disorientated, perform the closing procedures outlined below (p.244) and immediately return yourself to everyday existence by drinking some water and eating a sandwich or biscuit. This effectively seals off any strange feelings. If you still feel peculiar, seek the company of a friend or neighbour whose good sense you value, and just be with them until you feel restored to yourself. This sense of disorientation is not brought on by malign forces at work through the Tarot, but through sudden energy shifts.

A ritual aligns your defined space with the Otherworld. The Tarot cards are potent doorways for the flow of energy from one world to another and if you are meditating well, you will automatically align yourself. This is the value of the opening and closing procedures. They define which world you are in.

At all times, be respectful of the energies and powers you are encountering. They are not gods needing to be worshipped or appeased, but finely-tuned archetypes whose energy can affect our world. Sometimes unscripted things happen and you may find yourself in dialogue with, for example, the White Hart or the Grail Hermit. If you make a contact of this kind in a lone ritual, by all means pursue your dialogue. If you are working with others, then keep your dialogue silent and abandon it altogether if the time for mediation is past.

Working with others causes its own problems and it is best to designate a temporary leader for each session. Egos quickly get out of control around esoteric areas, and none worse than in ritual situations. Some rituals call for identification with and assumption of a Tarot power: this means one *temporarily* assumes or aligns with an archetype and then afterwards takes off the mask of that persona to become only oneself. If you suspect that you yourself or any other officer are still 'under the influence' of this archetype, either through careless closing procedures or through egotistical cussedness, then the effects will soon show. A high-handed and inhuman manner is the first sign, followed by outrageous behaviour in whatever archetypal department the power governs. The best method of releasing oneself from this temporary overlay of personalities is to calmly and matter of factly declare aloud one's personal identity and relationships on earth, and resolutely bid the overlaying archetype to return to its own world and nature. Of course, this is less easy in the case of someone actually *enjoying* this kind of possession. One can reinforce a similar message to this person, and if they persist in 'becoming the archetype' forbid them to work ritually with you until they sort out their own behavioural patterns more maturely.

Imbalanced individuals become more imbalanced during ritual stress; ordinary people with stable life-styles encounter the kinds of stresses the world already throws at them and with which they reasonably cope to the best of their ability. If your ordinary life is out of control, then retreating into a cosy ritual will not improve matters. You first need to have a clear perception of your own problems, limitations and potential. Instead of ritual, you will need to consult the *Hallowquest* pack in another way, perhaps by using the Mabon's Gate spread on p.231.

Ritual does not *in itself* cure all life's ills; the benefits of ritual are also side-effects to some degree, which you freely and incidentally experience. Ritual is alignment with the Otherworld first and foremost. It manifests on earth the archetypes which lie *in potentia* in the Otherworld. So although your understanding of the *Hallowquest* pack may be enhanced and you may meet exciting archetypes and experience a feeling of well-being, these are incidentals, for your major action has been to contact and mediate these Arthurian Powers in your own life.

Remember, you are always responsible for the experience which you have. If you do a ritual when you are not up to it, or resolutely refuse to follow the procedures outlined here, then it's no good blaming us or the Powers if things go wrong and you become confused as a result.

We, the authors, have discharged our responsibility to you, the reader, but this does not, as the packet says, 'infringe your constitutional rights'.

The ethics of the Otherworld are like those of the outer world, only on a higher arc. You do not have to abrogate common sense, accept fantastic things or condone silliness in any form just because this is a ritual. With these concepts firmly in mind, read on.

RITUAL PROCEDURES

The first thing we do in any ritual is to define our space and our reality. The room we have chosen should be clean, orderly and fit for a spiritual action. Outer mess is indicative of inner confusion. The next thing is to define our reality. In ritual we will be entering the Otherworld and leaving our outer world temporarily behind — or rather, the space we have prepared in the outer world will touch and contain the reality of the Otherworld for a short time. The two will be in alignment. We mentally and ritually define our purpose by *opening* and *closing* procedures. These simple affirmations begin and conclude each ritual action, just as the sign of the cross begins and concludes each celebration of the Eucharist. You can use the sample affirmations below, together with some ritual signal or gesture, or you can choose your own.

To Open:

World beyond world, this circle stands
The way lies open before my hands. (Open your clasped hands as though describing the opening of a pair of doors.)

To Close:

World within world, how lies the land?
The way is closed by either hand. (Bring your hands together as though describing the closing of a pair of doors.)

These procedures will, said with intention, see you in and out of the Otherworld.

Every culture has its ritual four directions, and the Arthurian Powers are no exception. The Hallows are the indicators and symbolic guardians of the four quarters and they can be set up in two ways. You can physically place each of the Hallows in their appropriate direction: Sword in the East, Spear in the South, Grail in the West, Stone in the North. Or you can ritually visualize them as being in each quarter. Of course you can combine these or even place replicas of the Hallows which you have made or purchased in the quarters. It is usual to formally acknowledge these powers as operative in your defined working space: e.g. 'I see in the East the Sword of Light. Its function is to cut through illusion and bring illumination to the world. May its shining strength protect and guard this circle.'

Before you start any ritual it is also good to perform the Centring Ritual, especially if you are working alone. This is a very short yet essential procedure which can be performed at the beginning of a ritual or at any time when you need to reorient or rebalance your energies. To perform the Centring Ritual:

Stand upright, with feet slightly apart and the body's weight evenly balanced. Breathe in and out deeply until you feel relaxed and comfortable.

Make your personal affirmation of intent and balance, e.g.

At the centre of the universe I stand
Between the worlds above and the worlds below.
I stand firm, I hold my way,
Wherever my steps are led,
In the harmonious unity
Of the worlds within and the worlds without.

At the conclusion of the ritual, before you actually close, it is respectful to acknowledge the help and guidance of the Four Quarter Guardians — in this case, the Hallows themselves, e.g.

By the Stone of Establishment we derive wisdom and blessing.
For guarding the northern quarter, we give thanks.

Many people imagine that rituals can only be performed by hooded people encumbered with ceremonial implements. The following rituals need only yourself, the *Hallowquest* pack and this book, anything else is an optional extra. Robes and magical emblems are aids to ritual, but they are not essential. The ability to work just as you are is a greater virtue than to distract yourself from the real purpose of deeper understanding. On p.272 there are suggestions for going beyond the basics outlined here. There are also far too many books available to help you establish a temple, make robes and implements if that is what you require. It is far better to buy some of the excellent works on ritual methods which are indicated in the bibliography.[12,67,69]

Read through the following rituals first before leaping into one. To draw upon the energies of the Arthurian Powers is no mean undertaking. When you have performed one of the rituals you will begin to understand that their effect upon your life is only just beginning.

SEASONAL RITUALS

Readers unfamiliar with the uses of ritual may find a way into this kind of work by the performance of seasonal rituals. The round of the year has been celebrated since time began, observed by rituals and ceremonies which brought the tribe together to observe and share the particular energies and powers which were available at that time.

In the West, two kinds of celebration using ritual forms are observable: the religious festivals such as Easter, Whitsun or Christmas, and the traditional festivals which predate these, such as May Day, Hallowe'en and Yule. Some of these have become inextricably mixed up, but no one seems to mind very deeply.

The Four Hallows are themselves emblematic of the four great seasonal changes which are marked by the two solstices and the two equinoxes, as we can see in Figures 11.1 and 11.2, where we see the Wheel of the Year. These four festivals are now only observed by religious festivals: Lady Day, St John's Eve, St Michael's Day and St Thomas' Eve, in the Christian calendar, although certain people, such as Druids and neo-pagans, hold these days as holy, for they mark the movement of the earth about the sun and define our seasons for us.

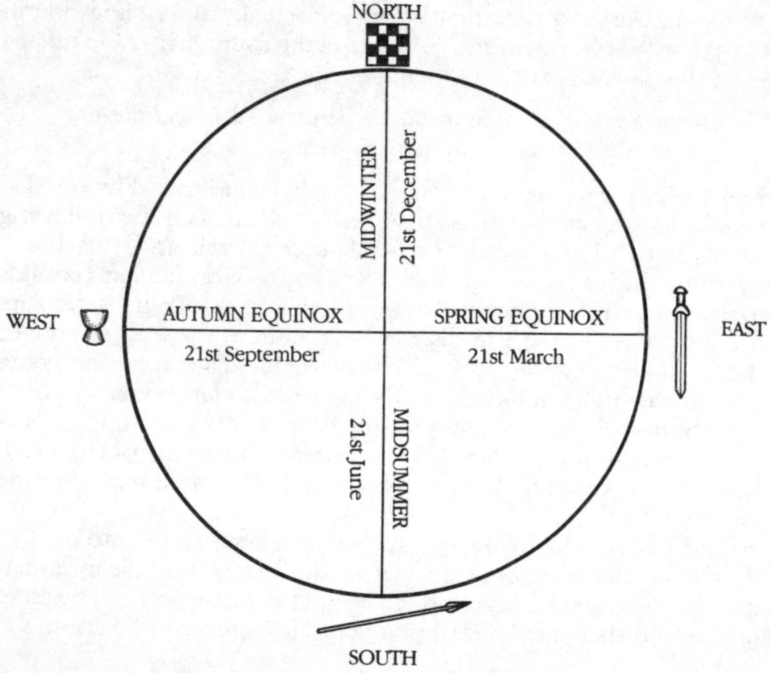

Fig. 11.1: The Wheel of the Year (Northern Hemisphere)

This diagram shows only the Wheel of the Year as it appears in the northern hemisphere. Readers in the southern hemisphere should alter the diagram to look like this, for their north and Winter position is geographically south.

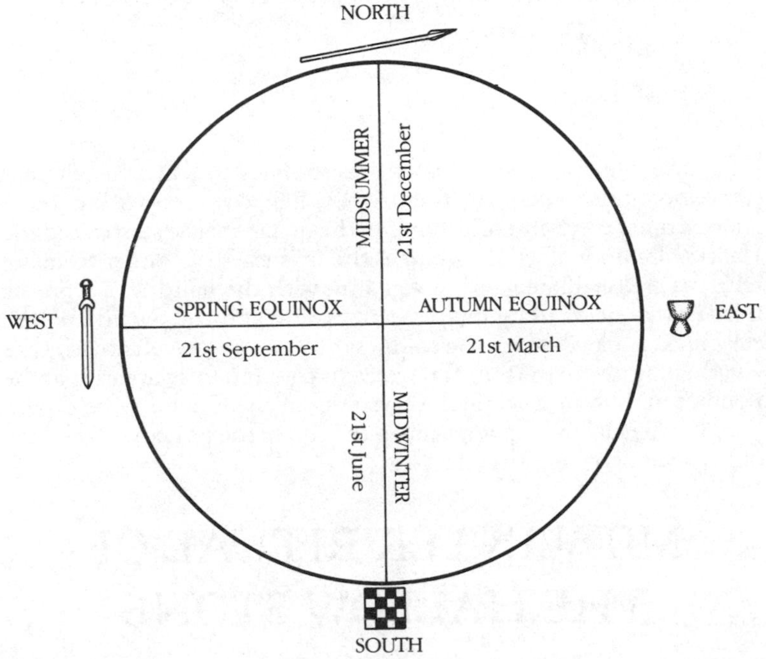

Fig. 11.2: The Wheel of the Year (Southern Hemisphere)

The four seasonal rituals which utilize the Hallows are as follows:

Spring equinox — Sword
Summer solstice — Spear
Autumn equinox — Grail
Winter solstice — Stone

Each ritual celebrates the inception of the Hallow Power in the seasonal round and allows the participants to interact with the incoming energy in an imaginative way. Such a set of rituals could form the basis of quarterly meetings of an esoteric group or they could be performed by the lone worker as a means of keeping in touch with the seasons while in a city. The shape of one ritual only is given, but this can be readily adapted for more or less extensive use, and the other three Hallow Rituals can easily be composed, following this outline.

The following ritual is set forth for the northern hemisphere and is arranged for one person, although it is easily adaptable for a number of people, if required. Each part of the ritual is tabulated for quick reference. It is a very simple ritual and can be performed with the minimum of magical regalia. If you have a robe, you can wear it, but what really matters is your intention.

Each ritual on the Wheel of the Year has its proper time of operation:

Sword	— Dawn	Spring
Spear	— Noon	Summer
Grail	— Twilight	Autumn
Stone	— Midnight	Winter

Of course, you can slightly adapt these times to suit your circumstances or indeed perform them when it is convenient, but these magical times precisely correspond to the quality of the season and the Hallow. Traditionally, for example, the mysteries of Winter in many religions are celebrated with a vigil and with the lighting of a fire, as in the ritual below. The mysteries of Spring and the Sword are best celebrated at dawn, when the coldness of Winter is driven away by the lengthening rays of the Sun. The Spear is triumphantly upraised at the noon of midsummer, while the mysteries of the Grail may be experienced as the Hallow cup appears on the rim of the horizon at the time of between light in Autumn.

MIDWINTER RITUAL OF THE HALLOW STONE

Let the area of working be decorated with evergreens and seasonally appropriate plants, flowers or fruits. At the four quarters, let there be representations of the Hallows. In the North, a suitable representation of the Stone Hallow is placed on a shelf/table/altar and given more prominence than the other three. (This could be stone, crystal or representation of the Hallow which you have made, or you could use the Hallow card itself.) Also on the altar should be a candlestick or oil lamp and some matches. This light is unlit at the beginning of the ritual. Let the room be as dark as possible without being dangerous. Place a chair or stool in the South, facing the Stone Hallow.

The next thing is to demark your working area: this is called 'the Making Sacred'. Your room is to become, however briefly, a temple of the Hallows. At each of the four quarters, you will have placed the elemental symbols of the Hallows:

East — some incense, either a stick or a charcoal block and a couple of good pinches of the real kind, for Air
South — a candle, for Fire
West — a chalice of freshly drawn water, for Water
North — a bowl of earth, for Earth

The Making Sacred

1. Starting in the East, visualize the Sword Hallow as strongly as you can and say:

> *In the East shines the Sword of Light. The hour is dawn and the sun is rising over the world. May the hallowed power of the Sword be manifest in this place.*

You offer the incense to the eastern quarter, then take it clockwise round the circle. (All movements are clockwise, unless otherwise stated. Don't worry if your circle is not entirely round.) You stop at each of the quarters and there offer incense to South, West and North, returning finally to the East where you set it down.

2. You pass to the South where you visualize the Spear, saying:

> *In the South speeds the Spear which heals and wounds. The hour is noon, and the sun is at its zenith. May the hallowed power of the Spear be manifest in this place.*

Then you offer the candle to the southern quarter and bear it round the circle, offering it as before, and returning it to the South.

3. You pass to the West where you visualize the Grail, saying:

> *In the West glows the Grail of Compassion. The hour is twilight, and the sun is setting. May the hallowed power of the Grail be manifest in this place.*

Then you offer the chalice of water to the West and bear it round the circle, offering it as before, and returning it to the West.

4. You pass to the North where you visualize the Stone, saying:

> *In the North stands the Stone of Knowledge. The hour is midnight, and the stars give their light. May the hallowed power of the Stone be manifest in this place.*

Then you offer the bowl of earth to the northern quarter and bear it round the circle, offering it as before, returning it to the North.

Invocation and Visualization of the Stone Hallow

You now invoke the protecting guidance of the Hallow guardian, which for the Winter and the Stone Hallow, is Merlin. (See p.118 for the other guardians.) Sit facing the North.

> *I call upon Merlin, the mighty guardian of the Stone Hallow, to aid and assist me in accomplishing this Midwinter ritual. He was the forerunner of the Pendragons, a sage councillor to Uther and Arthur. He withdrew into his Otherworldly abode from whence he watches the events of this world. In our time, he stands ready to give guidance*

and knowledge. At this dark Midwinter, I declare my intent to align with the Stone Hallow and seek its empowerment, for the benefit of all beings.

While you are speaking these words, strongly visualize Merlin bearing before him the Stone Hallow in his hands. He appears in his aspect of Hallow guardian, in full glory and strength. He looks compassionately upon you. Visualize a ray of warm light emanating from his heart. This falls upon the ground, forming a path of light between you. It also falls upon the Stone so that light is refracted to all directions. Be aware of that path and gratefully absorb the light which emanates from the Stone. Visualize it streaming impartially throughout the world to all people who desire knowledge with a true heart.

Meditation on the Midwinter Mystery

You now come to the heart of the ritual. Your meditation should reflect the nature of the season in your land: what follows is only an example.

We stand at one of the mighty portals of the year. This night is the longest night and we come in meditation to welcome in the power of the Stone Hallow at Midwinter. From this portal, the year is reborn at the time of greatest darkness. We close our doors and windows against the bitter wind, against the snows of the long cold, but we open this door to welcome in the restorer of light. It is not known, the time when the Courts of Joy shall be founded among us, but we wait in joyful hope, in expectation that many shall find ways to renew the world.

Now enter into silent meditation upon the nature of this season, visualizing the power of the Stone Hallow, as you have understood it, permeating the land. Visualize this power helping all who stand in need of knowledge: those without a spiritual tradition to sustain them, those who have become stale on their quest for truth; see family, friends, acquaintances, people unknown to you; include heads of government, those seeking effective ways of curing, preserving or restoring the creation. Do not forget yourself: this is a time of self-knowledge. Make your mediation impartial, including those people you do not get on with or actively dislike; include those responsible for perpetrating restrictive regimes in the world. Everyone is capable of change, but some people are fearful because of ignorance; thus they tend to be violent and disordered in their lives. The empowering knowledge of the Stone Hallow will help alleviate this.

The Epiphany of the Hallow

At the end of your meditation, approach the northern altar and strike a match to illumine your candle or lamp. Taking it to each quarter in turn, beginning East and ending North, say:

Behold the light which shines in darkness!

As you do so, visualize an encompassing swathe of radiance circling out from your temple into the world, taking the power of the Stone Hallow to all beings. Return the light to the altar.

Establishing the Stone Hallow Shrine (optional)

Each of the seasonal rituals has its ongoing effect. In token of this, a shrine to each of the Hallows may be established, the Stone Hallow shrine being operative from Midwinter to the Spring Equinox, when the Sword Hallow shrine may be established and kept operative, and so on. It may be inconvenient to have an obvious shrine arranged in your room, in which case, you can merely prop up your Hallow card in the appropate quarter as a visual remembrance of your ritual.

For the purposes of this ritual, your bowl of earth and a stone will form the basis of your shrine. Take up the stone or crystal and say:

Let this stone represent the powers of the Stone Hallow in this place. May it be blessed by the powers of the Great Above and the Great Below, the inhabiters of the ages before the ages. This shrine is established for the restoration of all the worlds.

Next, take it to each of the quarters, starting East and finishing North; elevate the stone and say at each quarter:

Behold the Stone Hallow, bringing knowledge to the world

Place it in the bowl of earth, saying:

May all who come here feel the indwelling power of the Stone Hallow in their hearts.

Conclusion

At this point you may wish to make music or sing a seasonally appropriate song. If you intend to leave your shrine up, let the light be left burning. Going to each quarter in turn, say:

We give thanks for the guarding presence of the Sword (or Spear, Grail, Stone) in this ritual. The Stone Hallow is now operative in this season of Winter. We await the coming of the Courts of Joy at every portal of the year's turning.

Finally, standing facing the northern altar, say:

Peace to all beings and the light of knowledge!
May the blessing of the Four Hallows guard us always.

THE EYE OF THE SEEKER RITUAL

The following ritual is derived from the Eye of the Seeker diagram on p.160 in which the triadic octaves of the Greater Powers are related. This ritual may be performed by three or 21 people, or else by the lone practitioner. The rules for working it will necessarily vary.

The lone worker will need a clear space, or a small uncluttered room. The four Hallows are set up in the quarters and the 21 Greater cards are placed circle-wise about the room, either on the floor or on convenient surfaces. There should be room to move without disrupting the spread. Starting at the centre, perform the centring ritual and acknowledge the powers of the Hallows about you in each quarter. You may, if you wish, hold the card of the Seeker or place it in a pouch about your neck.

Starting facing the Merlin position, approach Greater Power I and encounter Merlin. Vocalize your visualization as you do this, if necessary. When you have experienced the power of this card, face inward to the centre of the circle, holding the Merlin card in your hand. Feel the power of Merlin about you and gradually assume his guise. As Merlin, pace slowly until you reach the Gawain position, Greater Power VIII. As Merlin encounter Gawain: when you are ready, step into his position and assume his guise. Consciously feel the enhanced octave. Now slowly pace to Greater Power card XV and experience encountering the Green Knight as Gawain. Assume the guise of the Green Knight and step into his place. End by returning to the position of Merlin and allow the enhanced Arthurian Powers you have encountered and assumed return to the Merlin level.

Taking all three cards back with you into the centre, resume your own familiar shape and personality. If you wish, sit and rehearse in meditation, the combined qualities expressed by this triad. Salute the quarters and close as usual. Do not attempt more than one triad at each session, but slowly work your way through all seven, noting your experiences.

Three workers can also perform the ritual. Using the general framework of the ritual as outlined above, let each person assume one of the triadic positions — let us say the Lady of the Lake, the Grail Hermit and the Tower. Let each officer declare his or her function clearly and rehearse the quality of the Power each represents, in turn. Each officer should again assume the guise of their card. When all three positions are operative, let there be a period of quiet contemplation as the trio of officers feel their triune harmony and strength. It is not necessary to lay down the whole of the Greater Powers, although each officer may wish to hold their own card.

After a period of reflection and interaction, let each officer move one position to their left, so that the officer who was representing the Lady of the Lake becomes the Grail Hermit and so on. Again a short period of reflection in which each officer realizes the different octave of their triad. After this each moves on one position, until all officers have experienced each position. At the conclusion, let all three walk to the centre and facing outwards, assume their own guises again. Only one triad should be attempted at each session.

Twenty-one workers is a large number to find, but it is possible that a meeting of different esoteric groups might come together for a festival or other ritual purpose. Considerations of space will entail at least a very large room or small hall, or a secluded outdoor location for this form of the ritual to be effective. Let each person represent one of the Greater Powers and stand in order about the circle. The 22nd person will co-ordinate the ritual and represent the Seeker, and he or she stands at the centre, acting as interrogator. Let the Hallows be set up in each quarter. The Seeker will declare the purpose of the ritual, to better understand the harmony of the Greater Powers. Let the Seeker then state his or her purpose and function as questioner and quester. Then each officer will vocalize their function in turn in the following order:

I, VIII, XV
II, IX, XVI
III, X, XVII
IV, XI, XVIII
V, XII, XIX
VI, XIII, XX
VII, XIV, XXI

Each officer may hold their representative card and the officers in the primary octave of each triad i.e. I, II, III, IV, V, VI and VII may also denote the key theme of their triad. Each officer may likewise step forward into the centre as each triad unfolds until the Seeker is surrounded by each set of officers in each rotation, stepping back when the next triad starts. Each officer should seriously assume their Power and at the conclusion of the ritual divest themselves of their assumed personas to take up their own personal identity again.

In a ritual of the third kind, it is obviously beneficial and more convenient to simply script the whole thing, keeping some leeway for improvisation and developments. In working with more than 12 people this becomes imperative if the co-ordinating officer is going to be able to guide the ritual through successfully. This is not so important and indeed, is less powerful, if only working alone or with two others. With only one triad to work at a time, memory and resourcefulness are not so stretched.

RESTORATION OF THE COURTS OF JOY RITUAL

The following ritual was originally performed at a weekend course at Hawkwood College, Gloucestershire, entitled The Mysteries of the Grail, on 13 December 1987. We include it as an example of a fully-fledged ritual such as can be performed if there are sufficient numbers available. In this case, the ritual takes 21 people — not a number which most of us would ever be able to find to work with. However, the shape, movement and progression of the ritual are worth study, even if there are only two people available. Even a single person can learn a lot about ritual method and adapt this and other rituals for lone working.

The purpose of the ritual was and is to restore the Courts of Joy — to bring about the harmony of the worlds within and the worlds without, and to establish the energy, power and influence of the activated Hallows in the land of Britain. If you are a native of another country, adapt the ritual accordingly to your own physical geography. Alternatively, there is material here sufficient to adapt into a major meditation or magical piece of work which has its ongoing effect. The point about ritual is not that it leads us into fantastic and exciting parts of the Otherworld, but that we perform the ritual in order to *earth* the influence of the Otherworldly powers in our own world. This means starting with your own locality, village, town or city community and social network. The influence of the Courts of Joy must be felt by the world at large, not just strange esoteric people in robes. Magic and ritual, like prayer, are not performed for selfish ends: the idea is that everyone benefits, ordinary people as well as practitioners.

The props required need only be very simple. The elements are represented by incense (this can be an incense stick or smudge stick, or else a censer); a lighted candle or lantern will represent fire; a cup of water; and a bag or pot of earth. All of these should be easy to handle and unobtrusive. The Hallows themselves can be represented by actual implements — a Sword, Spear, Grail and Stone, as they were in our ritual at Hawkwood — or else by simple representations or by the Hallow cards themselves.

Although this is a long ritual, it is very orderly and logical in its working out. Perhaps the most important thing for performance is that it is not hurried, but allowed to unfold. The numerous circumambulations give it impetus and there is sufficient time for everyone to experience the influence of each of the Hallows. The pause for meditation on p.270 can be judged by whoever plays the Porter, but should allow everyone to mediate the energy raised by the ritual to those most in need of it, whether they be friends, enemies or people unknown to you. All movement within the ritual is clockwise, with the Knights and Maidens spiralling in and out.

The 'joy' may be announced by a horn or other wind instrument, or the entire company can chant a 'note of joy'.

Notes on the characters

Their symbolic resonances and functions —

The Inhabitants of the Four Cities Which Circle Clas Myrddin

Sword King — Air of Air
Sword Queen — Water of Air
Sword Knight — Fire of Air
Spear King — Air of Fire
Spear Queen — Water of Fire
Spear Knight — Fire of Fire
Grail King — Air of Water
Grail Queen — Water of Water
Grail Knight — Fire of Water
Stone King — Air of Earth
Stone Queen — Water of Earth
Stone Knight — Fire of Earth

The Kings of each quarter are the destined wielders of the Hallows.
The Queens are the keepers of the elemental tokens.
The Knights are the appointed representatives of their sovereigns, the Hallow questers, destined to succeed to the kingship. They also represent the Knights wandering in the forest in the Restoration of the Courts of Joy.

The Inhabitants of the Worlds Between (The Otherworld)

Morgan — Mistress of the Isles of the Dead, the Orcades. The Kingmaker.
Arthur Pendragon — Wounded King of the White Mount, once Emperor of Logres.
Guinevere — Wounded Queen of the Isle of Glass, once Empress of Logres.
Merlin Emrys — Master of the mound at Dinas Emrys. Keeper of wisdom.

All four inhabitants of the worlds between comprise the ancient Llys Arthur — the Court of Arthur — which is reconstituted in the action, when all four become the guardians of the elements.

The Inhabitants of the Realms Within (The Underworld)

Sword Maiden — Earth of Air
Spear Maiden — Earth of Fire
Grail Maiden — Earth of Water
Stone Maiden — Earth of Earth

The Maidens are the guardians of the Hallows, and are destined to become queens in their turn. They also represent the Damsels of the Wells in the Restoration of the Courts of Joy. (See p.156.)

The Gatekeeper of Clas Myrddin

Porter — the Keeper of the Gate to the Island of the Strong Door, or Logres, once gatekeeper to Llys Arthur.

Non-Speaking Participants

All non-designated participants represent the people of Logres.

All participants are responsible for mediating their specific roles. Kings and Queens represent their elemental quarter, Knights represent their sovereigns and the people of the kingdom of Logres, Maidens guard their Hallows and relinquish this duty only when the new guardians, the Llys Arthur officers, become operative as guardians and purifiers of the elements at the heart of the land. All officers and participants mediate the action to the land of Britain and to the world.

At the beginning of the action, all officers and participants are seated, except for the Hallow Maidens who wait outside the hall. Door is open.

Composition of Place

PORTER: See before you Logres, the inner realm of Britain that is faithfully reflected in the outer world when each is in alignment with the other. Long ago Merlin, the wisest of the land's many guardians, made a wall around this island which was called Clas Myrddin or Merlin's Enclosure. Assist me in the building of the wall, see it rise, clear and shimmering like a rainbow veil through which only those who wish the best for the land may pass . . .

Now see the land itself like a green quilt spread out before us. See the ancient centres of holiness, the guardian places of the Hallows, the ancient cities and standing stones, the forests and hills, the streams and rivers where once the seekers of the quest plied their way through the lands adventurous. See the cities that ringed the land in stone: in the East, Camulodunum, the ancient Colchester; in the South, Venta, the ancient Winchester; in the West, Caerleon, City of the Legions; and in the North, Luguvalium, the ancient Carlisle — great cities and centres which stand at the four quarters of the land of Logres.

Let us also now prepare to take up our parts in the quest for the

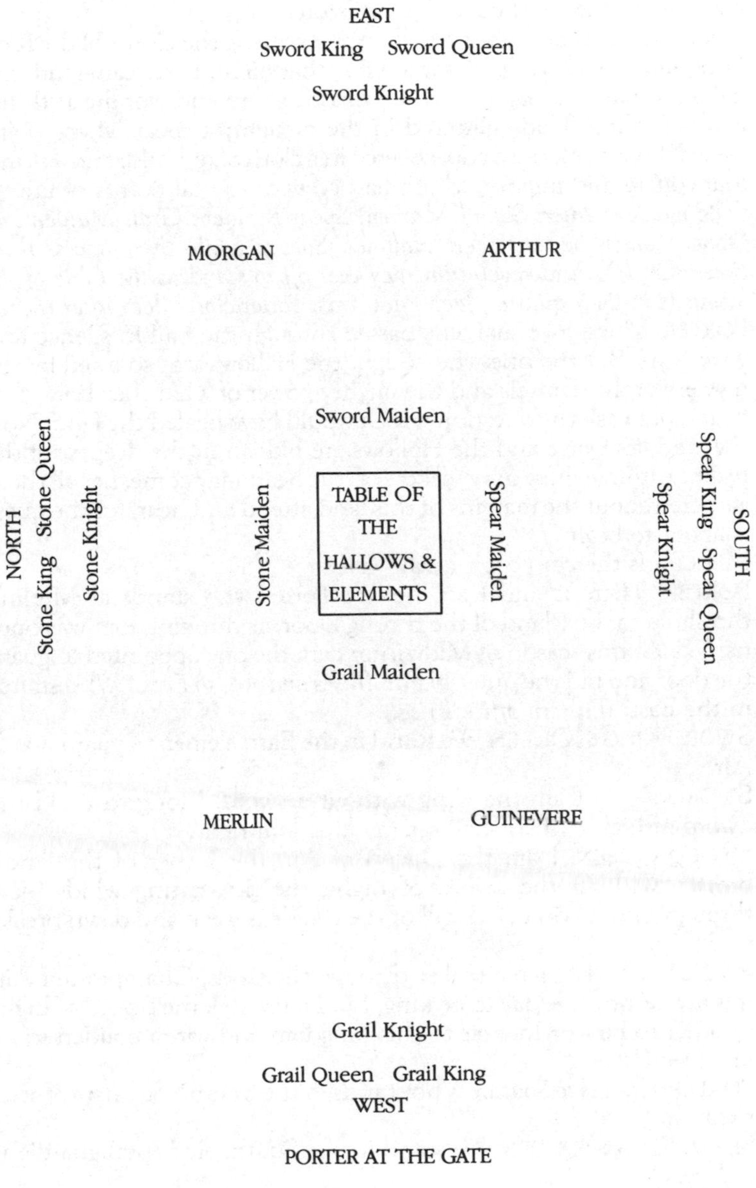

EAST

Sword King Sword Queen

Sword Knight

MORGAN ARTHUR

Sword Maiden

NORTH

Stone King Stone Queen

Stone Knight

Stone Maiden

TABLE OF THE HALLOWS & ELEMENTS

Spear Maiden

Spear Knight

Spear King Spear Queen

SOUTH

Grail Maiden

MERLIN GUINEVERE

Grail Knight

Grail Queen Grail King

WEST

PORTER AT THE GATE

Fig. 11.3: Restoration of the Courts of Joy Ritual: Starting Positions

Hallows that when these four holy and powerful objects are operative once more in the land, the Courts of Joy will be established and the balance of inner and outer lands restored.

For once, in times past, a knight came, seeking the Court of the Rich Fisherman. And while he sat at table that night, there came into the hall four maidens, each of whom carried a rare and wondrous thing: a sword whose blade glittered in the firelight; a spear whose point welled drops of blood; a cup, covered in a cloth of red gold; and a stone, four-square and mighty, which flashed with crystal points of fire.

(*The maidens enter: Sword Maiden, Spear Maiden, Grail Maiden and Stone Maiden bearing their Hallows. Silence while they process three times. On the third revolution they veer off to stand at the table of the elements in their quarter, facing inwards. Porter closes door after them.*)

PORTER: These four maidens passed through the hall in silence and were gone. But the one who sought the Hallows was so awed by the mystery of the damsels and the mighty power of what they bore, that he forgot to ask the question which would have healed the land. Now the land lies waste and the Hallows are hidden in the deepest of the realms within, where only seekers of true heart may come. Let all those gathered about the margins of this land attend and hear, for the quest is about to begin.

MERLIN: Is there a porter at the gate?

PORTER: There is and I am he, the Porter who stands at Merlin's threshold to the Island of the Strong Door, as this kingdom was once named. At this season of Midwinter I am the one appointed to guard the door and bid the quest begin. (*Rises and goes to East.*) Who stands in the East? (*Eastern officers rise.*)

SWORD KING & QUEEN: We stand in the East, elemental guardians of Air.

SWORD KING: I am the King without a sword. I long to wield the Sword of Light which shall set my kingdom right.

SWORD QUEEN: I am the Queen of Air, the keeper of the land's breath. Without the Sword of Light, the devastating winds blow through the kingdom, the will of the people is weak and dawn breaks to despair.

SWORD KNIGHT: I am a seeker through the lands, Champion of Air. It is my destiny one day to be king, but I must seek the Sword of Light in order to be worthy heir to this kingdom and win a maiden to be my queen.

PORTER: (*Moves to South.*) Who stands in the South? (*Southern officers rise.*)

SPEAR KING & QUEEN: We stand in the South, elemental guardians of Fire.

SPEAR KING: I am the King without a spear. I long to wield the Spear which Heals and Wounds, which shall set my kingdom right.

SPEAR QUEEN: I am the Queen of Fire, keeper of the blood of the land. Without the Spear which Heals and Wounds, the blood of the people is tainted and plague rages at noonday.

SPEAR KNIGHT: I am a seeker through the lands, Champion of Fire. It is my destiny one day to be king, but I must seek the Spear which Heals and Wounds in order to be worthy heir to this kingdom and win a maiden to be my queen.

PORTER: (*Moves to West.*) Who stands in the West? (*Western officers rise.*)

GRAIL KING & QUEEN: We stand in the West, elemental guardians of Water.

GRAIL KING: I am a King without a cup. I long to wield the Grail of Love which shall set my kingdom right.

GRAIL QUEEN: I am the Queen of Water, keeper of the waters of the land. Without the Grail of Love, the compassion of the people falters and twilight falls without a homecoming.

GRAIL KNIGHT: I am a seeker through the lands, Champion of Water. It is my destiny one day to be king, but I must seek the Grail of Love in order to be worthy heir to this kingdom and win a maiden to be my queen.

PORTER: (*Moves to North.*) Who stands in the North? (*Northern officers rise.*)

STONE KING & QUEEN: We stand in the North, elemental guardians of Earth.

STONE KING: I am the King without a stone of establishment. I long to wield the Stone of Knowledge which will set my kingdom right.

STONE QUEEN: I am the Queen of Earth, keeper of the body of the land. Without the Stone of Knowledge, the limbs of the people are weighted with lethargy and midnight comes without illumination.

STONE KNIGHT: I am a seeker through the lands, Champion of Earth. It is my destiny one day to be king, but I must seek the Stone of Knowledge in order to be worthy heir to this kingdom and win a maiden to be my queen.

PORTER: (*Circulates to his place in the West.*) The circle of Clas Myrddin is established, but there are other kingdoms in the worlds between. Who are they who stand at the crossing places, in the secret places, in the lands between?

MORGAN: I am Morgan, sometimes called Le Fay, sometimes shape-changer, but ever mistress of the worlds between. I rest between the worlds in the Isles of the Dead, the Orcades, where, in my turning tower, many are changed and remade. Now I watch the people of the land and await the coming of the Sword of Light, that there may arise one among them worthy to be sovereign in your realms and mine.

ARTHUR: I am Arthur Pendragon, once Emperor of this land and King yet to be. I rest between the worlds, at the White Mount, where once Bran the Blessed, wounded unto death, guarded the island until I fell in the Last Battle and took his place. Now I watch, wounded like him, awaiting the coming of the Spear which Heals and Wounds, that my wounds too might find healing.

GUINEVERE: I am Guinevere, once Empress of this island and Queen yet to be. I rest between the worlds in the Island of Glass, where once I was taken by my faery lover, Melwas the Winged. Now I watch, tormented by care, and await the coming of the Grail of Love, where all loves are reconciled.

MERLIN: I am Merlin Emrys, once magician of this island and its guardianship remains in my keeping. I rest between the worlds at Dinas Emrys where once I released the dragons to scour the kingdom of wrongdoing and evil kingship. Now I watch the people of this land and await the coming of the Stone of Knowledge, that there may arise among them new guardians of wisdom.

PORTER: The scattered circle of Llys Arthur is established, but there are other kingdoms in the lands beneath. Who are they who stand at the innermost earth, at the deep fountains, at the fissures of fire, at the fumes from the first rocks?

SWORD MAIDEN: I am the bearer of the Sword, its guardian and keeper. Whoever would seek the Sword of Light must fight with me. Whoever would win me must take me by the hand and claim me with a kiss.

SPEAR MAIDEN: I am the bearer of the Spear, its guardian and keeper. Whoever would seek the Spear which Heals and Wounds must learn of me. Whoever would win me must take me by the hand and claim me with a kiss.

GRAIL MAIDEN: I am the bearer of the Grail, its guardian and keeper. Whoever would seek the Grail of Love must ask of me. Whoever would win me must take me by the hand and claim me with a kiss.

STONE MAIDEN: I am the bearer of the Stone, its guardian and keeper. Whoever would win the Stone of Knowledge must answer me. Whoever would win me must take me by the hand and claim me with a kiss.

PORTER: the circle of the Underworld is established. With the circle of Llys Arthur and of Clas Myrddin, the worlds without, the worlds between and the worlds within stand ready. Is the company of one accord?

ALL: It is.

PORTER: Then let the quest for the Hallows begin. Let us look to the East of the lands adventurous. Champion of Air, stand forth!

(*Sword Knight turns to face Sword King and Queen.*)

SWORD KING: Champion of Air, we appoint you a wanderer in the lands adventurous, to seek and not to stay until you find the Sword of Light. For one day you shall be king of this land if you succeed.

SWORD QUEEN: Champion of Air, accept as token of your quest, this emblem of our kingdom. (*Gives incense stick.*) Let it be to you a breath

of hope until you find the Sword of Light by which the kingdom may be made bright.
SWORD KNIGHT: Lord and Lady, give your blessing on a wanderer in the wilderness.
(Sword King and Queen hold their left and right hands respectively over his head. He bows and departs towards the South, passing behind the Llys Arthur officers until he comes to the North East where he is challenged by Morgan.)
MORGAN: Champion of Air, you may not pass! Without the Sword of Light I can make no king.
SWORD KNIGHT: I have travelled in the Wastelands and in the wilderness but I have not found the Sword. Blessed Lady, do you know where it lies?
MORGAN: I am mistress of magics, the weaver at the web, queen of the turning castle. Within my orchard many knights lie mazed. Do you dare go where I will send you? To the places beneath, to the realms within? Then hold fast to your token, Champion of Air, knight yet to be king, and descend.
(Sword Knight spirals inward, in front of Llys Arthur officers, once, until he arrives at the eastern centre.)
SWORD MAIDEN: *(Turns to face East.)* Who approaches the realms within?
SWORD KNIGHT: A wanderer in the Wasteland.
SWORD MAIDEN: By what right do you come?
SWORD KNIGHT: By right of my sovereign lord, the King without a sword. By right of my sovereign lady, the Queen of Air. By right of the people of this land who need the Sword of Light. By right of the Lady Morgan, kingmaker.
SWORD MAIDEN: None may obtain the Sword of Light save the one who fights with me. *(She lifts the Sword for a blow but Sword Knight defends with his token.)*
SWORD KNIGHT: By virtue of this token I claim the Sword, that the keeper of the breath may be empowered, that the king may have his sword once more, that the people may find their way!
SWORD MAIDEN: You have triumphed, Champion of Air. Accept the Sword of Light in exchange for the token you bear, which I shall guard at the centre of the land, in the realms within.
(Sword Knight gives incense stick to Maiden who places it in eastern quarter of the Hallow table. She gives him Sword. Both bow to each other.)
SWORD KNIGHT: By this Sword of Light may my destiny be fulfilled. By its purpose may my children be directed. One day I shall be king; Maiden of the Sword, be queen of my kingdom in that day.
SWORD MAIDEN: I may not leave my guardianship yet, good knight. I am exiled here until another takes my place. If you find one willing to be keeper and guardian, bring her here and claim me with a kiss.
SWORD KNIGHT: I shall search the three worlds till I find a guardian,

that the Courts of Joy may be restored and all hearts set rejoicing. (*Sword Knight spirals round Hallow table until he comes to North East.*)
MORGAN: Bravely done, Champion of Air, you have gained the Sword of Light; yet your step falters, your mien is mournful. Come speak true, what ails you?
SWORD KNIGHT: I love the maiden who stands at the table of the Hallows in the place beneath, but she may not go from there until a guardian is found to take her place.
MORGAN: Then be cheerful, Champion of Air, for you have found her! When the Sword of Light is wielded in the lands, the king will come and my purpose be fulfilled. Conduct me from the Isles of the Dead, in the worlds between, to the realms within.
(*Sword Knight and Morgan spiral round Hallow table once until they arrive at the eastern centre.*)
MORGAN: Greetings, Maiden of the Sword, queen yet to be! (*To Sword Knight.*) Claim your lady with a kiss.
(*Sword Knight kisses Sword Maiden on cheek, Morgan joins their hands.*)
MORGAN: The quest for the Sword of Light is achieved, but there are other quests to accomplish. Until the finding of four Hallows of the land, the Courts of Joy cannot be restored, nor may you find your home until that day. I lay a destiny upon you that you wander in the worlds between until you come to the Isles of the Dead, sojourning there till the blowing of the horn of joy. I will guard the token of the kingdom of air that it may be purified in the realms within.
(*Sword Knight and Maiden spiral once round Hallow table until they come to North East where they stand.*)
PORTER: Let us look to the South of the lands adventurous. Champion of Fire, stand forth!
(*Spear Knight turns to face Spear King and Queen.*)
SPEAR KING: Champion of Fire, we appoint you a wanderer in the lands adventurous, to seek and not to stay, until you find the Spear which Heals and Wounds. For one day you shall be king of this land if you succeed.
SPEAR QUEEN: Champion of Fire, accept as token of your quest, this emblem of our kingdom. (*Gives candle.*) Let it be to you a beacon of light until you find the Spear which Heals and Wounds, by which the kingdom may be healed.
SPEAR KNIGHT: Lord and Lady, give your blessing on a wanderer in the wilderness.
(*Spear King and Queen hold their left and right hands respectively over his head. He bows and departs towards the West, passing behind the Llys Arthur positions until he comes to the South East where he is challenged by Arthur.*)
ARTHUR: Champion of Fire, you may not pass! Without the Spear which Heals and Wounds, my own wounds bleed still.
SPEAR KNIGHT: I have travelled in the Wastelands and in the

wilderness but I have not found the Spear. Dread Lord, do you know where it lies?
ARTHUR: I was lord of this land, its defender and champion. Do you dare to go where I once was? To the fires of Annwn, to the realms within? Then hold fast to your token, Champion of Fire, knight yet to be king, and descend.
(Spear Knight spirals inwards, in front of Llys Arthur positions, once, until he arrives at the southern centre.)
SPEAR MAIDEN: *(Turns to face South.)* Who approaches the realms within?
SPEAR KNIGHT: A wanderer in the Wasteland.
SPEAR MAIDEN: By what right do you come?
SPEAR KNIGHT: By right of my sovereign lord, the King without a spear. By right of my sovereign lady, Queen of Fire. By right of the people of this land who need the Spear which Heals and Wounds. By right of the Emperor Arthur whose wounds bleed yet.
SPEAR MAIDEN: None may obtain the Spear which Heals and Wounds save the one who learns of me. *(She holds the Spear point over his head.)*
SPEAR KNIGHT: I feel the pain and know the cure. *(He holds up his candle.)* By virtue of this token I claim the Spear, that the keeper of the blood may be empowered, that the King may have his spear once more, that the people may be healed.
SPEAR MAIDEN: You have triumphed, Champion of Fire. Accept the Spear which Heals and Wounds in exchange for the token you bear, which I shall guard at the centre of the land, in the realms within.
(Spear Knight gives candle to Maiden who places it in southern quarter of the Hallow table. She gives him Spear. Both bow to each other.)
SPEAR KNIGHT: By this Spear which Heals and Wounds may my destiny be fulfilled. By its wisdom shall my children flourish. One day I shall be king; Maiden of the Spear, be queen of my kingdom in that day.
SPEAR MAIDEN: I may not leave my guardianship yet, good knight. I am exiled here until another takes my place. If you find one willing to be keeper and guardian, bring him here and claim me with a kiss.
SPEAR KNIGHT: I shall search the three worlds till I find a guardian, that the Courts of Joy may be restored and all hearts set rejoicing.
(Spear Knight spirals round Hallow table until he comes to South East.)
ARTHUR: Bravely done, Champion of Fire, you have gained the Spear which Heals and Wounds, yet your step falters, your mien is mournful as my own when I returned with only seven from the confines of Annwn. Come, speak true, what ails you?
SPEAR KNIGHT: I love the maiden who stands at the table of the Hallows in the place beneath, but she may not go from there until a guardian is found to take her place.
ARTHUR: Then be cheerful, Champion of Fire, for you have found him! Lay but the point of the spear to my wounds and in return you

may conduct me from the White Mount in the worlds between, to the realms within.

(*Spear Knight touches Arthur's side with Spear point and both spiral round Hallow table once until they arrive at the southern centre.*)

ARTHUR: Greetings, Maiden of the Spear; queen yet to be! (*To Spear Knight*) Claim your lady with a kiss.

(*Spear Knight kisses Spear Maiden on cheek. Arthur joins their hands.*)

ARTHUR: The quest for the Spear which Heals and Wounds is achieved, but there are other quests to accomplish. Until the finding of the four Hallows of the land, the Courts of Joy cannot be restored, nor may you find your home until that day. Be heartened, no quest lasts forever. Until that time, I bid you wander in the worlds between until you find the White Mount, sojourning there until the blowing of the horn of joy. I will guard the token of the kingdom of Fire that it may be purified in the realms within.

(*Spear Knight and Maiden spiral once till they come to South East where they stand.*)

PORTER: Let us look to the West of the lands adventurous. Champion of Water, stand forth!

(*Grail Knight turns to face Grail King and Queen.*)

GRAIL KING: Champion of Water, we appoint you a wanderer in the lands adventurous, to seek and not to stay until you find the Grail of Love. For one day you shall be king of this land if you succeed.

GRAIL QUEEN: Champion of Water, accept as token of your quest this emblem of our kingdom. (*Gives phial of water.*) Let it be to you a sign of love in barren places until you find the Grail of Love by which the kingdom shall be made fertile.

GRAIL KNIGHT: Lord and Lady, give your blessing on a wanderer in the wildnerness.

(*Grail King and Queen hold their left and right hands respectively over his head. He bows and departs towards the North, passing behind the Llys Arthur positions until he comes to the South West where is challenged by Guinevere.*)

GUINEVERE: Champion of Water, you may not pass! Without the Grail of Love my heart is broken.

GRAIL KNIGHT: I have travelled in the Wastelands and in the wilderness but I have not found the Grail of Love. Sovereign Lady, do you know where it lies?

GUINEVERE: I was lady of this land, its mistress and its joy. Would you go where I was taken, to the courts of faery, to the realms within? Then hold fast to your token, Champion of Water, knight yet to be king, and descend.

(*Grail Knight spirals inwards, in front of Llys Arthur positions once, until he arrives at the western centre.*)

GRAIL MAIDEN: (*Turns to face West.*) Who approaches the realms within?

GRAIL KNIGHT: A wanderer in the wilderness.
GRAIL MAIDEN: By what right do you come?
GRAIL KNIGHT: By right of my sovereign lord, the King without a cup. By right of my sovereign lady, the Queen of Water. By right of the people of the land who need the Grail of Love. By right of the Empress Guinevere whose heart is sore.
GRAIL MAIDEN: None may obtain the Grail of Love save the one who asks of me.
GRAIL KNIGHT: What is the significance of the Grail?
GRAIL MAIDEN: It signifies service.
GRAIL KNIGHT: Whom does the Grail serve?
GRAIL MAIDEN: It serves all who serve the Grail.
GRAIL KNIGHT: By virtue of this token I claim the Grail, that the keeper of the waters be empowered, that the King may have his cup once more, that the people may learn compassion.
GRAIL MAIDEN: You have triumphed, Champion of Water. Accept the Grail of Love in exchange for the token you bear, which I shall guard at the centre of the land, in the realms within.
(Grail Knight gives phial to Maiden who places it in western quarter of the Hallow table. She gives him the Grail. Both bow to each other.)
GRAIL KNIGHT: By this Grail of Love may my destiny be fulfilled. By its fertility shall my children be engendered and nourished. One day I shall be king; Maiden of the Grail, be queen of my kingdom in that day.
GRAIL MAIDEN: I may not leave my guardianship yet, good knight. I am exiled here until another takes my place. If you find one willing to be keeper and guardian, bring her here and claim me with a kiss.
GRAIL KNIGHT: I shall search the three worlds till I find a guardian, that the Courts of Joy may be restored and all hearts set rejoicing.
(Grail Knight spirals round Hallow table until he comes to South West.)
GUINEVERE: Bravely done, Champion of Water, you have gained the Grail of Love! Yet your step falters, your mien is mournful as my own when I stood arraigned before the court. Come, speak true, what ails you?
GRAIL KNIGHT: I love the maiden who stands at the table of the Hallows in the place beneath, but she may not go from there until a guardian is found to take her place.
GUINEVERE: Then be cheerful, Champion of Water, for you have found her! Set but the rim of the Grail to my lips and mend my heart. In return you may conduct me from the Isle of Glass in the worlds between, to the realms within.
(Grail Knight gives Guinevere to drink and both spiral round Hallow table once until they arrive at the western centre.)
GUINEVERE: Greetings, Maiden of the Grail, queen yet to be! (*To Grail Knight*) Claim your lady with a kiss.
(Grail Knight kisses Grail Maiden on cheek. Guinevere joins their hands.)

GUINEVERE: The quest for the Grail of Love is achieved, but there is another quest to accomplish. Until the finding of the four Hallows of the land, the Courts of Joy cannot be restored, nor may you find your home until that day. Be happy, though you may not yet be one, for you may wander in the worlds between until you come to the Isle of Glass, sojourning there till the blowing of the horn of joy. I will guard the token of the kingdom of Water that it may be purified in the realms within.

(Grail Knight and Maiden spiral once round Hallow table until they come to South West where they stand.)

PORTER: Let us look to the North of the lands adventurous. Champion of Earth stand forth!

(Stone Knight turns to face Stone King and Queen.)

STONE KING: Champion of Earth, we appoint you a wanderer in the lands adventurous to seek and not to stay until you find the Stone of Knowledge. For one day you shall be king of this land if you succeed.

STONE QUEEN: Champion of Earth, accept as token of your quest this emblem of our kingdom. (*Gives him bag of earth.*) Let it be to you a sign of fellowship until you find the Stone of Knowledge by which the kingdom shall be made creative.

STONE KNIGHT: Lord and Lady, give your blessing on a wanderer in the wilderness.

(Stone King and Queen hold their left and right hands respectively over his head. He bows and departs towards the East, passing behind the Llys Arthur positions, until he comes to the North West where he is challenged by Merlin.)

MERLIN: Champion of Earth, you may not pass! Without the Stone of Knowledge I can teach no wisdom.

STONE KNIGHT: I have travelled in the Wastelands and in the wilderness but I have not found the Stone of Knowledge. Reverend Master, do you know where it lies?

MERLIN: I am master of magics, the keeper of the kingdom, the upholder of the law. I have been in many worlds, but do you dare to go where I will send you? To the places beneath, to the realms within? Then hold fast to your emblem, Champion of Earth, knight yet to be king, and descend.

(Stone Knight spirals inward, in front of Llys Arthur positions, once until he arrives at northern centre.)

STONE MAIDEN: (*Turns to face North.*) Who approaches the realms within?

STONE KNIGHT: A wanderer in the Wasteland.

STONE MAIDEN: By what right do you come?

STONE KNIGHT: By right of my sovereign lord, the King without a stone of establishment. By right of my sovereign lady, the Queen of Earth. By right of the people of this land who need the Stone of Knowledge. By right of the Master Merlin, Keeper of the Law.

STONE MAIDEN: None may obtain the Stone of Knowledge unless they answer me. Who is she who stands: a maiden, a warrior, a queen, a crone?
STONE KNIGHT: Who but Sovereignty, the true Lady of the Land?
STONE MAIDEN: Who represents her in the worlds without?
STONE KNIGHT: Who but the rightful sovereign, man or woman, who wields the Hallows for the good of the land and its people? By virtue of this token I claim the Stone of Knowledge that the keeper of the land's life may be empowered, that the king may have his stone of establishment, that the people may be made creative.
STONE MAIDEN: You have triumphed, Champion of Earth. Accept the Stone of Knowledge in exchange for the token you bear, which I shall guard at the centre of the realms within.
(Stone Knight gives her his bag of earth which she places on the northern quarter of the Hallows table. She gives him the Stone. Both bow to each other.)
STONE KNIGHT: By this Stone of Knowledge shall my destiny be fulfilled. By its law shall my children live. One day I shall be king; Maiden of the Stone, be queen of my kingdom in that day.
STONE MAIDEN: I may not leave my guardianship yet, good knight. I am exiled here until another takes my place. If you find one willing to be keeper and guardian, bring him here and claim me with a kiss.
STONE KNIGHT: I shall search the three worlds till I find a guardian, that the Courts of Joy may be restored and all hearts set rejoicing.
(Stone Knight spirals round Hallow table once until he comes to North West.)
MERLIN: Bravely done, Champion of Earth, you have gained the Stone of Knowledge, yet your step falters, your mien is mournful. Come, speak true, what ails you?
STONE KNIGHT: I love the maiden who stands at the table of the Hallows in the place beneath, but she may not go from there until a guardian is found to take her place.
MERLIN. Then be cheerful, Champion of Earth, for you have found him! When the Stone of Knowledge is wielded in the lands, the laws of the kingdom will be understood and my purpose be fulfilled. Conduct me from the heights of Dinas Emrys in the worlds between, to the realms within.
(Stone Knight and Merlin spiral round Hallow table once until they arrive at the northern centre.)
MERLIN: Greetings, Maiden of the Stone, queen yet to be! (*To Stone Knight*) Claim your lady with a kiss. (*Stone Knight kisses Stone Maiden on cheek. Merlin joins their hands.*) The quest for the Stone of Knowledge is achieved; there are no other quests to accomplish at this time. The Hallows of the Land are found and the Courts of Joy may be restored. None but we who stand at the elemental table of the Hallows may witness these mysteries. Go quickly and with joy to your

own lands, Knight and Maiden of the Stone, by way of Dinas Emrys. Knights and Maidens all, return to your own homes and present the Hallows to your Sovereigns.
(Stone Knight and Maiden spiral round Hallow table to North West and return to North. All Knights and Maidens pass directly to their home quarter, facing King and Queen.)
SWORD KNIGHT: Behold Sovereign Lord of Air, the Sword of Light! I give it into your hands. (*Sword King receives Sword.*)
SWORD KING: Thanks be to you, Champion of Air! You have done bravely and well.
SWORD QUEEN: Champion of Air, I gave into your hands a token of our kingdom; where is it now?
SWORD KNIGHT: Sovereign lady, I gave it into the keeping of this maiden.
SWORD MAIDEN: From my hands it passed into the keeping of the guardian in the realms within.
MORGAN: (*Facing East*) Greetings, Lord and Lady of Air! I hold the emblem of the kingdom of Air in trust where it shall be purified. Wield well the Sword of Light by which kings and queens are made, by which the people are empowered and the land restored. For now are the worlds without and the realms within aligned and operative. (*She holds up incense stick. Sword King and Queen raise the Sword between them.*) There stand before you two who will be king and queen in the years to come: let them be recognized in the kingdom of Air. (*Sword King invites Knight to sit beside him. Sword Queen invites Maiden to sit beside her.*)
SPEAR KNIGHT: Behold, Sovereign Lord of Fire, the Spear which Heals and Wounds. I give it into your hands. (*Spear King receives Spear.*)
SPEAR KING: Thanks be to you, Champion of Fire! You have done bravely and well.
SPEAR QUEEN: Champion of Fire, I gave into your hand a token of our kingdom; where is it now?
SPEAR KNIGHT: Sovereign Lady, I gave it into the keeping of this maiden.
SPEAR MAIDEN: From my hands it passed into the keeping of the guardian in the realms within.
ARTHUR: (*Facing South*) Greetings, Lord and Lady of Fire! I hold the emblem of the kingdom of Fire in trust where it shall be purified. Wield well the Spear which Heals and Wounds, by which kings and queens govern their lands, by which the people are healed and the land restored. For now are the worlds without and the realms within aligned and operative. (*He holds up candle. Spear King and Queen raise the Spear between them.*) There stand before you two who will be king and queen in the years to come: let them be recognized in the kingdom of Fire. (*Spear King invites Knight to sit beside him. Spear Queen invites Maiden to sit beside her.*)

GRAIL KNIGHT: Behold, Sovereign Lord of Water, the Grail of Love! I give it into your hands. (*Grail King receives Grail.*)
GRAIL KING: Thanks be to you, Champion of Water! You have done bravely and well.
GRAIL QUEEN: Champion of Water, I gave into your hands a token of our kingdom; where is it now?
GRAIL KNIGHT: Sovereign Lady, I gave it into the keeping of this maiden.
GRAIL MAIDEN: From my hands it passed into the keeping of the guardian in the realms within.
GUINEVERE: (*Facing West*) Greetings, Lord and Lady of Water! I hold the emblem of the kingdom of Water in trust where it shall be purified. Wield well the Grail of Love by which kings and queens rule with mercy, by which the people are taught compassion and the land restored. For now are the worlds without and the realms within aligned and operative. (*She holds up phial of water. Grail King and Queen raise the Grail between them.*)
GUINEVERE: There stand before you two who will be king and queen in the years to come; let them be recognized in the kingdom of Water. (*Grail King invites Knight to sit beside him. Grail Queen invites Maiden to sit beside her.*)
STONE KNIGHT: Behold, Sovereign Lord of Earth, the Stone of Knowledge! I give it into your hands. (*Stone King receives Stone.*)
STONE KING: Thanks be to you, Champion of Earth. You have done bravely and well.
STONE QUEEN: Champion of Earth, I gave into your hands a token of our kingdom; where is it now?
STONE KNIGHT: Sovereign Lady, I gave it into the keeping of this maiden.
STONE MAIDEN: From my hands it passed into the keeping of the guardian of the realms within.
MERLIN: (*Facing North*) Greetings, Lord and Lady of Earth! I hold the emblem of the kingdom of Earth in trust where it shall be purified. Wield well the Stone of Knowledge by which kings and queens rule with discernment and wisdom, by which the people are enlivened and the land restored. For now are the worlds without and the realms within aligned and operative. (*He holds up bag of earth. Stone King and Queen raise the Stone between them.*) There stand before you two who will be king and queen in the years to come; let them be recognized in the kingdom of Earth. (*Stone King invites Knight to sit beside him. Stone Queen invites Maiden to sit beside her.*) How stands the land, Porter at the Gate, Keeper of my Threshold?
PORTER: The trees are in bud, the fields gather their goodness, the waters flow, the hearts of the people awaken and the guardians stand ready.
MERLIN: (*To Hallow table guardians*) You who stand with me at the

land's centre, who have seen the Llys Arthur re-established in the realms within, is there hope for this land?
MORGAN, ARTHUR, GUINEVERE, MERLIN: There is.
MERLIN: Kings, queens, knights and maidens who stand at the four cities of this island, is there hope for this land?
ALL QUARTER OFFICERS: There is.
MERLIN: Good people, who stand about the borders of this island, my enclosure, is there hope for this land?
ALL: There is.
MERLIN: Then let the Courts of Joy be restored among us and a new quest begun. Porter at the Gate, let the horn sound to the four corners of the kingdom.
(Porter stands and blows horn at East, South, West and North, or the company chant the note of joy. Then Porter circulates back to his place in the West and sits.)
MERLIN: Let all within this land hear and obey the coming of Joy in the silent wondering of their hearts.

Mediation of the Courts of Joy

(There is a pause of at least five minutes during which the company mediate the energies raised by this ritual.)
PORTER: The sound of the horn goes forth through the land. The Hallows are established at the four corners of the Island of the Strong Door; the Maidens of the Wells and the Knights of the Wood no longer wander through the forests. There is peace on all peoples. See about us the land of Logres, with Llys Arthur at its midst where the ever-living guardians have their court. See, in every part of the land, the establishment of the Hallows, bringing that which is out of balance into alignment by the mighty power of their action . . .

Once I guarded the gateway into Llys Arthur, the Court of my lord the King. No longer do I guard the entrance to Clas Myrddin alone for there are many, seen and unseen, who assist me to hold the gate. All who are present here, through their participation in these rites, are made guardians with me . . .

I ask you all, will you share the guardianship of the land and help found among all peoples of the world the Courts of Joy?
ALL: We will.
PORTER: Then let these rites be ended. Guardians of the East, is the Sword of Light operative in the land?
EASTERN OFFICERS: It is.
PORTER: Guardians of the South, is the Spear which Heals and Wounds operative in the land?
SOUTHERN OFFICERS: It is.
PORTER: Guardians of the West, is the Grail of Love operative in the land?
WESTERN OFFICERS: It is.

PORTER: Guardians of the North, is the Stone of Knowledge operative in the land?
NORTHERN OFFICERS: It is.
PORTER: Guardian of the realms within, is the element of Air purified and operative in this land?
MORGAN: It is.
PORTER: Guardian of the realms within, is the element of Fire purified and operative in this land?
ARTHUR: It is.
PORTER: Guardian of the realms within, is the element of Water purified and operative in this land?
GUINEVERE: It is.
PORTER: Guardian of the realms within, is the element of Earth purifed and operative in this land?
MERLIN: It is.
PORTER: In token of this alignment of the worlds within and the worlds without let all partake of the Grail. (*Faces Grail King and Queen.*) Lord and Lady of Water, I ask that you give into my hands for a short while the vessel of the Grail, that all may drink. (*Grail King and Queen give it to him. He gives all to drink, starting at West. When all have drunk in outer circle, he spirals inwards to give Grail to Llys Arthur officers. Giving last to Morgan who gives him to drink, he spirals out again to the West and gives Grail back to Grail King and Queen.*) All have partaken of the Grail. Lord and Lady of Water, I give you thanks for your trust in me. (*He returns to his place.*) Lady Morgan, grant a blessing.
MORGAN: May all in this company be blessed by the dwellers in Avalon!
PORTER: Then let the Hallows be processed about Clas Myrddin and let their power go throughout the land. (*Porter opens door. Eastern Officers: King and Queen with Sword, followed by Knight and Maiden, circle clockwise, showing the Sword to each quarter, after East they circle and exit West.*)
(*Southern Officers: King and Queen with Spear, followed by Knight and Maiden circle clockwise, showing the Spear to each quarter: after South they circle and exit West.*)
(*Western Officers: King and Queen with Grail, followed by Knight and Maiden circle clockwise, showing the Grail to each quarter: after West they circle and exit West.*)
(*Northern Officers: King and Queen with Stone, followed by Knight and Maiden circle clockwise, showing the Stone to each quarter: after North they circle and exit West.*)
PORTER: Let all those who now guard Merlin's Enclosure with me, depart, bearing the Joy of the Court to their homes. On all, Peace and Blessing! (*All depart and are given gifts. When all are gone, central guardians depart and receive gifts with quarter officers.*)

EMPOWERMENT BY THE HALLOW GUARDIANS

Each *Hallowquest* user has in their hands the symbolic keys of personal and national empowerment. Empowerment does not mean aggrandizing, nor does it have any bearing on 'prosperity consciousness'. The Hallows are the deep inner elemental qualities by which lands and people are kept in balance. Our lives, our land and our society in this age are usually sadly imbalanced: everyone wants to get, no one wants to give. The rebalancing of matters as seemingly diverse as the right use of the earth's resources, the right adjustment of personality disorders or imbalances and the reanimation of spiritual values within one's own state or government are all part of the Healing of the Land which the Hallows effect.

Although it is nowhere suggested that the objects of the Hallows are physically buried, like treasure trove, in our own lands, they are indeed that which empowers those lands. In writing here solely about the Arthurian world we have employed only one possible set of symbols; these, as we see from p.130, are in turn derived from even earlier prototype symbols. Each land will have its own native mythos and set of power objects/symbols. If each person in each country in the world were to become aware of the inner balancing of which we are all capable, the earth would indeed be healed. Until that time, it is for each of us to find our own ways of empowerment.

This work may be best begun on a personal basis, bearing in mind that deep empowerment is not finally a matter of personal enriching — although of course that may happen along the way. In the last analysis, empowerment by the Hallows is a communication which rays out to affect all areas of one's own life and that of others; one's society, culture and country. All esoteric practitioners are engaged on the Great Work — the gathering in of all that is created for the good of all.

We might begin by making an inner journey or vision quest, either meditating on our own or using the Hallows pathworking on p.147. We should work and meditate over a period of months on each side of the Hallow symbols we have chosen to use, learning the inner symbolism of each of the elemental directions, qualities etc. By this work, we will find ourselves encountering the Hallow guardians themselves and so our inner communion will be deepened. The Hallow guardians are not figments of imagination, nor are they pathologies appearing in the deranged mind, but inner, living powers who hold in their keeping the great symbols by which our life is steered. They are not gods to be worshipped, but powers to be reverenced, as we would respect any great teacher who empowered us with wisdom, skill and knowledge. Finding ways of empowerment may prove to be a long journey, taking a lifetime of commitment, but we should appreciate that the work of the Hallow guardians transcends time; it is applicable in any age and is a power which they share with the companions of the Hallows. For in each age there are such companions who, in their own way, derive support and instruction in the guarding of the earth's wisdom. Just as the Hallow guardians communicate this lore to the companions of the Hallows, so do the companions communicate this teaching to the world.

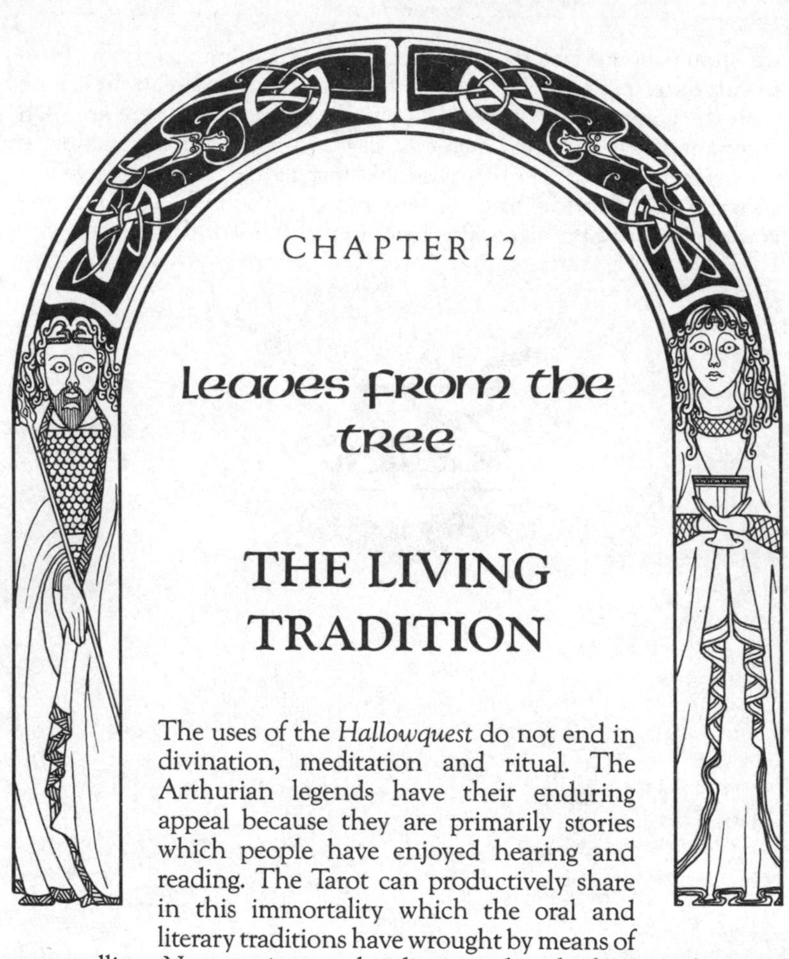

CHAPTER 12

Leaves from the tree

THE LIVING TRADITION

The uses of the *Hallowquest* do not end in divination, meditation and ritual. The Arthurian legends have their enduring appeal because they are primarily stories which people have enjoyed hearing and reading. The Tarot can productively share in this immortality which the oral and literary traditions have wrought by means of story-telling. New stories can be discovered with these cards, ones which will become non-canonical Arthurian legends.

Story-telling with the *Hallowquest* pack can be very exciting. New strands of the tradition emerge and characters stand out in totally different lights. The Arthurian Power in charge of this living tradition is, of course, Taliesin, for he holds the links of ancestral lore and esoteric wisdom in his hands. Whoever has heard his story becomes aware of other stories, because all his hearers are immediately connected with the springs of tradition.

The following exercises can be pursued on many levels: treat them as relaxation and enjoyment, allow the undiscovered humour of the Tarot to bubble up; treat Tarot story-telling in the light of an enjoyable teaching aid rather than as a very serious esoteric chore. The use of games and play within the history of spiritual wisdom is a somewhat forgotten art, but we can redeem the time by allowing ourselves the liberty to enjoy while we learn.

The parables of Jesus would never have been so popular with the people had he told them as esoteric aphorisms. The fact that they were stories which could be heard by everybody was the secret of their success, because no one need take them seriously but listened with an open heart instead.

The Tarot cards themselves have been used as playing cards: in Renaissance Italy large amounts of money changed hands in the game of *tarocchi*.

In Tibet, the Game of Rebirth was played by all kinds of people from monks down to children. It was a board game of the snakes and ladders variety on which many sacred and cosmological images from the Tibetan deities down to the levels of hell were ranged. The throw of a dice determined one's status upon the board, and the first one into nirvana won the game.[73]

Story-telling in one form or another has proved to be the mainstay of the spirit, whether it be tales from the Bible or the many novels our society greedily consumes. Stories reveal other pathways, different possibilities, and, as a species, humanity has a great interest and curiosity in how other people live and cope with life. The salvific stories of scriptures and mythology remain the living tradition for many — these are 'stories to live by'. Mundane story-telling nourishes us on other levels and serves as an accompaniment and pastime in our society, but its effects are nonetheless deep.

The suggestions outlined in this chapter can only present a few of the treasures of story-telling. Find your own stories, tell them, write them, become part of the living tradition.

THE 'TO BE CONTINUED' GAME

This game needs a circle of people. They do not need to have knowledge of the *Hallowquest*, nor indeed of any Tarot, to play, just a sense of fun and a quick imagination. Deal out the pack until all the cards are used up, or deal a determined number of cards per person so that everyone has an equal chance. There are no winners or losers in this game. The person to the left of the dealer starts the story off with a card chosen from their hand. At any point they can stop their story with the declaration: 'To be continued'. At which the next person on their left must take up the story using a card from their hand. The cards are shown to the circle at the beginning of each episode but after they have been used once they must be discarded in the centre.

The ingenuity of the players will be taxed not only by the challenge of each new episode demanded of them, but by their diminishing store of ideas. The rules are very flexible in this game. The circle may decide criteria at the outset, agreeing, for example, that unsuccessful continuations must retain their cards and forfeit their turn, and may only use that same card again on the next round. The rules will be dictated by the age and abilities of the players. Hardened story-tellers can make things very difficult for themselves by deciding that the story must have a particular theme or historical setting, for example. Garrulous players can be deterred from hogging the game by the imposition of a time or sentence limit. The unskilled player can be shielded from loss of face by allowing anyone in the circle to thread as little as just one sentence before handing on the story, for example. The person holding the last card must bring the story to a satisfactory conclusion.

This game certainly tests and improves one's skills as a raconteur. Lone players can switch on a tape recorder and see how they manage to string together a story from a determined number of cards.

TAROT IMPROVISATION GAME

This game calls for a number of ready and willing players, and can be quite an ice-breaker in Tarot workshops or seminars. It can have endless variations and applications, but basically each person draws a card and takes on the persona of the character depicted upon it. This may entail editing the pack down to the Arthurian Powers and the Court cards, for practical purposes. Individual cards can introduce themselves and quick character sketches of their life and attributes can be given, but the most effective use of this game is when the designated Tarot master or mistress becomes playwright and instructs his or her protagonists to improvise a short scenario. Esoteric workshops can also make this game the basis of a ritual encounter. The interaction of each card becomes immediately apparent and in the Tarot workshop, this game can be used as a practical demonstration of a reading. The Tarot master or mistress introduces each card and questions its actor from the floor, asking pertinent questions which surround the subject of the scenario, introducing fresh cards and instructing them to interact as necessary. Give time for each person to meditate on their card. The archetypes will do the rest. This game can provide challenging insights into the nature of the *Hallowquest* pack without the necessity for ritual prepration.

MAKING TAROT STORIES

For the lone player, the most rewarding way of making stories is probably by writing them down, although he or she can of course tell stories to others. The easiest method of making a story is to draw a number of cards from the pack and, just as though one was going to give a reading, lay them down in a spread. Alternatively, cards can be drawn randomly to provide the pegs on which the story hangs. The best number seems to be between eight and thirteen cards. Two examples conclude this book, showing how the *Hallowquest* need not automatically be used to create Arthurian stories. Obviously the imposition of Arthurian imagery upon the cards will dictate certain strictures for some people who might feel constrained to frame historical scenarios only. The cards are much more flexible than this, as are the concepts which animate them so demonstrably during divinatory spreads. With imagination and insight, stories of all kinds can emerge. The creation of a Tarot story is a good test of one's skills as a Tarot consultant, for exactly the same resources go into a reading as go into a story. One is constantly tracing the thread of the story and getting an overall picture.

Tarot stories are not considered to be a separate genre of literature, so you need not feel constrained to fit a certain style, for they are neither crime nor romance, not high literature nor penny dreadful. A Tarot story arises from the impulse of the cards alone and will dictate its own boundaries. It is also a rewarding way of exploring the cards in a more imaginative way and allows the creative springs underlying the images to work unhindered.

There follow two examples of Tarot stories, written by the authors. They were created in different ways. For 'The Peace King' by Caitlín Matthews, a sequence of 11 cards were drawn randomly from the pack. The story unfolded directly from the face images of the cards in the same sequence as the cards were drawn.

For 'The Maiden of the Spear' by John Matthews, the suit of Spears was deliberately chosen from the pack and then certain cards from that suit picked to form the story. The cards of the Grail Knight and the Washer at the Ford were also included as the story developed, since both these bore images which fitted the story.

Neither story is directly Arthurian in content, though their implications are close to the heart of the *Hallowquest*. Both authors are grateful to the writer and story-teller Rachel Pollack for introducing them to Tarot story-telling. You can read more such stories in *Tarot Tales* edited by Rachel Pollack and Caitlín Matthews.[40]

'THE PEACE KING'

My children, this story is for your remembrance and that of your own children. It is a tale from the period of the Days of Darkness, a story of retreat from oppression, of losing and finding. There are few who survive from those days but they, like your old grandfather, escaped the Death-bringers because they ran away. If there are heroic tales from those days, then there are none to sing them, for all who took up weapons against the outlanders, died upon the field and were buried where they fell.

It was April, in the year when the People's Voice was shackled to the Iron Fists. Throughout the land, city after city fell to their onslaught. All day, the troops of the outlanders had ringed the city, attempting to penetrate the walls. The high towers of the minster were now aflame with their fiery projectiles and at several points the walls had been breached. The city guard, under the command of York's captain, Peter Swallow, had held the marauders back where they could, but it was soon obvious that the outlanders outnumbered our forces.

I was no soldier, being but 13 years old, but I had a pointed stick and knew where to hide if the outlanders broke through our defences. My mother had turned off the radio because it could only transmit the Iron Fist's message of despair. All the free stations had gone off the air and that made our predicament worse, since my father worked at the Catterick Free Voice not 30 miles away. The radio's silence meant that he might now be dead or in enemy hands.

The firing grew worse, so we wrapped my sister in a blanket and took our emergency supplies down to the next level. She was crying quietly and shivering, so my mother began a story.

'There was once a tree that reached down to the roots of the world. Its branches were so lofty that it broke several stars and the pieces fell to earth. They fell so fast that they embedded themselves in different places all over the world. But the heart of the stars fell more slowly, turning over and over, round and round until they formed bowls, cups and dishes of crystal. These crystal cups were full of healing power and, it was said, there was one for every country. Whoever found one became its guardian for ever after and administered the healing power of the star-crystal to the people of that place.'

'What is crystal?' asked my sister. She had never left the city because

she suffered from the wasting sickness. It was only a matter of time before she would have to be carried everywhere.

My mother reached inside her smock and pulled out a golden chain with a green stone upon it. It was a precious jewel handed down in our family and there were many stories about it. Ruth took the bright jewel in her thin, transparent hands.

'This stone is said to be part of one of those cups. Perhaps one day it will be a part of one again.' She looked at me then with naked eyes — just as she sometimes looked at my father. 'Michael, you must take it and find your father.'

'And leave you here?' I cried.

She put a hand over my protesting mouth. I saw that she knew something very clearly; she had been a certified clear speaker before the days of the Iron Fists. The clarity of her thought burned me through. I looked into her dark eyes and saw what she meant me to do. Leave the city by the secret ways we both knew and find the truth of her story. That was why she had told it then in its barest form, to remind me.

She put the chain over my head. 'You are its bearer now. Go to the place and meet your father. Ruth and I will make our own way.' She clutched my sister to her thin side as though the two of them together would make a formidable opponent. I knew then the reason why she had given me extra rations, pretending that there had been a fresh allowance for boys of fighting age. She had stinted herself in order to feed me. The Iron Fists killed men but enslaved women and children. Ruth could not even run back to the city walls in times of danger; she would never survive a journey through the wilderness. I felt such torment and anger that I almost struck my sister for being ill. I would have argued with my mother but my words were lost as the walls above us crashed down, filling the cellar with brick dust.

When it cleared, my mother and sister were lying as though asleep under a heap of rubble. They were beyond the terrors of the Iron Fists and the cruel outlanders now. Ashamed of my former anger, and choked by tears, I squeezed my way down the air vent, emerging hot and grimy under the lowering sky of evening. The cherry trees in the lane were covered with a black blossom from the wreckage of the burning city. Everywhere people were scurrying in all directions, seeking safety and shelter.

Parties of outlanders were looting and killing. I stood no chance of escaping unless I was disguised as one of them. I found an Iron Fist soldier lying half-way over a fence, felled by a broken bottle. Struggling out of my tunic I pulled on his helmet and leather shirt. There was a dispatch satchel across his chest and I took that as well. It contained orders or messages of some kind.

After that I stopped running and walked with purpose to the East Gate. The helmet didn't fit, so I let it dangle from its strap over my shoulder. I was too short for a soldier, but the outlanders might mistake me for a messenger well enough. In the chaos there were men giving commands. I saw one, a tall fair man with a long nose. He looked impatient and angry and not a little disgusted. I looked at him too long, for he focused upon me and pointed:

'You, boy. I need you to run back to base.'

I hesitated a fraction, wondering whether I could kick him in the groin and run for it. He barked, 'Come here!'

I came. Shouting further orders at his lieutenant, he walked me into the crypt of the nearby chapel. It had been turned into a field operations room and dressing station combined. Transmitters were flashing, men screaming and groaning, while above, the last light filtered through the coloured glass on to the altar — now cleared of its cross and candles — where a map was laid.

'Do you have your map?' he asked me, looking over the enemy positions spread before him.

'Er, no sir.' I said, drawing myself to attention.

He felt in his greatcoat, 'Here, take this one. I'm sending you with a mobile unit. I've a message for Station B9 which you will deliver to Commander Foley.'

I could scarcely control my trembling. The man's impatience suddenly ran out of him, 'You're very young for this business. Here, drink some brandy.' I took a pull on his flask. 'When you've delivered the message, you're to accompany Count Erskine back to base after that. He's been severely wounded and I can't spare any able soldiers to attend to him. Our men seem to have shelled the city hospital by mistake and we have failed to capture any skilled surgeons.'

I nearly fainted with surprise. Count Erskine was a noble of our own royal house who had betrayed us to the enemy. My father had forbidden mention of the traitor's name in our home, he was so loathed by the people.

'What is your name, boy? I see you are of the public-spirited Flame Squadron.' I looked down at the flash on my leather shirt: a torch upheld in a clenched fist. This squadron had been formed from willing conscripts, so the radio said, but it was more likely that men joined in order to eat and have money for their families.

'I am Michael —' I searched for a different name, 'Michael Elder, sir.'

'Well, Elder, — you have an aged name for one so young!' I hated him for having time to joke while my mother and sister lay dead because of him. 'This is a heavy task, but you have a good driver. If you should be attacked or your vehicle immobilized, use this on Count Erskine. He would not wish to fall into enemy hands.'

He gave me a finely-wrought dagger, which I thrust into my belt. I could hardly believe my luck: transport out of York and a chance to kill our enemy!

'Commander Crozier, you are wanted on the walls. A message has just come in.' A grey-uniformed clerk in headphones handed him a dispatch. He studied the paper and directed me to some orderlies.

The infamous Count Erskine was lying on a stretcher. His well-known face was twisted in agony and a pool of blood welled up from under the sheet.

'If he screams, give him one of these,' directed one of the orderlies, giving me a phial of red pills. 'But only every hour or so. These are the last ones left.'

They thrust him into the back of a jeep. Erskine screamed sharply.

'What's wrong with him?' I asked.

'Bullet in the belly,' spat one, shortly.

'Internal bleeding as well, I shouldn't wonder,' said the other, with relish. I was amazed that they should hate him even as much as we did.

I swung up into the jeep beside the driver — a corpulent man with threads of black hair plastered across his brow.

'I'd put on that helmet, if I was you,' he suggested. 'Them shells is a bit close.'

XII the wounded king

He turned the jeep past a pot-hole and jack-knifed a three-point turn towards the East Gate. I turned to look at the city: the twin towers of the minster were no more. The river was full of burning vehicles and corpses. The setting sun was obscured by smoke.

While we waited at the check-point for clearance, the driver turned and offered a hand to me, 'Jack Tolland or Black Jack, to me mates. What's your manner of calling?'

I was worrying about the check-point, since I had no papers. An Iron Fist commando demanded my orders. I thrust them at him, one hand on the dagger.

He scanned the paper and glanced curiously at the stretcher in the back. 'Right, Michael Elder, escort and prisoner advance!'

Black Jack put his foot down as best he could against the incoming soldiery. As we bumped our way Eastwards, I pondered. Commander Crozier had obviously expected me to know that Erskine was a prisoner. In my ignorance, I had assumed that he was an honoured officer returning wounded to his unit.

'How far is Station B9?' I asked, as casually as I could.

'About another 40 miles at this rate,' said Black Jack. 'Why? You hungry or something? There's bread and sausage in the bag if you want it.'

I'd left my specially garnered rations in the cellar and even neglected to take the wounded soldier's water-bottle. I was too numb to even weep for the city of York. So I was cramming my mouth with sausage when I heard the news.

Peter Swallow, our great captain, had been captured. The word was being passed along the road by the oncoming troops. They were in triumphal mood. We heard of how Swallow and his men had attempted a charge on horseback across the other side of the river against the crack contingent of Iron Fist commandos. Our men had had no artillery left, no ammunition for guns. They had fought hand to hand with weapons from the museum walls

before being cut down by a hail of machine-gun fire.

'Well that's good news,' shouted Black Jack, heartily into the triumphal crowd. 'What's to do now?'

'They're putting up his head on Micklegate,' shouted one drunken bully.

My own groans were fortunately covered by the moaning of Erskine. I turned on him, 'You hear! you filthy traitor? Peter Swallow is dead because of you. And if you think I'm giving you these pain-killers, then you can think again!'

I almost flung them off the jeep, but Black Jack caught my hand: 'Steady, lad. We might need them ourselves yet.' But he didn't seem to think my outburst peculiar.

It was almost dark, too dark to see the roads without headlights and Black Jack refused to continue with them on because of possible ambush. But he pushed on for a few miles more.

Later, squinting at the map by the shaded light of a torch, I thought we were lost and said so.

Black Jack drove on still, ignoring me. He suspects me, I thought. He's going to hand me over to the Iron Fists. A few moments more and he stopped, pulling over by a great stone.

'Here we are — the Ploughstone. That's as far as I can take you, my lord. If you stay here with the boy, someone will come to pick you up soon.' He was talking to Erskine, and with respect.

'Aren't we going to Station B9?' I asked.

Black Jack flashed his teeth in the dark, 'Not anymore we're not. You didn't really want to join the enemy permanent, did you?'

I suppose my crest-fallen expression must have been visible under that moonless sky, for Black Jack gave a stifled laugh. 'You're no more a soldier of the Flame Squadron than I am. Crozier is on the inside, a double agent. He's a good man, trying to help us. As for poor Erskine here, I doubt he'll last the night. It was he who caused the trouble, but I doubt he'll be around to put the world right again. Stay here with

him and give him his tablets, there's a good lad, Michael — whatever your name is. Thank your lucky stars you're out of York! I've got to drive back again by morning and bring some other poor blighters out of it. It's the women and children I feel sorry for.'

The he helped me carry Erskine to the stone and with a wave, he was gone.

The night was chilly and though Black Jack had left the blankets and some food, I was far from comfortable. I huddled nearer to Erskine and cried for my mother and sister, for York, for my father — probably dead somewhere, or else worrying about us and me with no means of bringing him the news.

Erskine slept most of the time or else groaned. Towards morning was the worst time for me. I didn't know where I was nor what to do. I hadn't a notion of where to get food or how to live off the land.

Erskine finally stirred and spoke, 'Why do you weep, boy?'

I glared at him in the dawn light. 'You ask that of me? Crozier gave me a knife for your heart and I might use it, except that you'd die too quick. My mother and sister are dead because of you. You sold us to the enemy.'

Erskine sighed. There was blood in the sound, thick and crusty in his throat. 'Who is the enemy? The outlanders you were taught to hate as a child are one blood with us. This is civil strife, not invasion. They had many grievances against us, from times before times. I have not followed the best course, many think. I do not ask that you should hold my name in respect, boy, but that you should keep an open heart for the truth. Is there a tablet?'

I gave it to him, still grudgingly. His two-edged words were known in every home from transmissions on the People's Voice when he had spoken in favour of the outlanders' rights. After he joined them, no one would willingly listen to him again.

He lay still, waiting for the drugs to work. 'Keep your dagger against the wilderness, feed yourself as best you can from the land. I shall die before sunrise and will be no more trouble to you. When I am dead, check the stretcher poles. One of them has plans, papers and so forth in it. Take it to the Peace King. He will know what to do with it.'

It is hard to watch even one's enemy die when he is the only living thing to talk to. I did not believe then in the Peace King. He was a character from story: a mythical king appointed by the will of the people to balance the land without the need of war. One whose rule was perfect and heaven-guided, full of equity like the kings of old.

Erskine died, as he had predicted, before dawn. Death turned his features into a grey echo of his former nobility. He could almost be a Peace King himself etched on a tomb, like those in the minster. I found the stretcher pole with the papers in it. They made no sense to me, being in cypher. I thrust them back into the pole — it would serve as a suitable staff. I drew a corner of the blanket across Erskine's face. At least I did not need to use the dagger.

A thin persistent drizzle came with the dawn. Down from the dales came a party of men in full view. They were not Iron Fist soldiers, though they were dressed for combat. Their leader, a short rugged man, fell to his knees before the body and felt the artery for life.

'Did he leave no message for me?' he demanded.

'Sir, I do not even know who you are.'

He glanced at my borrowed harness, 'Remove that livery at once.' I obeyed him with alacrity. 'Now spit on it.' I did so willingly.

'Good, now come with us.'

The Men of the Bear, as they were called, served only Forgil. They marched me into their camp, tucked into the corner of the dales, inaccessible to road across miles of moor. Forgil and his lieutenants questioned me closely about the fall of York. They asked about details of supply lines and troop movements of which I was totally ignorant. Finally, Forgil called them off and gave me breakfast.

'He truly knows nothing. Let him alone.' Then turning to me, he said, 'You realize that if you attempt to leave here — even to find your father — that you could easily lead the enemy here? I cannot let you go. Which means I must swear you to my service. Are you ready to avenge York, for we fight against the Iron Fists wherever they go? If you follow me, you will learn arms and perhaps find your father in the days to come. Speak!'

'I have nowhere else to go, sir. I will join you gladly.'

'What, from necessity only? That is not the spirit! Those who follow me believe in the land beneath their feet and do its bidding. Those who follow me each bring a gift from their hearts. What have you to offer?'

He spoke lyrically, like a man reciting a poem, but sincerely, as though he were himself the poet and the words his own.

'Did Erskine truly say nothing of me before he died?' he demanded again.

I repeated what he had said about the Peace King and how I was to give the papers to him. 'But there is no such person, so how can I do it?'

Forgil's face brightened as though the sun had risen upon it, 'Then he did speak of me.'

'*You* are the Peace King?' I sounded incredulous, I suppose.

'I was and shall be,' he said, cryptically.

'But Peace Kings are supposed to be peaceful, I thought.' I no longer cared what happened to me.

'So they are. But peace comes through right will and true discernment. Without these two, nothing can be right in the land. When the Men of the Bear under my leadership have brought that understanding, then the times of peace will be with us.'

'You remind me of Count Erskine,' I said.

'That is not surprising, for we are brothers. When we were young, we planned great things for the land, but his way was not mine. He wanted all peoples under our dominion, but this will not happen in

stone two

our lifetime. Perhaps it will happen in yours?'

He took my chin in his hand and examined my face more closely. 'Yours is a strange destiny, boy. Do you know what way you want to go?'

My heart was moved by his touch and his voice.

'My mother said that in every land, a cup made of the crystal heart of a star is to be found and that whoever had it would bring healing. This stone is said to be part of one of these. If I give it to you, will you become the Peace King?'

I brought out the golden chain with its green jewel. A look of wonder crossed Forgil's face as he touched it. 'You offer me the heirloom of your house as a pledge of your service?'

'I have lost my family, my home and my honour. Boys younger than me fought and died today. If such a gift will make you the Peace King, then I give it to you.'

Forgil turned away, gazing into an inner distance just as my mother used to do when she practised as a clear speaker. 'You do not know me, yet you offer this thing? I say to you, when I am established on the King's Mound in the Place of the Bear, when I carry the sword of equity in my hand, then you, Michael Elder, and only you, shall place the crown upon my head and in that crown shall this stone be set on that day. Will that be bargain enough for you?'

Moved by his words, I sank on one knee and gave him my oath: 'I, Michael Elder of the city of York, swear to follow you, Forgil, Count of Britain.'

Then, my child, the great Forgil, King of Britain and the Outer Islands, knelt to your grandfather and said:

'Whatever is lost, I shall find. Whatever is wasted, I shall restore. Whatever is amiss, I shall set right. I swear this by the green stone, wrought of the heart of the stars in their first falling.'

And that has been for ever afterwards the oath of the Peace Kings. You who read this, safe in the sanctuary of the Bear, the long mercy

of the Peace Kings' rule, remember Michael Elder who lost a mother, a sister and a city, but found his father twice over in the service of his land.

CAITLÍN MATTHEWS

'THE MAIDEN OF THE SPEAR'

I am of the Clan of the Spear and I would tell how the destruction known as the Wasted Lands came to be, because of the breaking of a sacred trust and because of the love which I bore for one who was not of the Clan and who should not ever have laid eyes upon That which we guarded.

For the valley in which we lived was not like other parts of the land. Sickness and death were unknown, the corn grew tall and golden every year, the sun ever shone. This was because of the Spear, which stood at the centre of the valley, just as the valley, in turn, stood at the centre of the lands beyond. Some say, and I have no means to know otherwise, that while our land burgeoned, so did those beyond.

My father was a proud man, who took his duties as Guardian seriously. As Spear King he must not only care for the Sacred Weapon, but also take part in a yearly ritual. One which also involved my mother, the Queen, and me, the Spear Maiden, who must together and separately make offering in the secret way that was ever ours.

Every year, at the Feast of the Blessing of the Spear, the King heated the Fires of Life and brought out the sacred tools of the Smith and in full view of all, remade the head of the Spear and fitted it on to the shaft that was always the same, ancient and blackened from generations of handling, the pictures which once adorned it almost rubbed away, until they were no longer readable.

Then, when this was done, the Queen and the Maiden took the New Spear deep into the forest, and at a certain place known only to

them, passed from mother to daughter through the ages, the Queen ritually anointed the blade with her own blood. And when this was done, she would stretch out her arms and offer the Spear to the Gods above and the Gods beneath — and always, a shaft of sun would pierce the canopy of leaves above her and strike the blade until it splintered with light.

This done she would hand the Weapon to me, the Spear Maiden, who had come prepared with a bird from the Royal dovecots. This it was my task to dispatch, with the right words and the proper gestures, so that all should be well with the land. Once, it was said, the maiden would have made another kind of offering, after which she was maiden no longer, but the Bride of the Spear; and earlier even than that, in a time so long past it was scarcely a memory, the King himself would have given up his life for the good of the Land. But in the time of which I speak no such terrible offering had been demanded for longer than memory, and the land continued to prosper, and there was no death, and the corn grew tall in the fields beyond the walls of our village.

Each year, after the Blessing, the Spear was set upright on the hill that overlooked our homes, and garlands were placed upon it, and youths and maidens danced around it that both they, and the land, might be fertile.

And so it was, year upon year, without change — until the day when a stranger came into our lives who was to change them forever.

It was many years since we had last seen anyone from the world of men. Few came near the village, and those who did generally failed to notice it and passed by. This man was different. He had eyes that noticed things, great and small, with equal care. He moved with the grace of a warrior, yet he carried no weapon, only a harp slung across his back in a doeskin bag. And there was that about him which spoke of long dreaming, of one who was already less than half in the land of men.

I believe I loved him from the first, though such was forbidden to the Maiden of the Spear. I did my best to be formal and polite when

in his company, but I believe that my heart betrayed me whenever he came near. And so the pattern was set that was to lead to sorrow and death and the coming of the Wasted Lands.

It was in the Summer that he came, so that it was the better part of a year before the next Blessing of the Spear. It was not our way to turn away those whose steps lead them to our doors, and so the stranger, whose name was Lugaid, remained with us, playing and singing songs from the land of men to entertain us in the evenings.

He never spoke of his life before, of kith or kin or places he had known. Nor did we seek to probe his past, for such matters were his own possession and none other's. Yet sometimes I caught sight of a wistful look in his eyes which caused me to wonder for what he yearned, or why he had come to the Valley of the Spear.

Despite all I could do to prevent it we were sometimes alone in each other's company, and at such times a silence fell between us that said more than any words. Then one day as I walked in the woods Lugaid's path crossed mine, and in a little while, and with few words, we lay together beneath the trees of the sacred wood. And afterwards I wept for the shame of what I had done, for surely now the gods would curse us and the land would wither.

Throughout the year Lugaid and I continued to meet in the secret depths of the wood. Sweet were those days, and harder it became to keep silent and to hide the terrible secret that was ours. Nor, though we were as close as a man and a woman can be, did I learn anything more about him. His past remained forever undisclosed, as much to me as to the rest of the Valley.

Then, as the long chill nights of Winter drew upon us, an old woman of the Clan died, the first for many generations, and a shiver of fear passed through every one of us. Nursing my secret, part joy, part terror, I blamed myself for the death and for a time refused Lugaid. But the year turned, and as Spring drew near, I gave way again to the desire I felt for him, and once more we met whenever we might.

spear knight

But we grew careless, until at last word reached my father, the King, and though I heard afterwards that at first he refused to believe the tale, at length he was driven to follow me, and there he came upon us, Lugaid and I, locked in sweet embrace, and with a terrible cry leapt upon us with drawn sword.

My lover fled, being unarmed; and, fleet of foot and younger than my father, he drew away. Crying I knew not what, I followed them and came to the Hill of the Spear in time to witness a terrible deed.

My father had pressed Lugaid to the very place where the Spear stood, the ribbons and garlands long since gone from it, its blade tarnished and darkened by wind and weather. I saw without understanding as Lugaid pulled it from its resting place and turned it upon my father. The King fell bleeding from a wound in the thighs and seeing me cried out in a high and terrible voice to avenge him and the life of the Clan.

At such times a part of the mind that is older than the rest takes charge. I was no longer the lover of the man before me; his face no longer seemed sweet and familiar. I saw only one who had committed a deed of awful sacrilege. I took up the Spear from where he had let it fall and struck down the man I had lain with for almost a year with as little thought as I gave to one of the doves I had slain in the wood each year.

But already the damage was done. The Spear, which was in our sacred keeping, had twice been used to draw blood in a manner not of the rites. Rain began to fall from the moment the King received his wound, and kept up its beating for three weeks after, until the corn lay flattened and the land was barren. Many of the Clan fell sick of agues and began to die. The King lay in perpetual agony, his wound unhealing and his manhood dead.

At length the Queen, who had scarcely spoken to anyone since that terrible day, gathered those who remained of the Clan about her and said: 'We must leave this place and take the King to where he may be healed.' And so it was agreed. But when the wagons departed a few days after, with the King's litter in their midst, I did not go with them. This was my just punishment, that I should remain here alone until such time as one came who would heal the land. I have waited long since then — longer than I can remember, and few faces have I seen, and none that stayed to talk with the Hag of the swamplands.

You are the first who has spoken with me in all that time, so you must not be surprised if I am filled with hope that you are perhaps the one I have awaited. Last night I dreamed of a hill on which stood a house of gold. Before it was planted a new Spear, and as I watched I saw a blackbird settle at its feet and begin to peck at the earth, while from the tip of the Spear flew a white dove, that mounted into the sky . . .

JOHN MATTHEWS

afterword

Now that you have been with us on a journey through the realms of the *Hallowquest*, it is time for you to begin the journey for yourself. You will not be unaccompanied, since the archetypes of the *Arthurian Tarot* will be at your side throughout many adventures to come. We hope you will enjoy and learn from your experiences and would welcome hearing from you.

A *Hallowquest* course is in preparation through which you may wish to pursue the path begun in this book. A tape containing some of the meditations in this book will also be available. Write to us at the address below, sending two first-class stamps (for readers in the British Isles) or two international reply-paid coupons (for overseas readers), and we will keep you informed of future developments, as well as other related courses in the Arthurian, Native and Goddess traditions.

BCM — Hallowquest
London WC1N 3XX

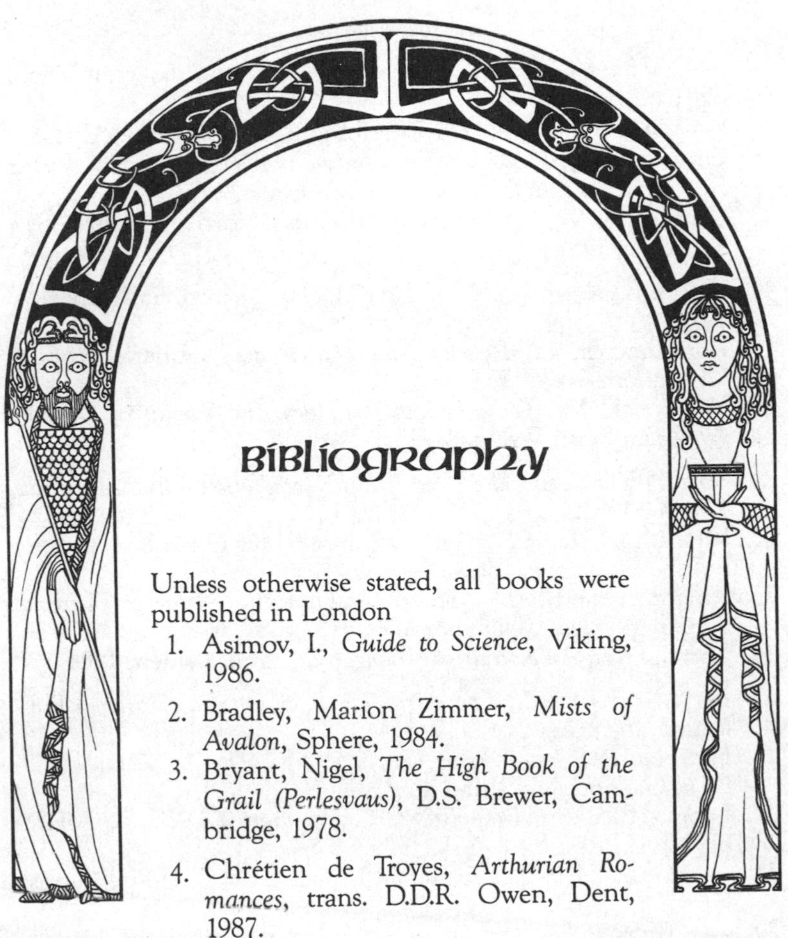

Bibliography

Unless otherwise stated, all books were published in London

1. Asimov, I., *Guide to Science*, Viking, 1986.
2. Bradley, Marion Zimmer, *Mists of Avalon*, Sphere, 1984.
3. Bryant, Nigel, *The High Book of the Grail (Perlesvaus)*, D.S. Brewer, Cambridge, 1978.
4. Chrétien de Troyes, *Arthurian Romances*, trans. D.D.R. Owen, Dent, 1987.
5. Cross, T.P. and Slover, C.H., *Ancient Irish Tales*, Figgis, Dublin, 1936.
6. Curtin, Jeremiah, *Hero Tales of Ireland*, Macmillan, 1894.
7. Fairfield, Gail, *Choice Centred Tarot*, Newcastle Publishing Co., Hollywood, 1984.
8. Geoffrey of Monmouth, *History of the Kings of Britain*, Penguin, Harmondsworth, 1966.
9. —, *Vita Merlini*, ed. and trans. J.J. Parry, Univ. of Illinois Press, Illinois, 1925.
10. Gilchrist, Cherry, *Circle of Nine*, Dryad Press, 1988.
11. —, *Divination*, Dryad Press, 1987.
12. Gray, W.G., *Magical Ritual Methods*, Helios Books, Toddington, 1971.
13. Greer, Mary K., *Tarot Constellations*, Newcastle Publishing Co., Hollywood, 1988.

14. —, *Tarot for Yourself*, Newcastle Publishing Co., Hollywood, 1984.
15. —, *Tarot Mirrors*, Newcastle Publishing Co., Hollywood, 1989.
16. Gregory, Lady, *Voyages of Brendan the Navigator and Tales of the Irish Saints*, Colin Smythe, Garrard's Cross, 1973.
17. Guss, David M., *The Language of the Birds*, North Point Press, San Francisco, 1985.
18. Hall, L.B., *Knightly Tales of Sir Gawaine*, Nelson Hall, Chicago, 1976.
19. Harf-Lancner, L., *Les Fées au Moyen age*, Librairie Honoré Champion, Paris, 1984.
20. Hashrouck, M. B., *Tarot and Astrology: the Pursuit of Destiny*, Aquarian Press, Wellingborough, 1986.
21. Karr, Phyllis Ann, *The King Arthur Companion*, Chaosium Inc., Albany, 1983.
22. Kitteridge, G.L., *A Study of Gawaine and the Green Knight*, Peter Smith, Gloucester, Mass., 1960.
23. Knight, Gareth, *The Secret Tradition in Arthurian Legend*, Aquarian Press, Wellingborough, 1983.
24. Korrel, Peter, *An Arthurian Triangle*, E.J. Brill, Leiden, 1984.
25. Lacy, Norris J., ed., *The Arthurian Encyclopedia*, Garland Publishing, Inc., New York, 1986.
26. Lacy, Norris J., and Ashe, Geoffrey, eds., *The Arthurian Handbook*, Garland Publishing Inc., New York, 1988.
27. Loomis, R.S., *Arthurian Tradition and Chrétien de Troyes*, Columbia Univ. Press, New York, 1949.
28. —, *Celtic Myth and Arthurian Legend*, Haskell House Pubns., New York, 1967.
29. —, *Wales and Arthurian Legend*, Folcroft Editions, 1977.
30. *Mabinogion*, ed. Lady Charlotte Guest, Ballantyne Press, 1910.
31. Malory, Sir Thomas, *Le Morte d'Arthur*, University Books, New York, 1961.
32. Maltwood, K.E., *The Enchantments of Britain*, James Clark & Co., Cambridge, 1982.
33. Markale, Jean, *Le Graal*, Retz, Paris, 1982.
34. —, *King Arthur, King of Kings*, Gordon Cremonesi, 1977.
35. Mason, Herbert, *Gilgamesh*, Houghton Mifflin, Boston, 1971.
36. Matarasso, P.M., *The Quest for the Holy Grail*, Penguin, Harmondsworth, 1969.
37. Matthews, Caitlín and John, *The Western Way vol I: The Native Tradition*, Arkana, 1985.
38. —, *The Western Way vol II: The Hermetic Tradition*, Arkana, 1986.
39. Matthews, Caitlín and Jones, Prudence, *Voices From the Circle*, Aquarian Press, Wellingborough, 1990.

40. Matthews, Caitlín and Pollack, Rachel, eds., *Tarot Tales*, Century, 1989.
41. Matthews, Caitlín, *Arthur and the Sovereignty of Britain: King & Goddess in the Mabinogion*, Arkana, 1989.
42. —, *The Elements of Celtic Tradition*, Element Books, Shaftesbury, 1989.
43. —, *The Elements of the Goddess*, Element Books, Shaftesbury, 1989.
44. —, *Mabon and the Mysteries of Britain: An Exploration of the Mabinogion*, Arkana, 1987.
45. Matthews, John and Green, Marian, *The Grail Seeker's Companion*, Aquarian Press, Wellingborough, 1986.
46. Matthews, John and Stewart, Bob, *Warriors of Arthur*, Blandford Press, Poole, 1987.
47. Matthews, John, ed., *The Arthurian Reader*, Aquarian Press, Wellingborough, 1988.
48. —, *At the Table of the Grail*, Arkana, 1987.
49. Matthews, John, *The Elements of the Arthurian Tradition*, Element Books, Shaftesbury, 1989.
50. —, *The Elements of the Grail Tradition*, Element Books, Shaftesbury, 1990.
51. —, *Gawain, Knight of the Goddess*, Aquarian Press, Wellingborough, 1990.
52. —, *The Grail: Quest for the Eternal*, Thames & Hudson, 1981.
53. Nennius, *British History and Welsh Annals*, ed. and trans. J. Morris, Phillimore, Chichester, 1980.
54. Parry, Idris, *Animals of Silence*, Oxford Univ. Press, Oxford, 1972.
55. Racoczi, Basil I., *The Painted Caravan*, L.J.C. Boucher, The Hague, 1954.
56. Raine, Kathleen, *Yeats the Initiate*, Dolmen Press, Portlaoise, 1986.
57. Ross, Anne, *Pagan Celtic Britain*, Routledge & Kegan Paul, 1967.
58. Skeels, D., *Romance of Perceval in Prose, (Didot Perceval)*, Univ. of Washington Press, Seattle, 1966.
59. Skene, William F., *The Four Ancient Books of Wales*, Edmonston & Douglas, Edinburgh, 1868.
60. Spence, Lewis, *The Mysteries of Britain*, Aquarian Press, Wellingborough, 1970.
61. Spenser, Edmund, *The Faerie Queen*, Oxford Standard Authors, New York, 1963.
62. Stafford, Greg, *Pendragon Game*, Chaosium, Inc., Albany, 1985.
63. Stewart, Bob and Matthews, John, *Legendary Britain: An Illustrated Journey*, Blandford Press, Poole, 1989.
64. Stewart, Mary, *The Crystal Cave*, Hodder & Stoughton, 1970.

65. —, *The Hollow Hills*, Hodder & Stoughton, 1973.
66. —, *The Last Enchantment*, Hodder & Stoughton, 1979.
67. Stewart, R.J., *Advanced Magical Arts*, Element Books, Shaftesbury, 1988.
68. —, *The Elements of Creation Mythology*, Element Books, Shaftesbury, 1989.
69. —, *Living Magical Arts*, Blandford Press, Poole, 1987.
70. —, *The Merlin Tarot* (illustrated by Miranda Gray), Aquarian Press, Wellingborough, 1988.
71. —, *The Underworld Initiation*, Aquarian Press, Wellingborough, 1985.
72. Sutcliff, Rosemary, *Sword at Sunset*, Hodder & Stoughton, 1963.
73. Tatz, M. and Kent, Jody, *The Tibetan Game of Liberation*, Rider, 1978.
74. Tennyson, Alfred, Lord, *Idylls of the King*, Penguin, Harmondsworth, 1983.
75. Tomberg, Valentine (Anonymously), *Meditations on the Tarot*, Amity House, Amity, 1985.
76. Treece, Henry, *The Great Captains*, Bodley Head, 1956.
77. Trevelyan, George and Marchatt, Edward, *Twelve Seats at the Round Table*, Neville Spearman, Jersey, 1976.
78. *Trioedd Ynys Prydein* [The Welsh Triads], trans. Rachel Bromwich, University of Wales Press, Cardiff, 1961.
79. Von Eschenbach, Wolfram, *Parzival*, trans. A.T. Hatto, Penguin, Harmondsworth, 1980.
80. Von Zatzikhovan, Ulrich, *Lanzelet*, ed. and trans. K.T.G. Webster, Columbia Univ. Press, New York, 1951.
81. Wang, Robert, *The Qabalistic Tarot*, Weiser, York Beach, Maine, 1983.
82. Webster, K.G.T., *Guinevere: a story of her abductions*, Turtle Press, Milton, Mass., 1951.
83. Weston, Jessie, *From Ritual to Romance*, Doubleday, New York, 1957.
84. White, T.H., *The Once and Future King*, Collins, 1952.
85. Williams, Charles, *The Greater Trumps*, William B. Eerdman's Pub. Co., Grand Rapids, 1978.
86. Willis, Tony, *Magick and the Tarot*, Aquarian Press, Wellingborough, 1988.
87. Yeats, W.B., *Mythologies*, Collier Books, New York, 1958.

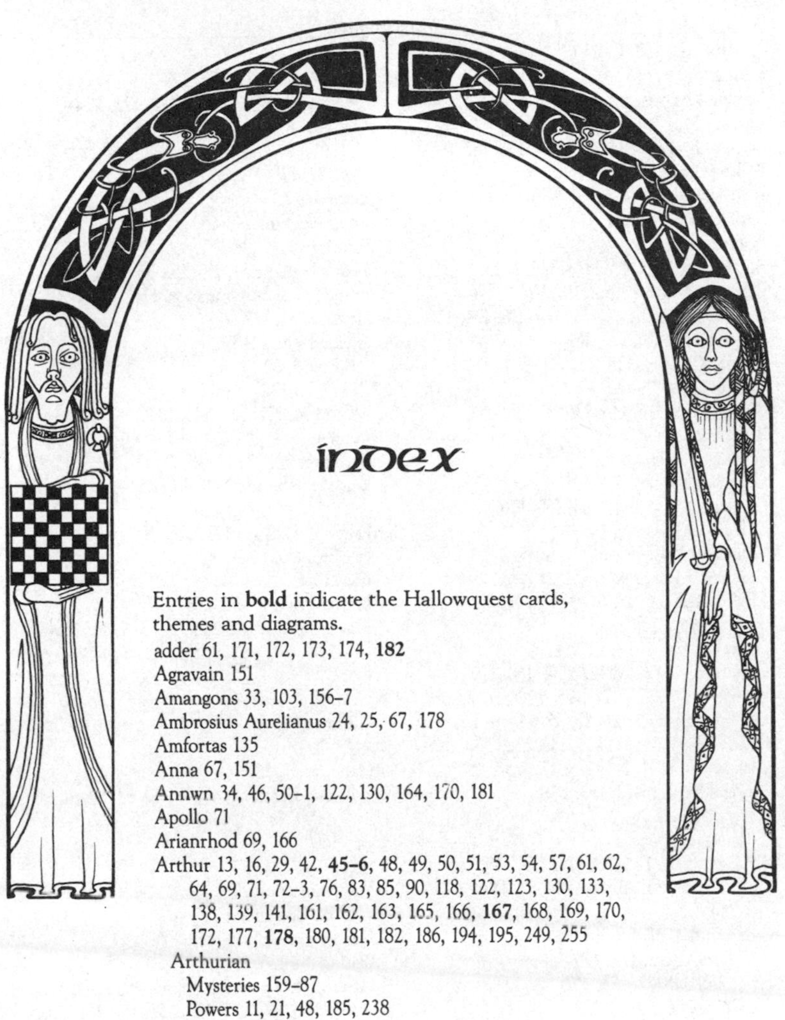

index

Entries in **bold** indicate the Hallowquest cards, themes and diagrams.